JUST WAR THEORY

JUST WAR THEORY
A REAPPRAISAL

Edited by
Mark Evans

Edinburgh University Press

© in selection and editorial matter, Mark Evans 2005
© in the individual contributions is retained by the authors

Edinburgh University Press Ltd
22 George Square, Edinburgh

Typeset in Palatino Light by
Koinonia, Manchester, and
printed and bound in Great Britain by
MPG Books Ltd, Bodmin, Cornwall

A CIP record for this book is available from the
British Library

ISBN 0 7486 2074 5 (hardback)
ISBN 0 7486 2075 3 (paperback)

The right of the contributors to be identified as authors
of this work has been asserted in accordance with
the Copyright, Designs and Patents Act 1988.

CONTENTS

CONCLUSION

NOTES ON THE CONTRIBUTORS

Helen Brocklehurst is Lecturer in Politics in the Department of Politics and International Relations, University of Wales Swansea. Her research interest is children and security and publications include *Who's Afraid of Children? Children, Conflict and International Relations* (Ashgate, in press). She is also completing an ESRC-funded research project on history and national identity, and co-edited *History, Nationhood and the Question of Britain* (Palgrave Macmillan, 2003).

Kateri Carmola is Assistant Professor of Political Science and Christian A. Johnson Fellow in Political Philosophy at Middlebury College, Vermont. She was formerly a post-doctoral fellow at the Travers Center for Ethics and Accountability in Government, University of California at Berkeley. She is currently writing a book on changing conceptions of death in wartime.

Neta C. Crawford is Associate Professor (Research) at the Watson Institute for International Studies at Brown University, Rhode Island. She is the author of *Argument and Change in World Politics: Ethics, Decolonisation and Humanitarian Intervention* (Cambridge University Press, 2002) and has published widely on topics in global ethics, including war and the ending of war.

Mark Evans is Senior Lecturer in Politics in the Department of Politics and International Relations, University of Wales Swansea. He has published widely on topics in political theory and is the editor of *The Edinburgh Companion to Contemporary Liberalism* (Edinburgh University Press, 2001) and *Ethical Theory in the Study of International Politics* (Nova Science Publishers, 2004). He is currently completing a book on *War, Morality and Humanity*. He is Associate Editor of the *Politics and Ethics Review* (Edinburgh University Press).

Patrick Hayden is Senior Lecturer in Political Theory at Victoria University of Wellington, New Zealand. He has written widely on international ethics, human rights and theories of war and peace, including *Cosmopolitan Global Politics* (Ashgate, 2005), *John Rawls: Towards a Just World Order* (University of Wales Press, 2002) and *The Philosophy of Human Rights* (Paragon House Publishers, 2001). He is also General Editor of the *Politics and Ethics Review* (Edinburgh University Press).

Anthony F. Lang Jr is Lecturer in the School of International Relations, University of St Andrews. He is the author of *Agency and Ethics: The Politics of Military Intervention* (SUNY Press, 2002), the editor of *Just Intervention* (Georgetown University Press, 2003) and (with Joel Rosenthal and Albert Pierce) *Ethics and the Future of Conflict* (Prentice Hall, 2004).

Brian Orend is Director of International Studies, and Philosophy Professor, at the University of Waterloo in Canada. He is the author of *War and International Justice: A Kantian Perspective* (Wilfrid Laurier University Press, 2000) and *Michael Walzer on War and Justice* (University of Wales Press, 2000) and a textbook on human rights entitled *Human Rights: Concept and Context* (Broadview Press, 2002).

Andrew Rigby is Professor and Director of the Centre for the Study of Forgiveness and Reconciliation, Coventry University. He is the author of *Justice and Reconciliation: After the Bloodshed* (Lynne Rienner, 2001) and numerous articles in scholarly journals on the problems of peace-building.

PREFACE AND ACKNOWLEDGEMENTS

War brings people to the very extremes of experience: confronting them with the awesomely terrible powers of destruction they can unleash, the raging and pitiless fury they can feel at fellow humans who have now become 'enemies', unimaginable fear at the precipice of death and uncomprehending horror at its carnage – and if they survive, maybe a bewildered joy at such a miracle, perhaps utter despair and grief at the remnants of lives wracked by injury and loss, a guilt, even, that they have survived at all … or, instead, a deadened sensibility, condemned to an existence no longer capable of relation to a world which has let loose such inhumanity.

For those of us fortunate enough never to have been subject to the rending realities of war, it can seem naïve and absurd, hubristic and disrespectful to its victims and survivors, to reflect from afar upon its nature and pronounce on its justifications and rules of conduct. 'How dare such people presume to judge matters that lie so far beyond the realms of their experiences and their imaginations?' Such is the complaint sometimes raised against the theorists of the just war who seem, to certain critics, to epitomise philosophers at their most unworldly, legislating from circumstances of insulated comfort for all-too-real events of which they have not the remotest grasp. According to these critics, no moral theory – which they may regard as by definition the creation of those who gaze upon harsh reality from afar – can have anything worthwhile to say on the nature of war.

Students of just war theory, which claims that war can and should be made subject to the considerations of morality – that even this phenomenon, at the far limits of what humanity may suffer, does not escape the realm of principles – should certainly approach the subject-matter with humility. But far from being justified in fearing they have no right to pronounce on the morality of war, I believe it is crucial for them – for all of *us* – to embrace the point that if our moral thinking cannot apply here then morality is a hollow thing indeed. It is *precisely* in such contexts that our appeals to the 'moral' ultimately matter most of all and this is evident in the fact that, far from being some otherworldly abstraction, just war theory is actually the product of experience, an extended effort to assert the claims of morality in the face of war's realities and against those who would regard such assertions as futile. This has yielded a tradition of thought to which people have appealed throughout the ages to rein in the temptations of conflict, to oppose those who succumb too easily to them, and to try to ensure that, when war proves unavoidable, its purposes and conduct remain tethered as tightly as possible to morality. Put another way: even if we believe that war is an inevitable feature of the human condition, as human beings we are also mandated not to let it slip totally free of the moral – if, that is, we are not to lose altogether the vestiges of 'humanity'. The precarious nature of our lives in the world today means that we are *all* liable to be touched by war: as victims, initiators, even as citizens in whose names our governments send others to fight or bystanders to conflicts waged by others. And just war theory seeks to minimise this liability, and keep us all somewhere in morality's realm when we are forced to suffer the affliction of war.

It is, however, a pertinent and perturbing question as to whether the tradition of just war theory bequeathed to us is at all adequate for upholding the demands of morality in the face of war. It has always had its critics, of course, and not just those who have disputed the very possibility of conjoining 'justice' and 'war' in moral thinking – the 'realists' on one side and the pacifists on the other. Its specifics have been contested even when its general moral aspirations have been accepted, not least by those who argue that in various ways the 'realities of modern warfare' require different approaches to that which it offers. This book aims to continue the contest – and recent events testify to the need to do so. We are living in an age of unprecedented political, social and technological change, but the phenomenon of war has hardly receded from our experience. In terms of war deaths the twentieth century was by far the bloodiest in history. Those who harboured millennial hopes that the twenty-first century would not be similarly disfigured have rapidly been disabused of such hopes: the shocking events of 11 September 2001 and the (equally shocking) ensuing wars in Afghanistan and Iraq have seen to that. Yet changes of the kind we are experiencing can affect how wars come about and are fought, even, indeed, what might count as a 'war'. The need, then, to reappraise our ideas about war and justice is politically, morally, *humanly* urgent.

Now and through the ages just war theorising can be found in many different cultures and traditions of thought and it would be a mistake to assume that there is a substantive generic pattern or content that they all share. Speaking of it in the singular is therefore in one sense misleading and an engagement with the entirety of its range would be necessary for a full appreciation of what the phrase 'just war' could denote. (I intend to turn to the varieties of just war theorising in a companion volume.) But there is considerable advantage to be gained from stating the theory as a general and timeless set of moral considerations. By abstracting from the conflicting particularities, nuances and qualifications of warfare's myriad concrete historical instances, we can clear away many potential obstacles to the presentation and analysis of a generalised moral framework which might orient a consistent set of judgements about war wherever and whenever it breaks out. This is the approach of this book: the chapters take up specific elements of the theory and analyse them in large part abstracted from specific traditions of thought in order to throw the clearest light possible on the issue of their general tenability. The approach does not imply that every contributor affirms precisely the same, generalised or abstracted version of just war theory; indeed, it is not the case that every author supports *any* particular version of just war theory. Nor is it pretended that this dissection of the theory is comprehensive; a lot more could be scrutinised and said. But enough is presented here to show that just war theory can and should be rigorously reappraised, and to advance that project.

In the Introduction, I first set out to provide a sketch of just war theory as an historical tradition in Western thinking. As much as anything, this conveys a sense of the remarkable longevity of the just war tradition, which perhaps should not be forgotten in any reappraisal of it. I then discuss some features of just war theory as a moral theory and present my own formulation of the theory as an example of how it might be stated sympathetically in a contemporary context.

The first three chapters discuss issues arising in the first part of traditional just war theory: *jus ad bellum*, or 'just cause'. First, Neta Crawford addresses the most controversial contemporary invocation of 'just cause': the 'preemptive defence' argument offered by George W. Bush in support of the 2003 invasion of Iraq. Distinguishing 'preemption' from 'preventive war', she subjects the putative justification for the most controversial war of recent times to penetrating theoretical critique. In Chapter 2, Anthony F. Lang Jr tackles the question of humanitarian intervention, which has arguably arisen recently as a norm to supplement self-defence as a possible just cause for war. Not least because of the tardiness with which some such interventions have been undertaken, he considers whether it is morally appropriate to attribute to them a punitive instead of a purely preventative goal.

In Chapter 3, I consider the question of who or what has the right to wage war. Traditional just war theory is highly state-centric: individual states are the sole relevant actors in this regard. It is clear, however, that this perspective – if ever it was justified – is too antiquated to be adequate in the modern world. But our institutions do not yet fully meet the requirements for authoritative direction here. I suggest a way, first of all, of thinking about this problem which I propose gives us some guidance. Controversially, perhaps, I also suggest that there is a democratic bias in just war theory which influences its accounts of legitimate political authority and 'just peace'.

The next three chapters turn to the second traditional part of the theory: *jus in bello*, or 'justice in the conduct of war'. In Chapter 4, Kateri Carmola points out that the concept of proportionality has always been difficult to operationalise. But there are certain aspects of recent conflicts which have exacerbated its indeterminacies and these are analysed in order to assess the continued utility of a concept that is all-too-readily set aside in the heat of battle. *Jus in bello* critically depends upon an ability to draw morally meaningful distinctions between those who are rightly liable to die in war (which includes the just as well as the unjust combatants) and the 'innocent', those whose deaths should be minimised as far as possible. It is a staple of debate about the theory that this distinction is difficult to draw, but Helen Brocklehurst's contribution in Chapter 5 forcefully stresses that the extent of this difficulty continues to be underestimated by neglecting the peculiarities of 'the child' as a moral and political subject in war. Through evocative examples and suggestive analyses her chapter proposes that some fundamental categories of just war theory may be significantly disrupted once we think properly about the role and status of children in war. In Chapter 6, Brian Orend discusses the 'supreme emergency exemption', which claims that the 'discrimination' criterion in *jus in bello* may be legitimately waived in certain extreme circumstances, for example when faced with attack from weapons of mass destruction.

As I suggest in the Introduction, an adequate just war theory must move beyond the traditional bipartite *ad bellum/in bello* structure to include a third part: *jus post bellum*. The goal of a just war is always in some sense a just peace, however, and it is plausible to argue that an adequate just war theory must attend not only to the content of this notion but also to the means by which a just peace might be secured. In Chapter 7, therefore, Patrick Hayden suggests that there is a human right to peace and analyses how this might sit in a theory of just war. Andrew Rigby, in Chapter 8, discusses the concepts of forgiveness and reconciliation, and the various practices by which these may be pursued in societies recovering from conflict.

I return implicitly to my version of just war theory in the concluding chapter, where I defend it against some of the most important and familiar criticisms it faces. I acknowledge, however, that it poses some very serious problems for the theorist attempting to render it coherent and cogent, which may well prove intractable. Yet my personal conclusion is that, if we are to take the normative evaluation of war at all seriously, it is hard to think of how we might do so without ultimately adopting some version of the just war theory. It is, of course, up to readers to consider whether my arguments satisfactorily support that claim, and assess whether the contributions of my collaborators bolster or detract from my own conclusion. What is difficult to deny, however, is the overall contention of this book that just war theory continues to demand close scholarly attention and not least because it is still very much 'out there', in real controversies about real wars.

As was the case for many other people, my interest in just war theory was dramatically heightened by the events of September 11th and their aftermath. To employ a cliché *de nos jours*, mine has been a steep subsequent learning curve with respect to the myriad issues the theory raises. My initial impression of it, that the theory was deeply flawed but presented an inescapable paradigm if we are to adopt any normative stance towards the phenomenon of war, has largely survived thus far (and is defended in the final chapter). I am under no illusion of having reached the top of this curve but, for having come thus far, I have been particularly reliant on the writings of, and discussions with, many of those who have directly and indirectly participated in this project. I would therefore like to thank Helen Brocklehurst, Kateri Carmola, Neta Crawford, Toni Erskine, Patrick Hayden, Tony Lang, Rex Martin, Alex Moseley, Brian Orend, Andrew Rigby, Peri Roberts and Peter Sutch. A number of graduate students in the Department of Politics and International Relations have helped me to develop the ideas discussed in this book. I would particularly like to mention Penny Lane, valuable conversations with whom prompted significant clarification in my thinking and the exposition of my ideas, and Christine Stender, who happily volunteered – without any prompting from me – to become in effect an unofficial (and hence unremunerated) research assistant, furnishing me with significant research material as well as valuable conversation on just-war issues. Her friendship and enthusiastic support have meant a lot in this endeavour. The staff of Edinburgh University Press, and in particular Nicola Carr, have been extremely supportive; and James Croft assiduously and constructively corrected errors and other infelicities in the typescript. Needless to say, apart from whatever my contributors themselves say in writing, no one bar myself has responsibility for what follows.

For financial assistance for the main conference at which the contents of this book were discussed, held under the auspices of the Department of Politics and International Relations and the Callaghan Centre for the Study of Conflict, University of Wales Swansea, I am very grateful to the British Academy for a conference grant (award number BCG 36807), the University of Wales Academic Support Fund, the Gregynog (University of Wales) staff colloquium fund and my own department. Albright College, Reading, PA and the University of Kansas independently provided assistance for Tony Lang and Rex Martin respectively, which was invaluable. My department granted me a sabbatical in the autumn of 2002 during which, among other projects, I was able to undertake the research of which this book is one of the products.

My most important debts are, however, first to my parents for their love and help over the years, and, above all, to Anne, whose love, forebearance, support and considerable assistance in preparing the manuscript have made this book possible.

Introduction

MORAL THEORY AND THE IDEA
OF A JUST WAR

MARK EVANS

⊂⊃

To begin the reappraisal of just war theory, it is helpful to gain a sense, albeit brief and partial, of how it has evolved to date. I shall thus say something about the history of the just war tradition in the West. To orient the subsequent discussions I then formulate one particular version of the theory, which I believe represents its most sympathetic contemporary exposition. As stressed in the preface, it must not be thought that the contributors to this book all accept my formulation or even the tradition in general. But the stated version will function to highlight both the almost generic features of the doctrines within the tradition as well as certain particular features that, I argue, may be included to remedy the defects of some alternative statements of the theory.

THE DEVELOPMENT OF THE JUST WAR TRADITION

War has been a central feature of civilisation throughout recorded time and it is hardly surprising, therefore, that a concern with – or indeed anguish over – its moral justifications should feature so prominently, across cultures, in so many past and present theories of morality. The term 'just war theory', however, is usually employed to denote that specific body of moral doctrine found within Christianity. Even though it can be presented with different theistic bases as well as in purely secular terms, then, the theory under review in this book can be thought of as the direct descendant of the Christian just war tradition. It is worth sketching the story of its historical unfolding.

The question as to whether Jesus himself was an absolute pacifist

1

remains a matter of perhaps unresolvable debate; there is, however, no doubting his general opposition to the use of violence. His teachings offer striking rejections of the celebration of martial virtues, according to which wars can be glorious and warriors heroic embodiments of humanity at its noblest: themes which were central to the ideology of the Roman Empire under which he lived. For Jesus, 'How blest are the peacemakers; God shall call them his sons.'[1] Rejecting the doctrine of retribution, he says, 'Do not set yourself against the man who wrongs you. If someone slaps you on the right cheek, turn and offer him your left.' Enemies should be loved and prayed for, not cursed – or, by implication, destroyed.[2] Crucial to his renunciation of violence is the idea that the supreme good ultimately lies not in this life but the (absolutely peaceful) 'after-life' in heaven, such that there is everything to be gained by suffering evil pacifically on earth. To Pilate he says, 'My kingdom does not belong to this world. If it did, my followers would be fighting to save me from arrest by the Jews.'[3]

Pacifism for Christians became increasingly difficult after the crucifixion, however. James Turner Johnson persuasively argues that early Christian rejection of war and violence was largely premised on the expectation that the Second Coming of Jesus, and the Reign of God, was imminent. As the years passed and this hope diminished, the problem of how to deal with the fact of war on earth could no longer be so easily sidestepped.[4] Certainly, by the end of the second century the sizeable presence of Christians in the Roman Army indicated that Jesus' pacific legacy had become significantly problematised: monks may have developed a form of existence in which its teachings could be lived to their ascetic full, but those Christians in 'ordinary' life could not so easily avoid the need to confront war in other ways. The challenge, then, was to work out which way of taking up arms could be rendered sufficiently compatible with Jesus' teachings.

The conversion to Christianity of the Roman Empire by Constantine in the fourth century gave further, powerful impetus to this project. Unsurprisingly, then, it is at this juncture that the just war tradition is thought to receive its major initial stimulus. Most significant in this process is *The City of God*, a monumental text by St Augustine of Hippo (354–430) which was written in response to those who believed that the sacking of Rome in 410 was due to its abandonment of paganism for Christianity. He draws a key distinction between the City of God, the perfection that is heaven, and the City of Man, the fallen condition that is mortal life on earth; this enables him to defend the strong disjunction between 'pure' Christian principles and the less-than-pristine norms with which we work in the tainted here-and-now. In the face of civil disorder, Augustine concludes that the resort to violence is justified but *regrettable*. To restore, as best one can, a just order, violence may be necessary if no alternative remains viable. But it must always be used as sparingly as possible, never wavering from its moral intentions and only ever to be deployed by legitimate civil authorities.[5]

Although the critical distinction between just cause (*jus ad bellum*) and justice in war's conduct (*jus in bello*) is far from fully worked out by Augustine, he lays down many of the moral criteria that frame the subsequent tradition. However, as Johnson argues, the fact that Augustine's corpus was subsequently neglected until Gratian's *Decretum* in the mid-twelfth century indicates the inaccuracy of placing him at the start of a *continuous* just-war narrative.[6] The barbarian influences in Europe following Rome's collapse yielded highly militaristic cultures based, once more, on the warrior code of glory and honour in battle, against which the Christian Church tried to react – most notably from the late tenth century with the idea of the Peace of God, a commitment to establish the immunity of non-combatants. The Crusades jarringly fused certain just war ideas with a sanctioning of morally unmitigated violence against unbelievers, but it is significant that the next figure often cited as key to the just war tradition's development, St Thomas Aquinas (1225–74), is reluctant even to discuss the concept of the 'Crusade'. His thought, too, does not clearly differentiate *jus in bello* independently from *jus ad bellum* but its overall implication, sanctioning war against infidels only when harm is threatened to Christians – and even then only when toleration of their existence is unsustainable – suggests that for him perhaps the Crusades, at least, were not sufficiently just in the first place for questions of their conduct's morality to arise.[7]

The failure of the Crusades did much (at least in the minds of many intellectuals) to discredit explicitly religious-based justifications for war. With the greater interaction (rather than sheer confrontation) in the Renaissance of Christian, Islamic and Jewish cultures, the idea of a doctrinally specific 'divine' order increasingly gave way to a putatively universalisable one of 'natural' order. Natural law, derived from an understanding of the nature of human personhood and the constraints of life in the material (mortal) world, made possible a new idea of

'international law' on which basis just war theory could be fundamentally recast. The savagery of the Spanish conquest of the New
World, for example, was thus opposed by Francesco de Vitoria (1492–
1546) on the grounds that no war could be just simply because one's
opponents did not share one's religion, for justice was rooted in a
natural law which was shared by all peoples.[8]

It is Hugo Grotius (1583–1645) who is generally accredited with the
completion of just war theory's secularisation in his comprehensive
treatment of a natural law-based account of international law in *The
Laws of War and Peace*.[9] His emphasis on defence against threatened or
actual attack as the just cause for war acquired refocused meaning and
increased resonance in the seventeenth century with the development
of the modern state and the international system of states from the 1648
Treaty of Westphalia. Consolidating the idea of international law as the
regulation of inter-state relations, nationalism, and the 'protection of
sovereignty' and national interests became increasingly prominent in
just war theory's concept of justice. This was dramatically epitomised in
the Napoleonic Wars which, according to the great theorist of war, Carl
von Clausewitz, initiated the era of 'absolute' or 'total' war, with huge
armies motivated by the causes of extended modern nation-states
supplanting the era of smaller battles fought for more localised causes.[10]
As technologies, communications and infrastructures developed through
the nineteenth and twentieth centuries, whole societies could place
themselves at war with each other. And, in democracies at least, more
people at least potentially had a say on the decisions as to whether to
wage war, and how: a development that helped to reframe just war
theory as a moral guide for leaders and citizens alike, laying out the
relevant moral considerations implied by acts of war for all those who
may be affected by them.

It would be misleading to think, from the rise of the nation-state,
that defence of sovereignty was offered as the sole possible just cause
for any length of time through the modern era. The natural law
tradition that grounded an account of natural rights, which has latterly
evolved into the theory of human rights, has always provided at least
the potential for a new 'crusading' cause: to spread such rights to those
societies which fail to respect them. And in opposition to this liberalism
(locating this survey now in the age of ideologies) other doctrines raised
the spectre of alternative political goals as morally justified ends to war.
Seeing this development as too often a dangerous abuse, those who

consciously invoked the just war tradition at this time therefore frequently tried to insist that just self-defence alone constituted just cause. But the separation of just cause from ideology was always difficult, and perhaps undesirable if not even conceptually incoherent. Few of the champions of just war theory had any problem with the idea that the Second World War, for example, was not merely a self-defensive war but a 'modern crusade' against the evils of the Axis powers and their fascist doctrines.

Just-war theory's ability to influence political leaders and military combatants has always been questioned. If, invariably, some have challenged the plausibility of the idea that those who matter in the making of war would really take heed of its principles, it would be wrong to think that just war arguments have been naïvely insulated from the realities of warfare. As may be gathered from the foregoing, the concept of an international legal order gained a very substantial part of its initial concrete embodiment through the enactment of just-war considerations: the Geneva and Hague Conventions established extensive sets of agreed laws and customs to regulate the conduct of war. Significantly, recognising the dangers spoken of above, the United Nations – set up after the Second World War to end the 'scourge of war' – established 'self-defence' as the only cause a state may legitimately cite for waging war unilaterally, without UN approval. Even then, the international community, particularly as represented in the Security Council, was deemed to have a vested and proactive overall interest with regards to the legitimacy of all warfare in the post-war order: Article 51 of the UN Charter insists that 'unilateral' self-defenders must account for their actions before the Security Council, which retains overall responsibility and authority for the maintenance or restoration of peace. Often breached though these requirements of international law have been (who could really think that the UN's mission against the 'scourge' has been all that successful?), their effect has nevertheless been far from negligible in determining the behaviour of, and relations between, sovereign states.

Another challenge to just war theory arose with the age of the nuclear bomb and other forms of weapon of mass destruction, which prompted many to regard it as hopelessly outmoded and irrelevant. For humanity now threatened itself with forms of war that in principle and practice could brook no determinate limit: truly 'total' war threatened literally complete annihilation. For some, the risks of escalation in any conflict to a full-scale nuclear exchange were always so great that no war of any kind could therefore pass moral muster. But if, for some Western thinkers especially, just war theory consequently seemed to have had its day, the realisation that Cold War conditions did not preclude the outbreak of all manner of smaller, conventional conflicts – whose nature again betrayed the severe limitations of the 'inter-state' paradigm of war – rapidly demonstrated the prematurity of its consignment to history's dustbin. In particular, the Vietnam War prompted a renewed and sustained engagement with the tradition that culminated in, for example, the publication of Michael Walzer's influential *Just and Unjust Wars*.[11] Protests against that war and other movements – such as the opposition to nuclear armament in Europe – helped to remind many of a feature central to the theory's purpose but too often neglected by commentators: it can serve not only to justify wars but also to *oppose* them, and to do so without committing one to an 'absolute', uncompromising pacifism.

The end of the Cold War and the collapse of Soviet-bloc communism was heralded by, among others, the first President Bush as the beginning of a new order in world affairs, which would be by implication a peaceful one. This, of course, has not come to pass. Reflecting changed perceptions and usages of military force and its purposes now that the constraints imposed by superpower confrontation have gone, the idea of humanitarian intervention seems to have moved decisively to the fore in the tradition as a just cause – a supplement to just defence. And the latter concept itself has now been significantly problematised by the 'war on terror', launched in the aftermath of the September 11th attacks in the USA on the World Trade Center and the Pentagon. Today's disputes over the nature of war – what kinds of conflict count as 'war' – and the role of just war theory in sanctioning and limiting its conduct are as complex and heated as they have ever been. Its tenets and assumptions have always been open to revisionary contest; this reappraisal, therefore, remains very much true to its spirit.

CONSTRUCTING A CONTEMPORARY THEORY OF JUST WAR

The fact that the just war tradition has managed thus far to evolve through changing historical circumstances and the consequent challenges to its relevance and tenability is, of course, not proof that it will ride through those that it faces today. Not all the contributors to this book might agree, but in my own chapters I present a case for saying that the tradition can and should adapt. Deferring defence of this claim to the final chapter, the rest of the present one is devoted to the explication of what I believe to be a suitable version of just war theory for contemporary conditions,[12] with a necessarily selective commentary on the reasoning behind some of its tenets, not least to flag up some continuities and discontinuities with the tradition summarised above.

First of all, as a justification for going to war, just war theory is no more an 'apology' or 'excuse' than it is supposed to be a purely descriptive explanation for why one has actually broken out. This is because if we *excuse* our doing of X, we are in general giving reasons for doing X when in fact X is *not* something that we should have done. There may be mitigating reasons that reduce our culpability in having done X but they do not fully *justify* it; that is, they do not show that we should have done, or at least permissibly did, X after all. Just war theory identifies the grounds on which we may justify waging war, the reasons which give us warrant – *good*, legitimising reasons – for this act. Of course it has been invoked in excuses for war, when there was no justification. But these have been *misuses* of the theory and it is important to stress that they do not necessarily impugn the theory at all. Any theory or principle can be misused, and the propensity for misuse cannot itself be a reason for rejecting it. As we will shortly appreciate more fully, just war theory is comprised of numerous criteria which pose stringent moral tests that a war has to pass in order to be morally justified. Two types of misuse from which the theory has suffered have, then, been:

1. *Misapplication of the theory's criteria.* For example, opponents of the 2003 invasion of Iraq believe that its attempted justifications exhibited this flaw: a factual error in believing that Saddam Hussein possessed weapons of mass destruction which thereby warranted his overthrow, when even the belligerent governments now concede that he didn't, and/or a moral error in thinking that mere possession (or potentiality of possession) of such weapons would anyway have constituted a sufficiently just cause for a war of 'regime change'.
2. *Incomplete application of the theory's criteria.* Supporters of a war sometimes appeal only to selected criteria of the theory on the assumption that these suffice to justify that war when in fact it requires that all the criteria be met before we can say it is justified.[13]

Again taking the 2003 war as an example, some evidently assumed that it was sufficient to have a just cause for it to be justified. But even if there *is* a just cause for a war, the just war theorist takes that to be a *necessary* but not *sufficient* condition for its justification; the other criteria have to be satisfied as well.

Next, I want to suggest that a fully cogent just war theory must make an assumption that many people today officially want to resist: it has to believe that the morality from which it draws its theory of justice (which informs, for example, its account of a just cause) is *objective*. It holds that there are right and wrong answers to the moral questions it poses and thus rejects the idea of moral relativism or 'equivalence' as far as its own principles are concerned. Further, I would urge that a concomitant feature of just war theory's moral objectivism is its *universalism*. The morality with which it works is deemed to be applicable to all human societies and situations, and provides a shared basis from which the morality of all conflicts may be assessed. Despite its actual origins within specific religious traditions, then, the theory can claim to eschew reliance on any purely particularistic and partisan creed. (I discuss the theory's universalism more fully in Chapter 3.)

Now of course the sides in a war will invariably claim justice to be on their side and it may be the case that 'local', culturally relative claims about justice are available to support such claims. But just war theory rejects the idea that these differences are sufficient to justify a subjectivist and relativised conception of morality, in which a moral belief is regarded as (merely) a statement of personal preference ('a matter of opinion', as some intend by this phrase) which has no independent authority over anyone else's alternative moral conviction. A key axiom of just war theory on my reading is that, in any war, at least one side ultimately has no justification to wage it, even if – as we should expect – it thinks it does.[14] (Often neither side is in the right, in which case the war is comprehensively unjustified: just war theory does not justify *those* wars.) And, to stress again the sense in which they are presented as objective, the theory's judgements are proffered as grounded independently of any one side's own beliefs. A war is not just because the just warriors say it is, but because justice is objectively and independently on their side; a just war is not 'victor's justice', as some have said, if this is to mean that 'justice' is only ever what the winners say. (As I note later, a just war could be a losing cause.)

This is not the place to enter into the well-worn meta-ethical defence of moral objectivity against its doubters. It should also be stressed that just war theory should indeed be sensitive to what can be regarded as *legitimate* cultural variety in morals. But such variety does not go all the way down, so to speak. As I shall argue in Chapter 3, just war theory is best conceptualised as operating with a minimal or 'thin' universalist morality, which sets certain boundaries to the toleration of conflicting accounts of morality that even those who are attracted to relativism (who think that their own moral judgements can't be said to be objectively correct against anyone who makes different judgements) are likely to find it hard to reject. If one is not already disposed to accept that there are such limits, however, then a separate reckoning with the debate about the objectivity of a universal morality may be necessary before one is likely even to engage with the idea of a just war.

Just War Theory as Non-Ideal Theory

Let us now consider a structural feature of the theory as I believe it to be best presented, which clarifies its overall attitude to the morality of war. Following John Rawls, we can distinguish between ideal and non-ideal theory, and place just war theory firmly into the domain of the latter.[15] In essence the distinction is a secularised version of Augustine's distinction between the city of God and the city of man, for it recognises that morality might still specify how we should act even in circumstances where it is impossible to live up to all of its fully realised demands. Ideal theory specifies the terms of the 'ideal world', defined as that in which it is possible to be fully moral. It is the world in which what ought to be the case actually *is* the case. Non-ideal theory specifies moral requirements and guidelines for a world in which this fully realised ideal situation has not been, and perhaps cannot foreseeably be, achieved.

Just war theory is non-ideal for the following reason: the goal of a just war is a just peace. In the ideal world there would be no war. Just war theory actually embraces pacifism at the ideal level, but eschews the absolute pacifist's rejection of the moral possibility of war at the non-ideal level. The fact that we need a just war theory arises from the assumption that, in our non-ideal world, war might at times be morally unavoidable. On such occasions it is justified in response to a very great injustice. At such times the principles which frame our conception of the ideal-world just peace simply cannot be applied in full: the requirements of justice pull away from the requirements of peace – and the just war theorist thinks that in principle there may be times when the former trump the latter.

The clearest expression of just war theory's non-ideal character, again echoing an Augustinian theme which has reverberated through the tradition, is its insistence that war is *the lesser of two evils*. When a war is just, it is right to wage it but, because the lesser of two evils is still an evil (and the theory can insist that it is still a very great evil), the rightness is severely tempered by the *tragic* character of the situation.[16] If we have had to resort to war, then we have found ourselves incapable of acting in ways which do not yield very significant wrongs. Just because a war is *just* does not mean that it is *good*, that there is nothing morally distressing about the decisions and actions of the just warriors. The essential point for the theory, though, is that even in such morally unpropitious circumstances moral considerations remain rigorously applicable. It is not the case that such moral tragedy leaves us with nothing but a set of morally equivalent evils as our options. There can still be just and unjust ways of dealing with tragedy, informed by a conception of how we might move a little further towards what would pertain in the ideal world.

Some fear that the language and sentiment of justice in just war theory make it prone to the encouragement of a messianic, zealous pursuit of war in which the morality of its goal is in effect allowed to sanction the most extreme violence. Yet just war, as the lesser of two evils, is acutely sensitive to the fact that dirty hands are indeed dirty, and they are not fully cleansed by any justice in a war's outcome. The stringency of its demands reflects an awareness of the awfulness of what it nevertheless justifies. Though within war there may be many acts of heroism, just war theory cannot, then, be said to glorify war or be ultimately blind to its moral horrors. Its tragic dimension should severely temper even the justified sense of righteousness of the just combatants, curbing the propensity of such to degenerate into hubristic narcissism. Further, in the non-ideal world when 'justice' and 'peace' cannot be fully combined, the evil of war makes even the just-war advocate more disposed *in general* to peace than justice. In other words, peace at the expense of justice tends to be the starting-point against which the just-war case for war has to be made – as will again be evident from the strictness of the justificatory criteria the case has to satisfy before winning the argument. Just war theorists are happy to recognise that sometimes – perhaps often – it is *peace* that is the lesser of two evils. All that they need to deny here is the strict pacifist claim that peace is *always* the lesser of two evils.

How To Use the Theory

Not least because the non-ideal world presents itself to us as morally perplexing and troubling, we cannot expect just war theory to be able to pronounce, with unambiguous certitude, on the justice or injustice of every war that is or could be fought. But in the whole field of moral thinking it is hardly alone in having to confront the possibility of genuine indeterminacy. Moral theories that do not recognise the possibilities of genuine moral dilemma and complexity as obstacles to definitive and decisive judgement are typically too simplistic in their depiction of certain aspects of moral reality. We thus need to be clear about what we can expect it to be able to do for us.

To be sure, at first sight the theory might seem to offer an 'algorithmic' procedure, which presumes that certain facts can be fed through its criteria in order to compute with precision the definite answer as to whether a war is justified. But, like many other prescriptive moral theories, it does not hold out such naïvely ambitious claims for itself. It is better thought of as a 'heuristic' tool, providing the set of moral criteria which should inform decisions as to whether to go to war and, if so, how it should be fought. It poses the questions that should be asked when we contemplate the morality of war but it does not absolve us of the responsibility to formulate the answers for ourselves, and there remains a perhaps unavoidable latitude in the degree of disagreement which reasonable answers to those questions may manifest. This is not to say there is complete licence in the answers we may give. The range of reasonable answers is constrained in the theory, otherwise it would indeed be of little value. But we should not expect the theory to force upon us one logically incontestable and irresistible conclusion.

Before stating my version of the theory, a final word about who 'we' are that might ask the just war questions. On one level it is obviously a theory of *political justification*, designed to govern the decisions of political and military leaders as to whether (and if so, how) they should use their armed forces in both initiating the use of force and responding to the threatened or actual use of force by enemy powers. They have a special and urgent moral responsibility to use the theory. But, as noted above, it has also become a morality for everyone: not just the leaders but the led, those who are asked to fight, those who face war, those in whose name war is fought, even those who are in some sense mere 'bystanders'. Particularly today, political leaders typically feel compelled to offer moral justifications to the international community in general for acts of war, and that community can use just war arguments to engage with their justifications. And of course many often think that those justifications fail – which shows how just war theory need not figure in our discourse only when we want to justify a war. As already noted, it can also frame the morality of opposition to war for those who do not believe in absolute pacifism. When we consider the arguments of many in what are called 'anti-war' movements, we see that this is indeed the position that they take: they are not 'anti-war' in general so much as 'anti-*this* war', and just war theory can provide the justification for their position. There is no irony or paradox in just war theory playing this kind of role in political argument.

In the rest of this Introduction, following my version of just war theory, I will briefly review its contents with a view to indicating where there may be latitude for reasonable dispute concerning its interpretation and application.

JUST WAR THEORY: A REPRESENTATIVE STATEMENT

1. *Jus ad bellum*: to have the moral right to wage war, the following conditions must be respected:
   (a) the cause is just;
   (b) the justice of the cause is sufficiently great as to warrant warfare and does not negate countervailing values of equal or greater weight;
   (c) on the basis of available knowledge and reasonable assessment of the situation, one must be as confident as one reasonably can be of achieving one's just objective without yielding longer-term consequences that are worse than the status quo;
   (d) warfare is genuinely a last resort: all peaceful alternatives which may also secure justice to a reasonable and sufficient degree have been exhausted;
   (e) one's own moral standing is not decisively compromised with respect to the waging of war in this instance;
   (f) even if the cause is just, the resort to war is actually motivated by that cause and not some other (hidden) reason;

(g) one is a legitimate, duly constituted authority with respect to the waging of war: one has the *right* to wage it;

(h) one must publicly declare war and publicly defend that declaration on the basis of (a) – (g), and subsequently be prepared to be politically accountable for the conduct and aftermath of the war, based on the criteria of *jus in bello* and *jus post bellum*.

2. *Jus in bello*: to fight a war justly, one must employ:

(i) *discrimination* in the selection of targets: avoiding the direct targeting of those not directly participating in the immediate conduct of war, and taking all reasonable measures possible to avoid casualties among such non-participants.

   (i₂) *Doctrine of double effect*: the foreseeable deaths of 'innocents' do not render a war unjust so long as they are not directly intended as the object of policy but are the unavoidable side-effects of a use of force justified by the other criteria of the theory.

(j) *Proportionality* in the use of force required to secure the just objectives;

(k) *just treatment of all non-combatants*: by which is intended prisoners of war as well as non-combatants in the wider arena of the war.

(l) One must observe all national and international laws governing the conduct of war which do not fundamentally conflict with the theory's other moral requirements.

3. *Jus post bellum*: to secure the justice sought in the resort to war, one must be prepared to:

(m) help to establish peace terms which are proportionately determined to make that peace just and stable as well as to redress the injustice which prompted the conflict;

(n) take full responsibility for one's fair share of the material burdens of the conflict's aftermath in constructing a just and stable peace;

(o) take full and proactive part in the processes of forgiveness and reconciliation that are central to the construction of a just and stable peace.

Supreme Emergency Exemption: in a situation of supreme emergency only, one may wage war in a way that suspends condition (i).

HOW TO APPLY THE THEORY

Much of this book is taken up with discussion of the issues arising from the attempt to utilise criteria such as these in moral judgements about war. Here, I give only a partial sense both of how the criteria might be applied and what problems might arise in their application, not only to illuminate how the theory may be intended to work but also to provide a foretaste of some of the reappraisals to come.

When to Apply the Theory?

We have observed that what counts as a war has been subject to revision in the history of the tradition, but it might nevertheless be thought that we need a settled definition of it in order to know when it is appropriate to apply the theory. Now in the final chapter I will adduce some considerations that suggest this may not be quite the critical question it could reasonably seem to be. However: straightforwardly we could say that war is the systematic use of military force by an organised social power to compel an enemy to submit to its will,[17] the objective being 'political' in the very broad sense that the enemy's exercise of power is intended either to be crushed or substantively altered. (Hence the pertinence of Clausewitz's observation that war is the continuation of politics by other means.[18]) The definitional difficulties are usually thought to arise when one considers by what kinds of 'organised social power' might wars be waged. There is, very familiarly, a state-based definition in which 'wars' have been the military conflicts fought by states, or alliances of states, against other states or alliances of states. However, wars have also been fought by 'peoples' – and not just when statehood is the desired objective of the conflict (a war of national liberation). And if we want to count the 'war on terror' as indeed a war, and not some other kind of conflict, we can see still further the inadequacy of exclusively statist-based definitions of war and why many now talk of there being qualitatively 'new' kinds of war.

David Rodin's recent critique is representative of the view that the theory is too conceptually tied to state-centrism and the morality of state sovereignty, leading it to an impoverished conception of 'just cause' as centred on nothing other than an aggression-against/defence-of-state-sovereignty dichotomy.[19] But just war theory can be readily recast to avoid reliance upon this: no fundamental alteration of the theory, at least in the form presented above, is required in order to accommodate the fact that bodies other than states can be said to go to war and are therefore subject to the constraints imposed by the theory. In Chapter 3, I sketch a theory which indicates how such state-centrism may be overcome in a discussion which also broaches the question of *what account of justice just war theory needs to employ*. In the first instance, this account identifies what constitutes just cause for war. But it is also reasonable to presume that it must inform the constraints upon warfare imposed by criteria I(b) onwards. The internal coherence of just war theory depends upon the availability of an account that successfully harmonises these features.

When is War Appropriate?

Any illusion that this harmonisation is a straightforward matter is dispelled once we see that *jus ad bellum* requires complex considerations even once the initial justice of the cause is established. The criteria from 1(b)–1(h) can be sub-divided into three: (b)–(d) seek to establish that the conditions are sufficiently serious to consider war; (e)–(f) ask questions about the 'ethical character' of those considering whether to wage a war; and (g)–(h) seek to establish their authority to be the ones to wage war. And for most of them, we can readily see what room there is for interpretive leeway. For example, consider what other values have sufficient weight in themselves to be judged as possibly counting against the values one seeks to promote through war. If we are fighting a war to achieve or restore a just peace, then in our non-ideal circum-stances we have opted for justice over peace. But we must consider the independent moral weight of peace, and the virtues it facilitates, in such circumstances – and the stringency of the theory's criteria help to explain the contention already stated that, contrary to the views of some of its critics, just war theory has a *pro tanto* disposition towards peace. This is not to insist, say, that just combatants must always be reasonably assured that they will *win* the war in question: perhaps it is possible, at least in principle, for it to be better to die fighting for justice than to live in extreme injustice (for it is false to think it follows from 'defeat of the just would be an unjust outcome' that 'the just would be therefore morally unjustified to fight a war they are likely to lose'). The inbuilt general bias towards peace, however, seems evident.

What counts as 'last resort' also leaves latitude for contest. It cannot literally be 'no alternative', because refusal to wage war is always a literal possibility. (The martyrdom this may imply is what we presume might be recommended by an absolute pacifist.) The point is whether there is a *reasonable* alternative – and controversy obviously arises over what 'reasonable' means in a specific context. If one's life and those of our families, friends, comrades in arms, say, are more likely to be lost without war, just war theory could argue that it is reasonable to hold our martyrdom and the victory of one's opponents not to be a morally superior outcome to the deaths which would be caused if we fought in self-defence instead. But we need not move far from this ostensibly simple judgement to see how problematic 'reasonable last resort' could be: is it really impossible, for example, for there ever to be no morally justified alternatives to martyrdom in such circumstances? (What if one's sole means of resistance was a weapon of mass destruction?)

It might also be thought that it matters greatly to the application of the theory as to whether one is initiating war, or whether one is responding to an act of war, or to a potential act of war. Some might believe that, though the decision to start a war should be regulated thus, the justification of one's response to attack – the enjoining of war – is not sensibly constrained by the theory's criteria in their entirety. Discussions of pre-emptive and preventive war and the supreme emergency exemption take particular angles on this issue and I raise it in the final chapter.

The Moral Character of Just Warriors

The next two criteria are 'ethical', invoking the Aristotelian idea of personal virtues of character – personal in that they specify how potential warriors should evaluate aspects of their own character in weighing up the justice of their cause. 1(e) is typically not found in traditional statements of just war theory, but I believe there to be sound reasons for its inclusion. The aggression by A against B may be a response to some past act by B which, whilst not constituting war itself, nevertheless created the reasons why A has felt compelled to resort to force. Even if A is wrong to believe that aggression is justified, B's launching of a defensive war is consequently morally problematic. For example, it might be wrong for a former, viciously oppressed colony to launch a revenge attack on their one-time rulers but it may not be straightforwardly justified for the latter to reply in kind given their direct responsibility for the grievance.[20]

Opponents of a decision to go to war will often impute motives to the decision-makers which are at immoral odds with the noble ends that the latter profess: control of oilfields in the Middle East, for example, as opposed to self-defence or the liberation of an oppressed people. And we surely would want to say that moral agents, particularly when contemplating something as devastating as war, ought to look to their own motives – and their own moral character more generally – in taking the responsibility they are required to shoulder in making such momentous decisions. But 1(f) might seem like self-regarding moral navel-gazing: what does it matter why people were really motivated to wage war, as long as there really is a just cause also available? This is not mere moral narcissism, however; actual but hidden motives can determine aspects of a war's conduct which the theory would not justify. Following the 2003 conquest of Iraq, critics noted how oil refineries were protected and other facilities were not when *jus post bellum* demanded that they should have been – a moral failing that they explained with reference to what they claimed to be the war's real motivating cause. Hence, there is not only intrinsic value to the criterion; it has instrumental utility in securing one to the requirement of justice.

Political Authority and the Waging of War

One of the reasons for the state-based bias of traditional just war theory is that, in the insistence that only states can fight wars, the possibility of mercenaries, brigands and other kinds of rabble having the right to fight was immediately rescinded. Having acknowledged that states are not the only kinds of organised political unit that could be said to wage 'war', and if just war theory wishes to permit the possibility that these other forms of conflict could be just, we clearly need an account of legitimate authority to accommodate this revision. The capaciousness of war's definition is likely, however, to problematise the idea of legitimate authority, and my discussion of it in Chapter 3 admits to these difficulties. But this does not necessarily lead to a case for abandoning 1(g), for we surely want to resist the claim that any body of people could constitute themselves as 'just warriors' and thereby, by default, acquire 'legitimate authority'. There are, for example, extremely small armed groups that claim to be fighting on behalf of a far larger group of people who do not actually support their methods, even if they are sympathetic to their cause. (The conceptual, as opposed to merely polemical, dispute over the categories of 'terrorists' and 'freedom fighters' might reflect the issue at stake here.) In these instances, it is surely incumbent on the group to reflect upon its own right to represent the group at all, particularly with the methods it employs – a point which, I suggest in the relevant chapter, should make us rethink how this criterion might be applied.

1(h) might be called the 'public justification' criterion, which I have strengthened from the more familiar 'public declaration' formulation by insisting that justificatory reasons should be given in some kind of recognised and appropriate political forum for the decision to go to war. Once again, I shall defer elaboration of this idea. But some might already, and rightly, see how this can give the notion of legitimate authority some distinctive content, for it implicitly commits just warriors to 'justificatory politics'. The requirement to justify one's actions implies not only certain responsibilities on the part of political decision-makers but also certain entitlements with respect to those on whose behalf decisions are taken: they are *owed* reasons. As I shall argue, this is already enough to set just war theory on a path to limit, if only fairly thinly, the type of political unit which could justifiably wage war.

Moral Restraints in the Conduct of War

The two main components of *jus in bello*, discrimination and proportionality, have probably produced more heated debate than any of the others. How can we distinguish between those whom the theory regards as rightly liable to be killed, and those whose lives must not be regarded as similarly forfeit (the 'innocent', as they are often called)? And what can 'proportionality' mean? I will not dwell long on the relevant criteria here, as forthcoming chapters will deal with these problems and I shall present some conclusions of my own on them in the final chapter. For now, I will merely note that 2(k) and 2(l) are not typically found in statements of *jus in bello*. They are often thought to be implicit in the other criteria, or at least in the ethos of the theory as a whole. This may be overly complacent, however: without being rendered explicit in the theory, an unjust licence for the neglect of law in practice might be unfairly attributed to it – and the frequency of such neglect indicates that the theory should not dismiss this as a trivial matter.

The Case for Theorising Jus Post Bellum

Traditionally, just war theory has been divided only into two parts: just cause and just conduct. But I think that there is a powerful case for insisting that a concern with the post-war situation be included explicitly into the justification of a war.[21] The case for *jus post bellum's* inclusion in the theory lies in the claim that 'crucial to winning the war is winning the peace'. If the goal of a just war is a just peace, it would be odd indeed if there were no requirement to address oneself as to how this may be promoted *when war is being planned and fought*. Put differently, *jus post bellum* consolidates the orienting presence of ideal theory in just war thinking. All just combatants are obliged to address questions of *jus post bellum* before war's conclusion; should they indeed be victorious, they are then obligated to act upon the fruits of their deliberations.

In his chapter, Patrick Hayden includes statements of *jus post bellum* criteria, emphasising the need for a just peace settlement and just discrimination in whatever punishments, compensations and reparations are at stake. I accept that all of these are necessary, but I would actually read them all into 3(m). The other two criteria emphasise, first of all, the peculiar responsibility of just warriors to take a fair (by which may often be meant 'substantial') share of the burden (which primarily but not exclusively denotes 'costs') of the construction of a just peace. Second – and this is the subject of Andrew Rigby's chapter – explicit attention is given to what, precisely, is involved in putting a just society together. It is not just a question of punishing wrongdoers, exacting reparations, and so on. All conflicts, to be permanently settled, require measures of reconciliation between former enemies, and in many circumstances (civil wars being notable examples) substantial mechanisms for forgiveness also have to be in place. The criticism of, for example, the West's post-war parsimony in reconstructive aid to Afghanistan can be seen to arise from this criterion. And as I write, the bloodily chaotic aftermath of the 2003 Iraq war has placed these considerations urgently on the table. This third part of the theory ultimately raises the question as to whether a failure of a putatively just warrior, initiating, say, a humanitarian war against a genocidal regime, fully to embrace *jus post bellum* criteria fatally undermines the warrior's justification for engaging in warfare to start with even when the other criteria have been satisfied.

The addition of any extra criteria obviously makes just war theory more demanding. Some might fear that, in its admirable desire to limit war in the name of morality, its requirements have set the bar so high that no actual conflict could possibly clear it when in fact we want to say that some wars (against Nazism, say) were morally justified, and/or that some decisions *not* to go to war (the West in Rwanda, perhaps, in 1994) were not. I believe this identifies one of the more serious problems with just war theory, and I shall take it up in the concluding chapter. From those chapters which precede it, to which we now turn, readers might of course conclude that the theory is sufficiently vitiated on other counts for this problem not to matter.

NOTES

1. Matthew 5: 9. It should also be noted that the God of the New Testament is an altogether more benevolent and pacific figure than the one found in the pages of the Old Testament. Biblical quotations from the New English Bible with the Apocrypha (1970).
2. Matthew 5: 39, 44. The doubt over Jesus' pacifism arises from the profound controversy over the meaning of statements such as this (Matthew 10: 34): 'You must not think that I have come to bring peace to the world; I have come not to bring peace but a sword.'
3. John 18: 36.
4. Johnson (1987), pp. 14–17.
5. Augustine [413–26 AD] (2001), Book 19, chapter 7.
6. Johnson (1987), p. 58.
7. Aquinas [1266–73] (1954), pp. 159–60.
8. Vitoria (1991), pp. 295–327. Vitoria takes the credit for significantly sharpening the *ad bellum*/*in bello* distinction.
9. Grotius (1925).
10. Clausewitz (1976), Book 3, chapter 17.
11. Walzer (1992).
12. Part of my intention is to demonstrate that the theory can be stated in a robustly unified and clear form, and is not the fuzzy morass suggested by Iain Clark's observation that the just war tradition is 'a mosaic of thought fashioned by theologians, philosophers, jurists, statesmen and soldiers': Clark (1988), p. 31.
13. Here, though, it should be noted that I raise some important questions about this feature in the final chapter.
14. I will, however, raise some questions about this axiom – which not every just war theorist accepts, at least in such stark form – in the final chapter.
15. Rawls (1999a), pp. 89–90.
16. In defining all just wars as a form of moral tragedy, I am using the latter concept

more liberally than does Brian Orend in his contribution to this volume.

17. This definition largely follows that of Shaw (2003), p. 18.

18. Clausewitz (1976), Book 1, chapter 1.

19. Rodin (2002).

20. On both sides of the Atlantic, some argued that the attacks of September 11th were the manifestation of 'blowback': the US suffering the consequences of its global behaviour. Whilst not condoning the attacks they would urge that this criterion should have been borne in mind when considering whether the subsequent war against the Taliban regime in Afghanistan was justified. See, for example, Honderich (2002).

21. It is worth noting that *jus post bellum* is detachable from the other two parts of the theory in the following sense: one could believe that there was no just cause for war, nor any just way of fighting a war and yet, given that wars nevertheless occur, embrace *jus post bellum* as non-ideal theory's moral criteria to govern the post-war situation given that (immoral) wars have been fought. It is one part of just war theory that a pacifist can – and perhaps should – embrace, as may be evident from the argument in Chapter 8.

JUST CAUSE

Chapter 1

THE JUSTICE OF PREEMPTION AND PREVENTIVE WAR DOCTRINES

NETA C. CRAWFORD

The Bush administration reacted to the horrific September 11th attacks by proclaiming a right to preemptive self-defence, making preemption official US military doctrine. A preemptive war doctrine is, so it argued, the only way to make the United States safe. The Bush administration rightly points to the changed nature of military threats and poses a dilemma for scholars of just war theory: how long, in an era of terrorism and weapons of mass destruction, can states afford to wait to use their military force in self-defence? But the administration's doctrine is actually also a preventive war doctrine. And although the doctrine seems compelling at first glance, the logic of the just war tradition's prohibition on preventive war still holds.

Preemptive military action is undertaken to eliminate an *immediate* and *credible* threat of grievous harm. Those acting preemptively believe that an adversary is about to attack, that the assault is inevitable, and that a preemptive strike can eliminate the threat or at least reduce the harm that the anticipated assault would cause. Just war theory and international law grant the legitimacy of self-defence in response to an armed attack, and if preemption is self-defence against imminent assault, it is legitimate. Thus, Michael Walzer argues, 'states may use military force in the face of threats of war, whenever the failure to do so would seriously risk their territorial integrity or political independence'.[1] Preemption may only be considered justified if one has a justified fear of imminent attack, where the potential attacker has a clear intent to cause injury, is actively preparing to do so, and when waiting until the threat is realised greatly increases the risk.[2]

By contrast, a *preventive* war is undertaken when a state believes that

25

war with a potential adversary is possible or likely at some future date and that, if it waits, it will lose important military advantages. In this case, the threat is not imminent or even certain to materialise in the near future. Rather, the preventive attacker has made a worst-case scenario their working assumption: their potential adversary will attack if they can at some point, and no negotiation or change in the adversary's goals will intervene to stop the assault. In sum: although preemption, when initiated under specific limited circumstances, is generally considered legal, legitimate, and prudent, preventive war is generally considered illegal, illegitimate and imprudent. Indeed, preventive war is often associated with aggression.[3]

Such strong language implies that it is easy to distinguish preemption, undertaken to thwart or mitigate an imminent attack, from preventive war, undertaken to make sure an adversary never becomes a significant threat. Yet, Walzer notes, there is a 'spectrum of anticipation: at one end is ... reflex ...; at the other end is preventive war, an attack that responds to a distant danger, a matter of foresight and free choice.'[4] But, following the September 11th attacks, the Bush administration compressed the spectrum to the point where it was difficult to see the poles.

Specifically, the Bush administration blurred the distinctions between preemptive action and preventive war by arguing that the existence of weapons of mass destruction and the dangers of terrorism and rogue states demand preemptive action. It argued, quite simply, that the nature of war has changed. In the past it took tremendous resources and time periods that could be measured in years to mount a threat to the United States or regional stability. States had time to mobilise their defences against a possible adversary. The administration's case is that the diffusion of technological capacities and the barbarism of terrorists has changed this truism: devastating attacks could come with little or no warning. Thus, President Bush said in June 2002, 'the gravest danger to freedom lies at the perilous crossroads of radicalism and technology ... If we wait for threats to fully materialise, we will have waited too long.'[5] In the September 2002 *National Security Strategy* the administration argued that 'we must adapt the concept of imminent threat to the capabilities and objectives of today's adversaries'.[6] And Bush Administration National Security Adviser Condoleezza Rice proclaimed that 'new technology requires new thinking about when a threat actually becomes "imminent". So as a matter of common sense, the United States must be prepared to take action, when necessary, before threats have fully materialised.'[7]

Yet because the Bush administration linked the announcement of its policy of preemption with an explicit drive for military 'preeminence' and a later war against Iraq – regarded by many during the run-up to the invasion as posing little immediate threat to the US – there was suspicion that the doctrine was not appropriately labelled preemptive. Indeed, Richard Betts accused the Bush administration of using the term preemption in a 'sloppy or disingenuous manner',[8] and Charles Kegley and Gregory Raymond have argued that 'what is problematic about the new Bush security strategy is its framing of preventive military action as preemption'.[9]

But is the Bush doctrine really a 'sloppy' formulation of preemption or a 'disingenuous' cover for a preventive war doctrine? The Bush administration's argument that the changed nature of war and mobilisation may require a new approach to security deserves careful consideration. If the claims are correct – if adversaries are implacable aggressors, if there is essentially no warning, if there is little or no time to mobilise defences, and there is no chance to avert a devastating future conflict – the Bush administration has indeed identified a challenge to the just war doctrine's prohibition on preventive war. Contemporary technology will have made the doctrine, at least with respect to preventive war, obsolete.

More fundamentally, the logic underlying the Bush doctrine potentially poses an even more significant challenge to just war theory. Specifically, just war theory rests crucially on the notion that it is possible to limit war. It assumes that it is possible to know, basically, when wars begin and end, who is a combatant and a non-combatant, and that we know where wars are occurring. Yet, if accepted, a doctrine of preventive war erodes and essentially explodes those limits. War becomes total in a sense that even Clausewitz did not anticipate or think possible.[10] The world is understood to have actually become more Hobbesian.

LAW AND ETHICS OF PREEMPTION AND PREVENTION

Three examples are commonly used to illustrate the distinctions between preemption and preventive war. Although widely described as preemptive, Israel's destruction of Iraq's Osiraq nuclear reactor in 1981 was an example of a preventive strike. The Israelis bombed the plant under the assumption that Iraq intended to use the plutonium that would be created in the not-yet operational reactor to build nuclear weapons, and under the further assumptions that Iraq intended use those weapons against Israel. The Iraqi weapons, under this logic, could not have been meant to deter Israeli nuclear weapons. In this case, though it was plausible that Iraq would gain fissile material suitable for a nuclear weapon, and that it might build a number of nuclear weapons, nuclear use against Israel was certainly not imminent or certain. What Israel sought was to maintain the balance of military power between itself and Iraq. The UN Security Council censured Israel for the attack, rejecting their claim of self-defence.

By contrast, many argue that when Israel launched war against its neighbours in 1967 the action was a case of justified preemption. Egypt and Syria had mobilised, closed the Straits of Tiran and had a history of harsh and threatening rhetoric toward Israel. Israelis believed that unless their country mobilised its reserves, it could not match Arab power.[11] Israel could not have relied on a defensive strategy of waiting until struck because an Arab offensive would be devastating. And, Israelis believed, if they had not struck first, the coming Arab offensive could have been the end of the Israeli state. Instead, because Israel moved first, the Six Day war resulted in Israeli victory.

In supporting their declared preemptive policy the Bush administration referred to a third famous case, Daniel Webster's arguments about 'anticipatory self-defence'. National Security Advisor Condoleezza Rice stated that 'Daniel Webster actually wrote a very famous defence of anticipatory self-defence.'[12] Yet, to the contrary, what Rice characterised as Webster's 'famous defence' was a *rejection* of British claims that they had attacked an American ship, the *Caroline*, in self-defence. The *Caroline* incident illustrates important distinctions between preventive war and preemption.

In December 1837 British military forces based in Canada learned that a private American ship, the *Caroline*, was ferrying arms, recruits, and supplies from Buffalo, New York, to a group of anti-British rebels on Navy Island on the Canadian side of the border. On the night of 29 December, British and Canadian forces together set out to the island to destroy the ship. They did not find the *Caroline* berthed there, but they tracked it down in United States waters. While most of the crew slept, the troops boarded the ship, attacked the crew and passengers, and set it on fire. They then towed and released the *Caroline* into the current headed toward Niagara Falls, where it broke up and sank. Most on board escaped, but one man was apparently executed and several others remained unaccounted for and presumed dead.

The incident brought the US and Britain to the brink of war when American citizens mobilised. War was averted only by the President sending troops to keep citizens from responding. The diplomatic correspondence over the incident continued for years after the event. British ambassador Henry Fox defended the incursion into US territory and the raid on the *Caroline*, arguing that British forces were simply acting in self-defence, protecting themselves against 'unprovoked attack' with preemptive force.[13]

US Secretary of State Daniel Webster rejected the British argument and articulated a set of demanding criteria for acting with a 'necessity of self-defence', a legitimate use of preemptive force. Preemption, Webster argued, is justified only in response to an *imminent* threat; moreover, the force must be necessary for self-defence and can be deployed only after non-lethal measures and attempts to dissuade the adversary from acting had failed. Furthermore, a preemptive attack must be limited to dealing with the immediate threat and must discriminate between armed and unarmed, innocent and guilty. Webster argued that the British attack on the *Caroline* failed miserably to meet these standards.

> It will be for that Government [the British] to show a necessity of self-defence, instant, overwhelming, leaving no choice of means, and no moment for deliberation. It will be for it to show, also, that the local authorities of Canada, – even supposing the necessity of the moment authorised them to enter the territories of the United States at all, – did nothing unreasonable or excessive; since the act, justified by the necessity of self-defence, must be limited by that necessity, and kept clearly within it. It must be shown that admonition or remonstrance to the persons on board the 'Caroline' was impracticable, or would have been unavailing; it must be shown that daylight could not be waited for; that there could be no attempt at discrimination between the innocent and the guilty; that it would not have been enough to seize and detain the vessel; but that there was a necessity, present and inevitable, for attacking her in the darkness of night, while moored to the shore, and while unarmed men were asleep on board, killing some and wound[ing] others, and then drawing her into the current above the cataract, setting her on fire, and, careless to know whether there might not

be in her the innocent with the guilty, or the living with the dead, committing her to a fate which fills the imagination with horror. A necessity for all this the government of the United States cannot believe to have existed.

Webster concluded that 'if such things [as the attack on the *Caroline*] be allowed to occur, they must lead to bloody and exasperated war'.[14] Thus, he articulated what became the standard view of preemption in international law and points to the dangers of preemption as a doctrine.

Webster's standards are analogous to the *jus ad bellum* criteria of just war. For war to be legitimately undertaken according to just war theory, the cause must be self-defence, war must be a last resort and necessary in the sense that no other methods would work, the attack must be proportionate, and the war must have a chance of success. The legitimate preemptive use of force was strictly limited in Webster's view. Preemption is justified when resort to it is confined to a response to imminent threat, when force is necessary after attempts to dissuade the adversary from acting and non-lethal measures had failed. Webster's arguments also recall the *jus in bello* injunctions of proportionality and discrimination between combatants and non-combatants, where non-combatants are not legitimate targets. Webster specifies that the conduct of such a preemptive strike should be limited to dealing with the immediate threat and discriminate between the armed and the unarmed and the innocent and the guilty. On the other hand, while one can make a case for preemption under limited circumstances, the legal and ethical case for preventive wars – those waged to prevent unfavourable changes in the balance of power – is much weaker and most scholars want to keep firm distinctions between self-defence, preemption and preventive war.

An ostensible exception to the widespread legal and scholarly aversion to preventive war is Immanuel Kant, who allows both preemption, in cases where another state prepares its military for attack, and preventive war. Kant argues that in the state of nature 'even the mere menacing increase of power (*potentia tremenda*) of another state (through the acquisition of new territory) can be regarded as a threat, inasmuch as the mere existence of a superior power is itself injurious to a lesser, and this makes an attack on the former undoubtedly legitimate in a state of nature'.[15]

But it must always be kept in mind that Kant thought that international politics was not a simple state of nature. Rather, in *Perpetual*

Peace and the *Metaphysics of Morals*, he argues that international relations were already closer to international *society* where the rule of law and economic interchange and interdependence provide the conditions for a potential system of peace.[16] Thus, fully considered, Kant implies that resort to preventive war should be increasingly rare as international society developed. Further, conduct in war should promote international law: 'right during a war would, then, have to be the waging of war in accordance with principles that always leave open the possibility of leaving the state of nature among states (in external relation to one another) and entering a rightful condition'.[17]

Indeed, Kant's argument implies that states that have a preventive war doctrine are unjust:

> But what is an *unjust enemy* in terms of the concept of the Right of Nations, in which – as in the case in a state of nature generally – each state is a judge in its own case? It is an enemy whose publicly expressed will (whether by word or by deed) reveals a maxim by which, if it were made a universal rule, any condition of peace among nations would be impossible and, instead, a state of nature would be perpetuated.[18]

In other words, while preemption might be justified in specific and limited circumstances, a preventive war doctrine, in this view, fails to promote peace, which is a key element of the just war tradition.

JUSTIFIED PREEMPTION

Under what conditions might preemption be justified?[19] Preemptive war, even in the case of what appears to be an imminent attack, is obviously a grave step, fraught with risks and costs, and should only be undertaken if it is both prudent and morally justified. Building on Webster and just war theory, I argue that legitimate preemption could occur if four necessary conditions were met: if preemption was truly in self-defence, where the self is narrowly defined; if preemption was based on a credible fear of imminent attack; if preemption would succeed in reducing the threat, and if military force was necessary. Further, to be justified, the conduct of a preemptive action must adhere to traditional just war limits of proportionality and discrimination.

'Self' Narrowly Defined

First, the party contemplating preemption should have a narrow conception of the 'self' to be defended in circumstances of national self-defence.[20] On the face of it, the self-defence criterion seems clear. When our lives are threatened, we must be able to defend ourselves using force if necessary. But self-defence could come to have a thicker sense when our 'self' is expressed not only by mere existence, but also by our free and prosperous existence.

For example, even if a tyrant would allow us to live, but not under institutions of our own choosing, we may justly fight to free ourselves from political oppression. But how far do the rights of the self extend? What values may actors legitimately defend with military force? If someone threatens our access to food, or fuel, or shelter, can we use force? Or if they allow us access to the material goods necessary for our existence, but charge such a high price that we must make a terrible choice – between food and health care, or between mere existence and growth – are we justified in using force to secure access to a good that would enhance the self?

If economic interests and vulnerabilities are understood to be global, and when the moral and political community of democracy and human rights are defined more broadly than ever before, self-conceptions become greatly enlarged. Great powers with imperial aspirations tend to have enormously large conceptions of their interests, in line with this expansive view of the self.[21] They may or may not then think it is legitimate to use lethal force to protect or extend their expansively understood self-interests.

The US has increasingly defined its 'self' in broad terms. According to the 2001 *Quadrennial Defense Review,* the 'enduring national interests' of the United States, which are to be secured by force if necessary, include 'contributing to economic well-being', which itself includes 'vitality and productivity of the global economy', and 'access to key markets and strategic resources'.[22] Further, the goal of US strategy is to maintain 'preeminence'. As the President said at West Point, 'America has, and intends to keep, military strengths beyond challenge.'[23] The National Security Strategy also fuses ambitious political and economic goals with security: 'the U.S. national security strategy will be based on a distinctly American internationalism that reflects the fusion of our values and our national interests. The aim of this strategy is to help make the world not just safer but better.'[24] And, perhaps most strikingly, the administration claims that 'Today the distinction between domestic and foreign affairs is diminishing.'[25] If the self is defined so broadly and threats to this greater 'self' are met with military force, at what point does self-defence begin to look, at least to outside observers, like aggression? As Richard Betts argues,

> When security is defined in terms broader than protecting the near-term integrity of national sovereignty and borders, the distinction between offence and defence blurs hopelessly ... security can be as insatiable an appetite as acquisitiveness – there may never be enough buffers.[26]

A broad conception of self is not obviously legitimate and neither are the values to be defended necessarily apparent. When the self is defined expansively, too many interests become vital. Threats to those seemingly vital interests seem to abound. The policy of making war (or setting up military bases) to protect a vast network of ostensibly self-interests tends geographically to enlarge the self. Preemption is justified in cases of true self-defence: defence of homeland and citizens abroad. Preemption is not justified to protect what becomes, by virtue of an expansive definition of the self and self-defence, imperial interests or assets.

Justified Fear of Imminent Attack

Second, to justify preemption there would have to be strong evidence that war was inevitable and likely in the immediate future. Immediate threats are those which can be made manifest within hours or weeks unless action is taken to thwart an imminent attack. This requires clear intelligence showing that a potential aggressor has both the capability and intention to do harm in the near future. Capability alone is not a justification.[27] Nor is mere blustering.

As Michael Walzer argued persuasively in *Just and Unjust Wars*, simple fear cannot be the only criterion for launching a preemptive attack. Fear, already omnipresent in world politics, increases in the context of a terrorist campaign and in a world of weapons of mass destruction. Further, the nature of fear in the wake of a devastating assault may mean that a government and people will, justifiably, be vigilant. Indeed they may, out of this heightened fear, be aware of threats to the point of hypervigilance – seeing threats that are small as being large, and squashing potential threats with enormous brutality. The fearful may then overreact to threats that do not risk the territorial integrity or political independence of a state. Or the threat of 'uncertainty', may trigger preemptive attacks. In sum, if the threshold for credible fear is necessarily lower in the context of contemporary counterterror war, when terrorists have the advantage of surprise, the consequences of lowering the threshold of evidence for justified fear may be increased instability and the premature use of force. If this is the case, if simple fear justifies the assault of preemption, then preemption will have no limits since, according to the Bush administration's own arguments, we cannot always know with certainty what the other side has and where it might be located or when it might be used. And if fear of a surprise attack was once clearly justified, when and how will we know that a threat has been significantly reduced or eliminated? Thus, if fear of what others might do is the sole determinant of justified preemption, then states might preempt threats that do not exist or have ceased to exist.

If simple fear is not enough to trigger action, how much of what kind of fear justifies preemption? There is a fine balance to be struck. The threshold of evidence and warning cannot be too low, where simple apprehension that a potential adversary might be out there somewhere and may be acquiring the means to do harm, triggers the offensive use of force. This is not preemption, but paranoid aggression.

We must also avoid the tendency to exaggerate the threat and inadvertently to heighten our own fear. For example, though nuclear weapons and long-range delivery technologies are more available nowadays than in the past, they are not yet widely so. To suggest that chemical and biological weapons pose the same threat as nuclear weapons is also to exaggerate. A policy that assumes such a dangerous world exists now is, at this point, paranoid. Rather than assuming this is the present or inevitable future, we must work to make this outcome less likely by limiting access to technology and resolving the disputes and underlying tensions that lead to armaments and war. Humans must, as psychologically stressful as this is, accept some vulnerability and uncertainty. Just as terrorists and rogue states are not perfect enemies with all the advantages of the offence and no vulnerabilities, we cannot be perfectly secure from military threats. True security will not be gained by military force in any case.

On the other hand, the threshold of evidence and warning for justified fear cannot be so high that those who might be about to do harm get so far along in their preparations that they cannot be stopped or the damage limited. So what is required, assuming a substantial investment in intelligence gathering, assessment, and understanding of potential advisories, is a policy that both maximises our understanding of the capabilities *and* intentions of potential adversaries, and simultaneously minimises our physical vulnerability. While uncertainty about intentions, capabilities and risk can never be eliminated, it can be reduced.

Aggressive intent, coupled with a capacity to do immediate harm, is the threshold that may trigger justified preemptive attacks. We may judge aggressive intent if the answers to the following two questions are 'yes':

1. Have potential aggressors said they want to harm us in the near future? Or have they harmed us in the recent past?
2. Are potential adversaries moving their forces into a position to do significant harm?

And while it might be tempting to assume that secrecy on the part of a potential adversary is a sure sign of aggressive intentions, secrecy may simply be a desire to prepare a deterrent force that might itself be the target of a preventive offensive strike. For example, in the case of the plans for the September 11th attacks, on these criteria, which assume intelligence warning of preparations and clear evidence of aggressive intent, a preemptive strike would have meant the arrest of the hijackers of the four aircraft which were used as weapons would have been justified. If the hijackers violently resisted arrest they might have been the targets of lethal force. Or after the planes had been successfully hijacked a preemptive action would have been to shoot down the aircraft before they were used as missiles. But, prior to the September 11th attacks, taking the war to Afghanistan to attack, for instance, al-Qaeda camps or the Taliban could not have been justified preemption unless it was clear that such action could have thwarted imminent terrorist attacks.

Preemption Likely to Succeed

Third, to be justified, preemption should be likely to succeed in reducing or eliminating the threat. Specifically, there should be a high likelihood that the source of the military threat can be found and the damage that it was about to do could be greatly reduced or eliminated by a preemptive attack. If preemption is likely to fail on either of those counts it should not be undertaken. The prosecution of a successful counter-terror war is very difficult. Terrorists operatives are hard to find because they are generally few in number, mostly inactive and concealed, and tend to be co-located with civilians. Preemption may be easier against 'rogue' states simply because the preparations of governments, even for surprise attacks, tend to involve larger scale mobilisations which therefore tend to be more visible.

Military Force Required

Fourth, for military preemption to be justified, military force must be necessary. In other words, no other measures have time to work or would be likely to work to avert a devastating attack, the preparations for which are already under way. If arrest of a potential terrorist is an option, for example, then it is preferred to military strikes because military strikes can harm innocents (whose relatives and friends may then become your enemies). The requirement that military force be necessary thus puts the onus on defenders to work to resolve conflicts with potential adversaries. The threat of weapons of mass destruction and terrorism can be dealt with through other means than preventive war, although preemption may sometimes be advisable.

Conduct of Military Preemption

Once the four criteria for undertaking a justified preemptive strike are met – a limited conception of the self to be defended, knowledge of imminent threat, likelihood of success, and military necessity – the use of preemptive force should also meet *jus in bello* criteria of proportionality and discrimination. Specifically, the damage caused by the preemptive strikes should not exceed what was put at risk by the strike one was trying to preempt. For example, when the Bush administration suggests in its 2002 strategy to combat weapons of mass destruction that nuclear weapons could be used to preempt the acquisition of chemical and biological weapons, it proposes a disproportionate response.[28]

Preemptive action should also avoid killing innocents and the use of measures which harm the prospects of future peace. As Kant argued more than 200 years ago, 'it must still remain possible, even in wartime, to have some sort of trust in the attitude of the enemy, otherwise peace could not be concluded and the hostilities would turn into a war of extermination'.[29] Discrimination is extremely difficult in the case of counterterrorist preemption because terrorists do not live as regular armies do, in separate garrisons, but among civilian populations who may not even know they are there. Civilian deaths are thus both unavoidable and foreseeable even if the preemptive strike involves the use of precision guided weapons or commando raids.

Further, preemptive actions must have limited military objectives, and the preemptive action should cease when the threat is eliminated or significantly reduced. A legitimate preemptive motive does not give license to actions that go beyond reducing or eliminating an immediate threat.

THE LOGIC OF THE BUSH DOCTRINE, OR THEY (ALMOST) HIT ME FIRST

If a war is initiated when the threat is not imminent and grave, but rather undertaken against a possible future threat, then the war is preventive and hence unjust. But, as noted above, it is possible to blur the line between present and possible future threats. The Bush administration, which began laying the groundwork for a preemptive strategy that blurs the distinction between imminent and potential threats in the immediate aftermath of the September 11th attacks, argues that its strategy of military preemption against potential threats is legal, moral and prudent. Specifically, Donald Rumsfeld argued repeatedly in the fall of 2001, that the nature of war had changed and that this justified preemption. For example, he said,

> I will say this, there is no question but that the United States of America has every right, as every country does, of self-defence, and the problem with terrorism is that there is no way to defend against the terrorists at every place and every time against every conceivable

technique. Therefore, the only way to deal with the terrorist network is to take the battle to them. That is in fact what we're doing.
That is in effect self-defence of a preemptive nature.[30]

By the time of President Bush's West Point speech of June 2002, the
argument about preemption had expanded in two respects: it was no
longer an ad hoc response to threats, it had become a doctrine, and the
right to preempt had been expanded from terrorists to rogue states and
'tyrants' who seek weapons of mass destruction. In other words, the
threat was both terrorists and rogues, and the distinction between them
had collapsed. As President Bush said,

> When the spread of chemical and biological and nuclear weapons,
> along with ballistic missile technology – when that occurs, even
> weak states and small groups could attain a catastrophic power to
> strike great nations. Our enemies have declared this very intention,
> and have been caught seeking these terrible weapons. They want
> the capability to blackmail us, or to harm us, or to harm our friends
> – and we will oppose them with all our power.

Therefore, he went on, 'our security will require … a military that must
be ready to strike at a moment's notice in any dark corner of the world.
And our security will require all Americans to be forward-looking and
resolute, to be ready for preemptive action when necessary to defend
our liberty and to defend our lives.'[31]

The preemptive war logic of the Bush administration was given fuller
articulation in its *National Security Strategy* of September 2002:

> Given the goals of rogue states and terrorists, the United States can
> no longer rely on a reactive posture as we have in the past. The
> inability to deter a potential attacker, the immediacy of today's
> threats, and the magnitude of potential harm that could be caused
> by our adversaries' choice of weapons, do not permit that option.
> We cannot let our enemies strike first …
>
> For centuries, international law recognised that nations need not
> suffer an attack before they can lawfully take action to defend
> themselves against forces that present an imminent danger of
> attack. Legal scholars and international jurists often conditioned
> the legitimacy of preemption on the existence of an imminent

threat – most often a visible mobilisation of armies, navies, and air forces preparing to attack …

We must adapt the concept of imminent threat to the capabilities and objectives of today's adversaries …

The United States has long maintained the option of preemptive actions to counter sufficient threat to our national security. The greater the threat, the greater is the risk of inaction – and the more compelling is the case for taking anticipatory action to defend ourselves, even if uncertainty remains as to the time and place of the enemy's attack. To forestall or prevent such hostile acts by our adversaries, the United States will, if necessary, act preemptively.[32]

The administration has been clear that old strategies are insufficient to face the threat of terrorism. President Bush said at West Point that, 'For much of the last century, America's defense relied on the Cold War doctrines of deterrence and containment. In some cases, those strategies still apply.' The key to the administration's claim that a preemptive doctrine is necessary is their arguments that the nature of war has changed and that deterrence and containment cannot work against certain kinds of adversaries. But:

new threats also require new thinking. Deterrence – the promise of massive retaliation against nations – means nothing against shadowy terrorist networks with no nation or citizens to defend. Containment is not possible when unbalanced dictators with weapons of mass destruction can deliver those weapons on missiles or secretly provide them to terrorist allies.[33]

THE SHIFT FROM IMMINENT TO IMMANENT THREAT

The Bush administration's argument for preemption thus rests on three assumptions about the character of war in the contemporary era. First, the adversaries of the US cannot be deterred because, by their nature, they are the kinds of combatants that do not respond to deterrent threats. Implicit and sometimes explicit in this view is the belief that rational civilised states can be deterred, while irrational barbarians cannot be deterred; terrorists and rogue states only respond to force. Second, due to changes in the technology of war, these terrorists and rogue states are able to strike without warning – we won't see them mobilise – and they can deploy weapons of mass destruction. It is not possible to rely on good intelligence or warning of imminent attack; the consequences of waiting for unambiguous evidence of a grave threat can be devastating. Third, the administration assumes that there is no effective alternative besides war: neither deterrence nor law enforcement will work with sufficient reliability.

The Bush administration assumes that terrorists are capable of the sort of total war or absolute war of extremes of effort and capability described by Clausewitz in *On War*. As Clausewitz argued, if one assumes the other will act without limits, you must of course maximise your own effort: 'But the enemy will do the same; competition will again result and, in pure theory, it must again force you both to extremes.'[34] Yet, Clausewitz argued that effort and outcomes in war were necessarily limited by the realities of politics, resources and will. Clausewitz's point was to emphasise that commanders realise that their own efforts will not be without 'friction'. Clausewitz was also arguing that the opponent can never be absolutely perfect in capabilities and will: 'War never breaks out wholly unexpectedly, nor can it be spread instantaneously … Such shortcomings affect both sides alike and therefore constitute a moderating force.'[35] Thus, if we assume that the opponents are overwhelming in capacities and ratchet up our effort in response, we tend to drive the preparations and the conflict toward extremes.

The reasoning of the Bush administration is thus a serious challenge to the distinction between preemption and preventive war because it collapses the crucial distinctions between imminent and immanent threat. If a grave threat is immanent – always present – then preemption is always justified and the distinction between preemption and preventive war is essentially erased. If the administration is right that the nature of war has changed, then perhaps a doctrine that in effect erases the distinction between preemption and preventive war is justified. As Michael Walzer recently noted,

> the old argument … did not take into account weapons of mass destruction or delivery systems that allow no time for arguments about how to respond. Perhaps the gulf between preemption and prevention has now narrowed so that there is little strategic (and therefore little moral) difference between them.[36]

While Walzer and others have correctly argued against the US war in

Iraq on the grounds that it was not a preemptive strike made in last resort against an imminent threat, the challenge posed by the changing nature of war that the Bush administration has identified has not yet been fully addressed.

But the argument for a preventive war doctrine (or a preemption doctrine that is a de facto preventive war doctrine) must still be rejected, even in contemporary circumstances, because the logic of preventive war undermines the limits that help maintain the already precarious limits to war. Preventive war doctrines can lead to limitless war-making under the ever-expanding logic of prevention. Under the assumption of an environment of immanent threat, self-defence requires immediate and constant action to reduce the omnipresent threat. If the interests of the self are defined broadly, and in the case of the Bush administration, in global terms, then the self is potentially under threat everywhere. If 'rogue' states are serial aggressors, who cannot be deterred or negotiated with, then regime change is the only logical option. The distinctions between imminent and immanent, actual present and possible future, war and peace, self and other, combatant and non-combatant, thus blur to the point of collapse. The state with a preventive war doctrine thus has no way to limit its wars of 'preventive' self-defence: potential future threats are many and grave and must, if possible, be eliminated.

CRITICISMS OF PREEMPTIVE AND PREVENTIVE WAR DOCTRINES

Of course the Bush administration's preemptive war doctrine has not been without its critics. Testifying before Congress, Michael O'Hanlon of the Brookings Institution criticised the preemptive war doctrine of the US by arguing that it created problems not just for international stability but also for the ability of the United States to achieve its political and military objectives. O'Hanlon's critique is thus based on an argument of self-interest and expediency: the Bush doctrine undermines US policy goals.

Elevating the preemptive option to a policy doctrine can have serious negative consequences. For one, it reinforces the image of the United States as too quick to use military force and to do so outside the bounds of international law and legitimacy. This can make it more difficult for the United States to gain international support for its use of force, and over the long term, may lead others to resist U.S. foreign policy goals more broadly, including efforts to fight terrorism. Elevating preemption to the level of a formal doctrine may also increase the administration's inclination to reach for the military lever quickly, when other tools still have a good chance of working ...

Advocating preemption warns potential enemies to hide the very assets we might wish to take preemptive action against, or to otherwise prepare responses and defences. In this tactical sense, talking too openly about preemption reduces its likely utility, if and when it is employed. Finally, advocating preemption may well embolden other countries that would like to justify attacks on their enemies as preemptive in nature.[37]

But the problems with a preemptive/preventive doctrine go beyond the fact that it is potentially counterproductive to the interests of the state that holds it. International lawyers and scholars of international security point out the general problems of preemption and preventive war doctrines. In late 2004, UN Secretary General Kofi Annan argued that the Iraq war, in particular, was illegal. But a year before, the Secretary General criticised the preemption doctrine itself at the opening of the UN General Assembly by pointing out that unless authorised by the UN Security Council, a doctrine of preemption can create international instability. The first element of Annan's argument was a brief for the legitimising function of the UN itself:

> Since this organisation was founded, States have generally sought to deal with threats to the peace through containment and deterrence, by a system based on collective security and the United Nations Charter. Article 51 of the Charter prescribes that all States, if attacked, retain the inherent right of self-defence. But until now it has been understood that when States go beyond that, and decide to use force to deal with broader threats to international peace and security, they need the unique legitimacy provided by the United Nations.

Yet, Annan's most important criticism was more fundamental and shows a clear appreciation of the challenge that the Bush doctrine poses to the distinction between preemption and preventive war:

Now, some say this understanding is no longer tenable, since an 'armed attack with weapons of mass destruction could be launched at any time, without warning, or by a clandestine group. Rather than wait for that to happen, they argue, States have the right and obligation to use force preemptively, even on the territory of other States, and even while weapons systems that might be used to attack them are still being developed. According to this argument, States are not obliged to wait until there is agreement in the Security Council. Instead, they reserve the right to act unilaterally, or in ad hoc coalitions. This logic represents a fundamental challenge to the principles on which, however imperfectly, world peace and stability have rested for the last fifty-eight years. My concern is that, if it were to be adopted, it could set precedents that resulted in a proliferation of the unilateral and lawless use of force, with or without justification.[38]

In sum, Annan's criticism is that a preventive war doctrine undermines international law and diplomacy. It short-circuits non-military means of solving problems, because it ignores the just war requirement of last resort. If all states reacted to potential adversaries as if they faced a clear and present danger of imminent attack, tensions would escalate along already tense borders and regions.

ARE PREVENTIVE WARS JUSTIFIED?

Despite these criticisms, is the Bush administration right to extend the logic of justified preemption as authority for preventive offensive wars? If *all* threats are immediate and grave, then the answer is yes. But although the threat of use of weapons of mass destruction with little or no warning has transformed war, not all threats are immediate. And even if the world were so dangerous, the dangers of a preventive war doctrine, as Annan suggests, are likely to outweigh the ostensible benefits of a preventive war.

Specifically, while the threat posed by terrorism is significant, and governments must be alert to the dangers of attack, the world is not poised on the abyss of absolute destruction at the hands of terrorists. In other words, as the Bush administration argues, it is true that unconventional adversaries, prepared to wage unconventional 'asymmetric' war, can conceal their movements, weapons and immediate intentions and may conduct devastating surprise attacks.[39] It is also true that nuclear weapons, though not widely held, are more widely held than they were in the recent past. And of course, the 'everyday' infrastructure of the US or any industrial state can be turned against it as were the planes the terrorists hijacked on September 11th. Terrorists in particular are extremely flexible: unlike conventional militaries, they can project power with great efficiency since they do not have to develop weapons and delivery vehicles, they may live among their target populations, and they require comparatively little in the way of logistical support. It is also true that, although physical risk to terrorism could certainly be reduced in many ways, as Rumsfeld acknowledges, it is impossible to achieve complete invulnerability. Though the US was open to serious threats in the past, Americans are perhaps more emotionally aware of that exposure today since, as Condoleezza Rice says, '9/11 crystallised our vulnerability'.[40] When combined with the advantage of surprise, terrorism is a formidable military strategy which costs many times more to defend against than it costs terrorists to conduct.

On the other hand, terrorists do not hold all the cards, nor should their threat be exaggerated. For example, their sources of funding, often tied to illicit transactions and black market economies, are vulnerable to disruption through determined law enforcement. And while terrorists can piggy-back on the infrastructure of their targets, they are also vulnerable to detection via that same infrastructure as they use phones, faxes, the internet and other electronic media. Finally, although there are far too many leaks in the containment of technologies for weapons of mass destruction, many of those weapons are still relatively expensive to acquire and difficult to produce in any quantity. Nuclear weapons material can still be secured if sufficient resources are devoted to the task.

Those who argue for the preemptive/preventive war doctrine assume that even if terrorists do not, for example, have nuclear weapons capabilities now, they might soon get them. However, much more important than capabilities that 'might' be employed by someone, are the intentions of a likely adversary. In other words, the character of potential threats becomes extremely important in evaluating the legitimacy of the administration's new doctrine and thus the assertion that the US faces rogue enemies who 'hate everything' about it must be carefully evaluated. While there is certainly strong evidence that al-Qaeda members desire to harm the US and American citizens, the national security strategy makes a questionable leap when it assumes that 'rogue states' also desire to harm the US and pose an imminent military threat. Moreover, the administration blurs the distinction between 'rogue states' and terrorists and essentially erases the difference between terrorists and those states where they reside: 'We make no distinction between terrorists and those who knowingly harbor or provide aid to them.'[41] But these distinctions make a difference.

The advocates of preventive war fail to grasp how a preventive war doctrine undermines the limits that underpin restraint in world politics. First, while a preventive war doctrine tends to move not only time horizons forward – acting before the other can get the capacity to act – it also moves 'borders' out away from the homeland as the fight is taken abroad. As President Bush said at West Point:

> We must take the battle to the enemy, disrupt his plans and confront the worst threats before they emerge ... Our security will require ... a military that must be ready to strike at a moment's notice in any dark corner of the world. And our security will require all Americans to be forward-looking and resolute, to be ready for preemptive action when necessary to defend our liberty and to defend our lives.[42]

Indeed, since September 11th and the Bush administration's gradual articulation of the preemptive/preventive offensive war doctrine, the US has sent troops to fight terrorists not only in Afghanistan but in the Philippines, Yemen, Indonesia and former Soviet Georgia and, of course, has invaded Iraq. The self to be defended thus expands spatially with the need to provide force protection for these forward-deployed elements of the preventive war state.

A preventive offensive doctrine thus entails an expanding list of force deployments, 'commitments', which might spread military forces thin while at the same time risking escalating military conflicts and becoming imperial in appearance if not aspiration. Such uses of force, while seemingly necessary in an atmosphere of perceived heightened vulnerability, may at best be unnecessary. At worst the state engaged in preventive wars risks a backlash fuelled by fear and resentment, not least because discrimination between combatants and non-combatants is difficult in preventive war and any wars of occupation that follow.

Further, preventive war doctrines make it impossible to adhere to just war criteria of necessity, last resort, proportionality and discrimination. Because preventive doctrines assume that today's potential rival will certainly become tomorrow's adversary, it weakens diplomacy and ignores the possibility that some other factor (such as a change in economic power or the growth of empathetic relations between peoples) could work to change the relationship from antagonism to accommodation. As Bismarck said in 1875, 'I would ... never advise Your Majesty to declare war forthwith, simply because it appeared that our opponent would begin hostilities in the near future. One can never anticipate the ways of divine providence securely enough for that.'[43] Indeed, because they have not yet made an aggressive act, nearly all those killed or injured by a preventive war will be non-combatants. The distinction between combatants and non-combatants is thus eroded conceptually, as those who might harm us are seen as 'legitimate' targets, and practically, as preventive wars inevitably kill civilians who happen to live, work, or worship near potential combatants.

In sum, by the logic of preventive war doctrines, as Annan argues, the strategy undermines the concepts and distinctions that buttress the stability of the international system. Further, the important distinction between war and peace itself is eroded as preventive war logic promotes a constant state of mobilisation and justification for war. The preventive war tends to expand the occasions for the use of preventive force: the preventive logic may justify embargoes, assassinations (so-called targeted killings), torture, and indefinite detention of prisoners of war and 'unlawful combatants' on the grounds that others might someday become a threat and we must do all we can to thwart their potential.

THE IMPRUDENCE OF PREEMPTIVE AND PREVENTIVE WAR DOCTRINES

Foreign policies are not only judged on grounds of legality and morality, but also on grounds of prudence. Preemption is only prudent if it is limited to clear and immediate dangers and if there are constraints on its conduct – proportionality, discrimination and limited aims. If preemption becomes a regular practice or if it becomes the cover for a preventive offensive war doctrine, then it may become self-defeating as it increases instability and insecurity.

Specifically, a legitimate preemptive war requires that states identify that the potential aggressors have the capability *and* the intention of doing great harm. However, while capability may not be in dispute, the motives and intentions of a potential adversary may be misinterpreted. States may mobilise in what appear to be aggressive ways because they are fearful or because they are aggressive. Some states may defensively arm because they are afraid of the 'preemptive/preventive' state; others may arm offensively because they resent the preventive war aggressor who may have killed many innocents in their quest for total security. A preemptive doctrine which has – because of great fear and a desire to control the international environment – become a preventive war doctrine, is likely to create more of both fearful and aggressor states. In either case, instability is likely to grow as a preventive war creates the mutual fear of surprise attack. In the case of the US preemptive/preventive war doctrine, instability is more likely to increase because the preventive war doctrine is coupled with America's goal of maintaining global preeminence and where the US has said it will discourage any military rivals from challenging its 'preeminence'.[44]

One can understand why any administration would favour preemption and why some would be attracted to preventive wars if they believe preventive war could guarantee security from future attack. But the psychological reassurance promised by a preventive offensive war doctrine is at best illusory, and at worst, preventive war is counterproductive. Preventive wars are imprudent, because they bring wars that might not otherwise happen and increase resentment. They are also unjust because they assume, as Bismarck said, perfect knowledge of an adversary's ill intentions when such a presumption of guilt may be premature or false. But the most dangerous aspect of preventive war doctrines is the world it makes through its own assumptions and the logic of insecurity. The limits and distinctions that provide the possibility for peace – distinctions between war and peace, between actual and potential threat, between combatant and non-combatant, and between narrowly defined self-defence and an expansive notion of self – are undermined and eroded by a preventive war doctrine. By assuming a world of immanent threat, of limitless war, preventive war doctrines create a state of nature more thoroughly than has ever existed in history.

Preemption can be justified if it is undertaken under immediate threat, where there is no time for diplomacy to be attempted, and where the preemptive action is limited to reducing the immediate threat. There is a great temptation, however, to slide over the line from preemption to preventive war, because that line can be vague in the world of asymmetric war and weapons of mass destruction and because the stress of living under the threat of terrorist attack or war is great. But the temptation of preventive war should be avoided. The stress of living in fear should be assuaged by true prevention: arms control, disarmament, negotiations, confidence-building measures, and the development of international law.[45]

NOTES

1. Walzer (1992), p. 85.
2. Ibid., p. 81.
3. Ibid., pp. 74–85.
4. Ibid., p. 75.
5. Bush (2002).
6. National Security Council (2002), p. 15.
7. Rice (2002).
8. Betts (2003), p. 18.
9. Kegley and Raymond (2003), p. 389.
10. See Clausewitz (1976), Book One.
11. See Walzer (1992), pp. 82–5; Betts (2003), pp. 19–20.
12. Quoted in Sanger (2002).
13. Henry S. Fox, British Ambassador to the United States, in a letter to Daniel Webster, 12 March 1841, in Shewmaker (1983), p. 42.
14. Webster in a letter to Fox, 24 April 1841, in ibid., pp. 62, 67–8.
15. Kant [1780] (1999).
16. Kant (1991a), pp. 93–130.
17. Kant [1785] (1991b), p. 153.
18. Ibid., p. 155.
19. The discussion in this section is based on Crawford (2003a).
20. For an interesting discussion of the analogy between individual self-defence and national defence, see Rodin (2002). Rodin does not agree that the analogy is useful.
21. Perhaps this formulation should be written another way: those states with all-encompassing conceptions of themselves and their rightful place in the world tend to have correspondingly large conceptions of their 'interests' and a possessive view of how those interests are to be secured.
22. United States Department of Defense (2001), p. 2.
23. Ibid., pp. 30, 62; Bush (2002).
24. National Security Council (2002), p. 1.
25. Ibid., p. 31.
26. Betts (1982), pp. 142–3.

27. Yet current US military doctrine is to defend against potential and actual military capabilities, not against likely threats.
28. See the 'National Strategy to Combat Weapons of Mass Destruction', December 2002, http://www.whitehouse.gov/news/releases/2002/12/WMDStrategy. pdf.
29. Kant (1991a), p. 96.
30. From remarks at a stakeout outside the ABC TV Studio 28 October 2001, at www.defenselink.mil/news/Oct2001/t10292001_t1028sd3.html.
31. Bush (2002).
32. National Security Council (2002), p. 15.
33. Bush (2002).
34. Clausewitz (1976), p. 77.
35. Ibid., p. 78.
36. Walzer (2004), p. 147.
37. O'Hanlon (2003).
38. Address to the United Nations General Assembly, 23 September 2003.
39. I spell out the nature of this transformation in Crawford (2003b). See also Betts (2002).
40. Rice (2002).
41. National Security Council (2002), p. 5.
42. Bush (2002).
43. Bismarck, quoted in Craig (1955), p. 255.
44. United States Department of Defense, pp. 30, 62.
45. I thank participants in the 2003 conference on 'Just War Theory Reappraised' (Department of Politics and International Relations, University of Wales Swansea) for their comments. I thank Toni Erskine and Tony Lang for their comments on a later draft. I also benefited from conversations with Henry Shue.

Chapter 2

PUNITIVE INTERVENTION: ENFORCING JUSTICE OR GENERATING CONFLICT?

ANTHONY F. LANG JR

Humanitarian intervention, while controversial, has become more acceptable as a reason for using military force in the last twenty years. But humanitarian intervention may be giving way to a related, yet distinct, form of intervention. This new form of intervention is characterised by a desire to punish wrongdoers, whether they are individual leaders or whole states, a phenomenon I call *punitive intervention*. Punitive intervention can be defined as the use of military force across national boundaries to alter the internal affairs of a state that has violated inter-national law or other widely recognised international norms. A punitive intervention aims to deter future violations, to rehabilitate the offending state (usually by replacing its government), or to exact retribution.

US interventions in Panama (1989), Haiti (1994) and Somalia, especially to capture Mohammed Farah Aideed (1993), could be called punitive, as could the use of air power in Libya (1986) and Iraq (1993, 1998). The ongoing Russian intervention in Chechnya has a punitive dimension. The belated French intervention in Rwanda (1994) had punitive aspects. The NATO intervention in the former Yugoslavia has generated debate over whether or not the major powers should be in the business of capturing war criminals. The use of coercive air power by NATO against Serbia in 1999 sought to halt the violations of Albanian human rights but also to punish those responsible, particularly Slobodan Milosevic. The Israeli incursions into Lebanon (1982, 1996), like its campaigns since 2000 in the occupied territories, were partly designed to punish those who threaten Israeli security. The calls for intervention in Liberia in 2003 were in part humanitarian, but there was also an underlying desire to capture and punish President Charles

Taylor. Finally, the US interventions in Afghanistan and Iraq following the attacks of 11 September 2001 have been couched largely in terms of punishing the states that allowed terrorists to operate on their territory and capturing those directly responsible. Indeed, the war on terrorism, which the Bush administration argues will be a long-term conflict, is punitive as well as preventive.

This use of military force to punish reflects an important normative shift in the international system. International law prohibits the use of force to punish; indeed, the concept of punishment is largely absent from international law. The UN Charter allows for the use of force only in self-defence, or when the Security Council authorises it to protect 'international peace and security'. This latter reason might suggest a punitive justification, but in the most recent Security Council authorisation of a full-scale war – the 1991 Gulf War – the purpose of the use of force was not to punish Iraq but to force it to leave Kuwait.

While the use of military force to punish appears to be gaining normative legitimacy, in this chapter I focus on a particular type of military action: intervention in the territory of a sovereign state. Punitive interventions are not entirely new, especially for the US; its 1916 intervention in Mexico was designed to capture and punish Pancho Villa for his raid into the US.[1] But the recent resurgence in calls for punishing terrorists, dictators and other violators of human rights suggests a shift in the normative structure of the international system. Three questions suggest themselves:

1. Is there in fact a normative change in the use of force, one that is more oriented toward punishment?
2. What explains this shift in the normative structure of the international system?
3. How should this shift be evaluated?

The two traditional standards by which to evaluate international affairs are peace and justice. The debate about punishment arises at the intersection of these criteria because, although the use of force to punish might advance the cause of justice, it is also a source of conflict that can undermine the search for peace. I explore this dilemma below.

This chapter will focus on the third question, using the just war tradition to evaluate what I believe to be a shift in the international normative structure of the system, although in so doing I will also provide some evidence in response to the other questions. The just war tradition is useful in evaluating this new normative structure for a number of reasons. First, it does not disavow the use of military force, as does pacifism, but allows for it in certain specific situations. The tradition can therefore be used to evaluate different uses of force according to general criteria. Second, it pays attention both to the consequences of using force and to the norms governing that use. Third, using war to punish is actually part of the classical idea of the just war as articulated by Augustine, Aquinas and Grotius.

But the just war tradition is not only about finding a just cause. It includes other criteria, such as comparative justice[2] and proper authority. When considered in terms of these other criteria, the just war tradition leads one to the conclusion that using military force to punish fails to conform to generally accepted principles of conduct in warfare. I conclude that the just war tradition not only gives us an important tool to evaluate the use of force to punish; it also helps to explain some of the consequences of using force in this way, particularly the negative reactions from many around the world when such actions are undertaken by the United States.

Moreover, focusing on punishment allows us critically to examine the function of the just war tradition in public discourse. When invoked by political leaders, especially in the United States during the past twenty years, the tradition has invariably been boiled down to two primary elements: identifying a just cause and avoiding the targeting of civilians. It seems to be assumed that if one meets these criteria, one can use force punitively. In fact, however, the idea of punishment highlights the importance of other just war criteria, in particular legitimate authority and comparative justice. The rise of punitive intervention lays bare how American political leaders have distorted the just war tradition and reminds us of the importance of taking the full tradition into account when evaluating the use of force.

The chapter proceeds as follows. The next section describes the concept of punishment generally and then provides a brief overview as to how punishment can be seen as a norm motivating recent military interventions. Following this, I evaluate punishment from the standpoint of international law and the just war tradition. I find that it is both illegal according to international law and problematic within the framework of just war thinking. Punitive intervention may conform to certain just war criteria, but it fails to fulfil others, rendering it highly suspect as a tool for creating justice and order in the international system. I also suggest how a critical analysis of punitive intervention can help us to see the just war tradition as a coherent system of principles, and not – as so often appears – as a set of disconnected precepts to be applied selectively to rationalise the use of force. I conclude with some suggestions as to how we might counter this urge to punish with military force yet continue to seek enforcement of human rights norms.

PUNISHMENT

A punishment, in the sense relevant to this chapter, is a penalty imposed by a state, according to its judicial procedures, on someone who has violated the criminal law. Its moral basis can be found in three ideas: deterrence, retribution and rehabilitation. Deterrence is the idea that by punishing criminals, the authorities can deter future violations. It can be either specific or general. If it is specific, it is an attempt to deter a particular criminal from violating the same law again. If it is general, it is an attempt to deter others from violating the law by using the individual case as an example. Punishment premised on deterrence is unconcerned with the welfare or character of the criminal. Instead, the practice aims simply to alter his behaviour and to demonstrate a larger point to the community. Deterrence can be evaluated in terms of whether or not the same crimes continue to occur. If they do, the deterrence approach may not be working; if they do not, one would have a reason, though not a conclusive one, for thinking that deterrence does work.

A rehabilitative theory of punishment seeks to change the moral character of the criminal. While a deterrent effect may result from this approach, the primary focus is on making the person more law-abiding. Unlike a deterrent approach, however, a rehabilitative approach to punishment provides means by which the criminal can change his behaviour not as a result of fear but through a genuine change in attitude. The evaluation of this form of punishment is similar to specific deterrence; its success depends on whether that individual criminal commits further crimes. More importantly – and it is difficult see how this could be observed – the criminal would have to refrain from crime because he believed crime was wrong and not because of a fear of getting caught.[3]

Retribution as the moral idea underlying punishment is more difficult to capture. It is, perhaps, the most common-sense notion of punishment. As one author suggests, it is the 'idea that wrongdoers should be "paid back" for their wicked deeds'.[4] This idea seeks to restore a sense of balance to a community by punishing wrongdoers. It differs from deterrence in not seeking to use the criminal to teach a larger lesson. It differs from rehabilitation in not seeking to change the character of the criminal. An underlying principle of retributive punishment is justice; that is, retribution seeks to create a system in which there exists a fair distribution of security in a society. Ironically, retributive punishment respects the moral autonomy of the criminal more than does punishment aimed at deterrence or rehabilitation. Retribution assumes that the criminal is not a tool to be used to teach society a lesson (deterrence), nor that the criminal is a pliant entity that can be coercively shaped into a new person (rehabilitation); instead, a criminal is someone presumed to be morally autonomous and therefore responsible for his or her actions. This is one reason that Kant held retribution to be the only justifiable reason for punishment.[5]

These three ideas underlie most forms of punishment in domestic legal systems. It is probably the case that most legal systems incorporate all three purposes, though different systems weigh them differently. Highlighting their distinctive features allows us to see punishment where we might not otherwise notice it – such as in the use of military force.

INTERVENTION AS PUNISHMENT

What evidence do we have that military intervention has become a form of punishment in the twenty-first century? The two uses of military force by the United States in recent years – in Afghanistan and Iraq – provide the clearest evidence for this new model. Before laying this out, however, a brief review of the past few decades suggests that the trend toward punitive military action has been growing.

The following examples cover a wide range of military actions, from bombing campaigns to fully-fledged military interventions. In none of these cases have US policy-makers explicitly invoked punishment as the reason for using military force. This does not necessarily undermine the point I am making, however. Any state using military force will have a number of intentions or motives. The use of force can be simultaneously punitive and defensive. In all the cases I will suggest, a punitive element exists, although it may not be the primary element. Some of these uses of force might be called reprisals, a legal term defined as 'an act of self-help on the part of an injured state, an act corresponding after an unsatisfied demand to an act contrary to the law of nations on the part of the offending state'.[6] Strictly speaking, a reprisal must aim at forcing that state to comply with international law. But the term is also used more broadly to cover actions that are thought to be justified merely on retributive grounds – that is, as acts of vengeance aimed not at reinforcing an underlying law or norm but simply at striking back against one who has acted in a hostile way. I wish to distinguish punitive reprisals from acts of vengeance and, before turning to humanitarian intervention, to explore a wider range of cases in which there is a punitive element because force was used to instantiate a larger norm. Two such cases are the Reagan administration's bombing of Libya and the Clinton administration's strikes against Sudan and Afghanistan in 1998.

The Reagan administration used military force to punish Libya for its support of terrorism with a bombing raid in 1986. Framing the attack as a response to terrorism, it specifically targeted the Libyan regime in a clearly punitive action.[7] In 1989, the first Bush administration used military force to arrest and then punish Manuel Noriega. This attack was framed as a response to Noriega's support for drug trafficking, part of a larger US effort to punish those in this business. The other reason suggested, that the regime was harming US soldiers protecting the Canal, also suggests a punitive purpose behind this intervention.

The Clinton administration began to frame the debate about the use of force in a mildly punitive way by articulating a national security doctrine focused on combating 'rogue states'. To articulate foreign and defence policy in this way is to suggest that those against whom force is used are criminals who deserve punishment.[8] One of its first uses of military force – the bombing of the Iraqi intelligence services in 1993 in response to an attempt to assassinate the first President George Bush – embodied a punitive ethos. Cruise missile strikes against Sudan and Afghanistan in 1998 were explicitly framed as responses to the terrorist attacks on US embassies in Kenya and Tanzania – further examples of punishment. The NATO-led attack against the former Yugoslavia in 1999 to force compliance with human rights norms in Kosovo was a combination of coercive diplomacy and punishment. In a speech in Chicago in April 1999, British Prime Minister Tony Blair defended the attacks in terms that could be interpreted as manifesting a deterrent approach to punishment:

> This is a just war, based not on any territorial ambitions but on values. We cannot let the evil of ethnic cleansing stand. We must not rest until it is reversed. We have learned twice before in this century that appeasement does not work. If we let an evil dictator range unchallenged, we will have to spill infinitely more blood and treasure to stop him later.[9]

This brings us to the current campaigns against Afghanistan and Iraq. On one level, these two military actions are unique, since they come in response to an attack on the United States. But that attack and the American response falls into a pattern that has developed over the last few years: disgruntled terrorists strike at the United States or its allies, leading to a punitive military action. Interestingly, those punitive military actions embody all three elements of punishment: deterrence, rehabilitation and retribution.

American actions in Afghanistan, while certainly an attempt to eliminate al-Qaeda, and thus a form of self-defence, took on a punitive character as the desire to avenge the attacks of September 11th filtered through not only popular culture but the military as well (as evidenced by US soldiers there carrying American flags that were found at 'ground zero' in New York City). The intervention in Afghanistan sought to punish not only al-Qaeda but also the Taliban as well, a regime that did not itself threaten America in any way. The only reason for using such force against it was to punish it for assisting terrorists.

All three elements of punishment are evident in this attack. First, the administration explicitly stated that this action should be seen as a warning – a deterrent – to those states that believe harbouring terrorists is a legitimate policy. Although perhaps speaking to Iraq, the use of deterrent language to justify the bombing of Afghanistan was un-doubtedly meant to apply more broadly.

Rehabilitation is a bit harder to locate here. One might argue that uses of military force aimed at changing the internal governance of the target state, are forms of rehabilitation; that is, in such cases military power is used to punish a state for certain actions and, in the process, change the 'character' of that state. The quick turn toward reforming Afghanistan's government suggests that there might be a rehabilitation model at work in the intervention there. On the other hand, there seems to be no inclination to rehabilitate al-Qaeda as an organisation or its individual members. One might argue, though, that some in the Bush administration aspired to 'rehabilitate' Islam by turning it away from the kind of radicalism on which al-Qaeda draws.

Finally, retribution in the Afghanistan case may be difficult to identify, but it does exist. A retributive approach to the use of military force would need to be disconnected from any specific outcome: it would be the use of military force simply to hit back at a state that had undertaken (or supported) armed aggression. The military campaign against the Taliban and, especially, al-Qaeda can be interpreted as a form of retribution – that is, as an effort to rectify the injustice of the September 11th attacks conducted by al-Qaeda and supported by the Taliban.

Can these three punitive objectives be seen in the military campaign against Iraq? First, in terms of deterrence, the action against Iraq might seem to be a unique case, one that will end here. But there appeared to be an internal debate in the Bush administration as to whether or not this action should be seen as deterring other 'rogue states' or was wholly concerned with Iraq alone. Secretary of State Colin Powell seemed to argue the latter case, that once the campaign against Iraq was finished, the war against states supporting terrorism would be over. Secretary of Defense Donald Rumsfeld, in contrast, seemed to believe that the Iraq war was a lesson to others, such as North Korea, warning them to avoid challenging the United States. Furthermore, the war in Iraq was to serve not only as a deterrent to other rogue states but as an incentive to other Middle Eastern states to become democratic. For all these reasons, it would appear that the Bush Administration saw the war as part of a strategy of deterring Islamic radicals from attacking the United States or American allies and interests elsewhere in the world.

The rehabilitative aspects of the war in Iraq are also evidenced by the change of regime. In this case, one could argue that attacking Iraq was conceived by the US government as punishment for its continued violations of UN resolutions concerning its weapons of mass destruction. (I leave aside here the issue of whether the US had the authority to do this and therefore whether its war on Iraq can qualify as punishment in the strict sense of a properly authorised use of coercive force against a criminal.) Rather than punish the state in the hope of deterring future actions, the United States decided that the regime could not be deterred but needed to be replaced. Since its aim was regime change, then, one might argue that the war against Iraq was a form of rehabilitation.

Finally, retribution is also evident in the war against Iraq. Some have condemned the war as motivated by misplaced revenge for September 11th. Leaving revenge aside, however, we might find evidence of retribution for Iraq's failure to comply with UN demands to permit open inspection of its capacity to produce weapons of mass destruction.

In this admittedly brief list of punitive military actions, distinctions need to be made between war, intervention and coercive diplomacy. Only in Panama, Afghanistan and Iraq has a traditional intervention been evident; that is, the use of ground troops that cross sovereign borders to change a political system. The other cases are more accurately categorised as coercive diplomacy (Libya, Serbia, Iraq in 1993 and 1998). Some have argued that interventions can include the use of air power alone, especially if that air power is designed to force radical changes in the target state.[10] Punitive intervention is one manifestation of a larger scale change in the international system: the growth of punishment as a legitimate normative purpose for the use of military force.

So, it would appear that in the past twenty years, intervention has evolved, at least in some cases, to be at least sometimes a form of punishment. But should it be so? Will this development strengthen the international system?

INTERNATIONAL LAW AND PUNISHMENT

To evaluate the concept of punitive intervention, let me turn to two traditions of normative international thought: international law and the just war tradition. We can use these traditions to ascertain whether the growth of punitive intervention has improved the prospects for peace and justice in the international system.

According to international law, any use of armed force by one state to punish another is illegal.[11] Upon examination, however, international law is seen to contain little about punishment as an explicit concept. In fact, in one place where punishment was explicitly discussed, in the drafting of articles on state responsibility, the concept was rejected. In the recent International Law Commission (ILC) draft of Articles on Responsibility of States for Internationally Wrongful Acts, the drafters rejected proposed rules providing punitive measures against states that violate their obligations under international law. Such violations should result not in punishment but in 'reparations'. An earlier version of the articles had included (in Article 19) the term 'crime' to describe a breach of the law. The drafting committee removed this reference after pressure from various member states. In effect, then, the concept of reparations and countermeasures moves the idea of state responsibility away from the sphere of criminal law to that of civil law. Moreover, the rejected draft that referred to crimes did not mention the use of military force to enforce compliance with the law or to punish criminal states.[12]

In the law governing the use of military force, such actions are allowed only in two cases: (1) if necessary for self-defence and (2) if authorised by the Security Council to 'enforce peace and security'. Punishment is not self-defence as self-defence is defined by international law. Self-defence is military action in response to an attack by another state and aimed at thwarting that attack. So, self-defence is not punishment.

Security Council-authorised uses of force, however, might include cases in which the force authorised was punitive. If enforcing peace and security means creating the conditions in which attacks are kept to a minimum, punishment of those who violate that norm might be a means to the end of keeping a peaceful and secure system. At the same time, because international law is reluctant to embrace punishments, Security Council actions are more like those of a police officer than those of a court. Police officers do not punish: they stop crimes in action and seek to keep the peace by being continually vigilant. They also bring those suspected of crimes before a court that can then punish those crimes, but their primary job is not punishment. In the same way, the Security Council is in the business of law enforcement, not punishment.

JUST WAR AND PUNISHMENT

According to international law, then, military force cannot be used to punish. But international law is not the only source of standards by which to evaluate the use of force. The just war tradition, which helped create international law, does provide some support for those who argue that force may justly be used to punish states that violate its standards.

Punishment as a Just Cause

In the just war tradition, punishment is one of the three classic just
causes: defence against attack, retaking what has been unjustly taken,
and punishment of wrongdoing. James Turner Johnson notes that
although modern international law has narrowed the just causes of war
to one, self-defence, the just war tradition has historically envisaged
other justified uses of military force:

> A retaliatory second strike, for example, would classically have
> been called 'punishment of evil;' today it is categorised as 'defense'
> ... So the underlying ideas remain, though the vocabulary has
> changed to reflect twentieth-century sentiment that first use of
> force in a developing country is morally suspect, while second use
> is not.[13]

Moreover, punishment fits the classic model of the just war tradition,
which was to create a *tranquillitas ordinis*, or state of ordered peace. This
can only happen if those who violate the public order are punished so
that the injuries they have inflicted on the community are redressed.
Both Augustine and Aquinas addressed the topic of war in a political
context of potential anarchy brought on by brigands. They saw the use
of force as a means to ensure justice in a world where it was often
frighteningly absent. Punishing those who violate those norms is central
to the defence of the political order.

The idea of punishment continued to inform thinking about the use
of force. Hugo Grotius, who influentially stated new principles of war
during the formative period of the modern states system, argued that
punishment could have a role to play in that system.[14] In *The Law of War
and Peace*, he offers a philosophical defence of punishment against the
view that a Christian cannot support it in light of Jesus' admonitions to
forgive. Turning from this general defence, he asks whether one king
can punish the subjects of another for violating natural law and not
simply for crimes against them or their own subjects. He argues that
kings can punish in response to violations of natural law, that is, in
situations where the king or state is not directly affected by a criminal
action. A king can rightly use force to punish those who are not his own
charge, but to defend the general peace and tranquility of international
society.[15]

This argument parallels almost exactly those made by the Bush administration for its wars in Afghanistan and Iraq. Jean Bethke Elshtain agrees that punishment is a justified reason for using force, especially in response to the attacks of September 11th: 'examining the evidence, we can see that the US military response in Afghanistan clearly meets the just cause criterion of being a war fought with the right intention – to punish wrongdoers and to prevent them from murdering civilians in the future'.[16] The Bush administration defended its use of force in both Afghanistan and Iraq as self-defence, but the appeal of these military actions for much of the American public lies in punishing those who harmed Americans.

Others argue that punishment can no longer serve as a just cause. The US Catholic Bishops stated in their 1983 letter on nuclear weapons that war is permissible only to confront a 'real and certain danger' – that is, to protect innocent life, to preserve the conditions necessary for decent human existence, and to secure basic human rights. As both Pope Pius XII and Pope John XXIII made clear, if war of retribution was ever justifiable, the risks of modern war negate such a claim today.[17] While retribution is not the same as punishment, the overlap between the two concepts is close enough to indicate that the Catholic Church condones the use of force only for much more limited reasons which do not conform completely to the classical tradition. Others have reiterated this position on what legitimates a just cause, emphasising that the just war tradition has a 'presumption against war', rather than a focus on enforcing justice. Some hold that a foundation of modern just war thinking is that it embodies a 'presumption against the use of force' and that just war criteria are 'impediments to which exceptions might be made in a specific case'.[18] Joseph Boyle argues that the Catholic Church's recent move to restrict just cause to defence is a 'genuine development of traditional just war doctrine'.[19] Others contend that this modern Catholic thinking has distorted the tradition by focusing on peace rather than justice.[20]

Punishment, then, does appear to be at least potentially a just cause. Although the challenge offered by Boyle that punishment can no longer play a role in the justification of force must be taken seriously, the hegemonic power of the United States and new threats from terrorists would suggest that punishment might at some point again become relevant as a just cause. So we can ask: should punishment again become a legitimate reason for using force? If just cause were the only criterion of just war, one could easily be led to this conclusion. But, the tradition includes reflection on more than the cause for using force. Indeed, the just war tradition speaks powerfully to questions of war and peace precisely because it does not rest solely on determining whether a cause is just. Even within the *jus ad bellum* criteria, there remain important impediments to allowing punishment to become a reason for using military force. Two in particular raise serious questions about punishment: legitimate authority and comparative justice.

Legitimate Authority

The just war tradition argues that only a legitimate authority can use military force. This focus on authority was essential in the formative period of the tradition; Augustine, who explores the use of force most explicitly in Book 19 of *The City of God*, wrote this book in the context of the breakdown of the Roman Empire. His sermons and letters were often addressed to military and political leaders who were seeking to impose order in the Northern African context of the fifth century.[21] Aquinas highlighted legitimate authority as the central criteria of the tradition, stressing the difference between *bellum* and *duellum*, the distinction between sovereign authorities waging war versus private vendettas between individuals. In the context of thirteenth-century Europe, Aquinas was also seeking to locate authority and limit the ability of non-sovereign figures to use force.

The intent of this condition is to limit the kinds of entities permitted to wage war, and to ensure that the decision to wage war is made by a legitimate authority. The difficulty, obviously, is identifying what is the sovereign authority in the current international system. According to current international law, only the UN Security Council can authorise the use of force. Even in cases where a state needs to respond in self-defence, preemptively or otherwise, the state is obligated to take its case back to the Security Council for retroactive approval. This stipulation, and the general adherence to it by most states in the post-Second World War period, suggests that the Security Council has a legitimate claim to being the proper authority.

If this is the case, then punitive intervention by states appears to violate that authority. This conclusion is based not on any statement by the Council or the international community but on a review of those interventions that the Security Council has authorised. In almost every humanitarian intervention, the state using military force has received authorisation from the Security Council: the United States in Somalia (1992), France in Rwanda (1994), Australia in East Timor (1999) and Great Britain in Sierra Leone (2000) are all cases in which the Security Council encouraged states to undertake military action on humanitarian grounds. But in cases of punitive intervention, the Security Council has not given its authorisation, and has, in fact, ruled against the use of force: the United States was able to evade Security Council control in its interventions in Panama (1989), Sudan and Afghanistan (1998), Afghanistan (2003) and Iraq (2003). The Security Council condemned other cases of punitive uses of force, such as the coercive bombing of Serbia in 1999. It would appear that the UN Security Council does not advocate punitive interventions since it has yet to approve one.

Some have argued that the Security Council is not the legitimate authority when it comes to using force, but that individual states retain this role. Indeed, the Security Council may not have a separate agency apart from the states that constitute it, in the sense that it cannot act without their consent and cooperation. Moreover, the fact that states continue to use force without authorisation by the Council suggests that the Council has not yet become an effective authority. The view – articulated by Johnson and George Weigel among others – that the UN Security Council does not have the capacity to govern the system, either de jure or de facto, does have merit, especially in the current international system where threats to security demand an immediate response. The nature of the Security Council is such that political conflicts are not necessarily resolved by its deliberations; indeed those conflicts may be exacerbated. If this is the case, the hope that the Council will be able to authorise the use of military force in time to defend a threatened state may be wishful thinking. Not until cosmopolitanism takes stronger hold on the global imagination will states be able to move their sovereignty to a new entity. For the time being, the need to respond to threats to security remains, in large part, the responsibility of individual states and their leaders.

But while it might make sense from within the just war tradition for states to retain the status of legitimate authority when it comes to self-defence, this makes less sense when we speak of punishment. Here the case is more complex. In law, punishment must be undertaken by a 'public authority', that is, a sovereign. If the agent using force is not a sovereign power, actions that are intended to deter, rehabilitate or enact retribution should not be called punishment; rather, they should be considered a form of revenge or retaliation. Saying that states can punish is like saying that individuals in a state of nature could punish by coercing those who violate their natural rights.[22] This violates the definition of punishment as a legally authorised sanction.

At the international level, states have the authority to defend themselves but not to enforce international law. Unlike Augustine and Aquinas, who could see a potential cosmopolis in the Church, most contemporary just war theorists are persuaded that the current international system remains divided. In this system there is no global sovereign and therefore no subjects to punish. The notion that individuals can punish, whether they are citizens in a civil community or states in international society, makes little sense. Only an acknowledged sovereign authority, which acts to uphold the law, can engage in punishment. Although it may be an open question as to who the legitimate authority is when it comes to matters of self-defence, it is logically impossible for a sovereign state to engage in punishment.

Comparative Justice

Punishment might be a possible just cause, but the absence of a body authorised to punish makes the practice of punitive intervention suspect. One other criterion from the tradition also challenges the right to punish: comparative justice. The idea of comparative justice is that absolutes do not exist when it comes to judging the justice of a war. No one party can epitomise absolute good or be completely and unequivocally in the right. Conversely, no party can be considered absolutely evil or completely and unequivocally in the wrong. As the US Catholic Bishops wrote in the 1983 pastoral letter on nuclear weapons:

> in essence, which side is sufficiently right in a dispute, and are the values at stake critical enough to override the presumption against war? ... In a world of sovereign states recognising neither a common moral authority nor a central political authority, comparative justice stresses that no state should act on the basis that it has 'absolute justice' on its side. Every party to a conflict should acknowledge the limits of its 'just cause' and the consequent requirement to use only limited means in pursuit of its objectives.[23]

In a sense, this criterion represents the just war tradition's recognition that considerations of justice are not only extremely complex but also that they cannot be entirely divorced from those of political prudence. Recognising that no actor in a war can claim certainty in defining right or wrong should discipline political leaders who are quick to use the tradition to support their cause.

This caution can be found in ancient as well as in current articulations of the tradition. Augustine, for example, rejects the Greek and Roman belief that 'true justice' (the Latin *justitia*) can be found in the human political community. Political communities are established and sustained by human beings engaged in the pursuit of earthly goods, a pursuit that leads to destruction and violence. The failure to create the City of God means that human beings cannot judge the contending parties. As a result, they cannot with certainty determine what is just and what is unjust in the context of a war. As Paul Ramsey has written,

> The just war theory cannot have meant for him [Augustine] the presence of justice (i.e., temporary order and form of these divided loves) on one side, its absence on the other ... Christian ethics may attribute to ordinary men, and to their political leaders, a capacity to know more clearly and certainly the moral limits pertaining to the armed action a man or a nation is about to engage in, than they are likely to know enough to compare unerringly the overall justice of regimes and nations.[24]

In other words, no human can make a judgement about who deserves death, especially when it comes to deciding that an entire community should suffer violence. Because human judgement is so flawed, Augustine suggests that the criterion of comparative justice prudently limits the propensity of leaders to use military force.

Doubts about just cause can be found in other classical sources. As noted above, Grotius argued that punishment could have a role to play in international society. But, even while allowing that military force might be used to punish, he goes on to hedge that permission with cautions against its abuse. After laying out a series of such cautions, he concludes, with the following words:

> Finally, to avoid repeating often what I have said, we must add this word of warning, that wars which are undertaken to inflict

punishment are under suspicion of being unjust, unless the crimes are very atrocious and very evident, or there is some other coincident reason. Perhaps Mithradites was not far wrong in saying of the Romans, 'They assail not the faults of kings but the power and authority of kings.'[25]

Michael Walzer expresses similar doubts in *Just and Unjust Wars*, although he does not invoke the idea of comparative justice. He argues that there exists a tension at the heart of the just war tradition: namely, if a war is undertaken because it is just, why should there be any limits on defeating the side that is unjust? If moral righteousness belongs to one side, why give the other side any standing? Walzer argues that the just war tradition avoids this dilemma by insisting on keeping the *jus ad bellum* criteria separate from the *jus in bello*. That is, no matter how just the cause, the rules of just conduct in the way a war is waged continue to apply:

> there are rules of war, though there are no rules of robbery (or of rape or murder). The moral equality of the battlefield distinguishes combat from domestic crime. If we are to judge what goes on in the course of a battle, then, 'we must treat both combatants' as Henry Sidgwick has written, 'on the assumption that each believes himself in the right.'[26]

By making this point, Walzer reminds us that the core principles of *jus in bello* protect against treating the enemy as evil, not by distinguishing the opposing soldiers from their leadership, but by stressing that both sides have some legitimate claims for using force. This emphasis reinforces the concept of comparative justice.

Yet not all agree that comparative justice is a core component of the tradition. In *Morality and Contemporary Warfare*, Johnson does not list comparative justice as one of the principles of *jus ad bellum*. On the contrary, he argues that limiting the use of force by emphasising 'prudential' factors fails to acknowledge some important just causes. Another defender of the classical approach argues that the principle of comparative justice requires that 'War should not be waged unless the evils that are fought against are grave enough to justify killing.'[27] This formulation of the criterion suggests that we can determine the 'evil of certain acts' and that our determination can then justify the use of force.

Such a formulation would support a move toward punishment as a just cause.

When seen in terms of the comparative justice criterion, the practice of punitive intervention stands exposed as highly problematic for the tradition. The assumption in undertaking an intervention is that the opposing government has become so faulty that it can no longer be treated as an equal. In one case it might be possible to keep the comparative justice criterion in place when undertaking a punitive intervention, that of deterring future actions. The other two purposes, rehabilitation and retribution, however, would violate this criterion. In these two models, the existing political authority in the target state deserves nothing less than to be destroyed and replaced by a new government and legitimate political authority.

It would appear, then, that punitive intervention violates the criteria of comparative justice. Here it is also useful to point out how the current justifications for interventions in Afghanistan and Iraq can be said to violate this criterion as well. Although the overall 'evil' to be defeated is terrorism in general and al-Qaeda in particular, the Bush administration labelled the Taliban and the regime of Saddam Hussein as beyond the pale of acceptable international society. In so doing, these regimes are no longer comparatively legitimate or even worthy of respect. Rather, they are seen as evil and worthy only of destruction.

By focusing solely on the element of just cause, the Bush administration ignored comparative justice. This is natural for a political leadership seeking to use force. But the just war tradition supports a more stringent standard. It is not acceptable simply to find evil in the world and punish it; political leaders, and more importantly citizens, must ask questions about the legitimacy and comparative justice of their states' policies if they are serious about the justice of those policies.

CONCLUSION

I have argued that neither international law nor the just war tradition justify punitive intervention. If this is the case, how can human rights be protected? If there is no way to punish individuals and communities that violate these rights, won't they become a dead letter? Both individual states and the Security Council can be said to enforce international law, yet we lack the one thing that seems necessary for punishment: an effective international court. The International Court of Justice does not issue judgements that include instructions to punish. Rather, it makes judgements that must be enforced by the parties before the Court – not a very effective way of ensuring that judgements will be carried out.

The development of the International Criminal Court might seem to be a move in this direction, but there are problems here as well. Leaving aside the fact that the most powerful state in the system refuses to sign the treaty establishing the new court, that treaty has no provisions for punishment. There has been little discussion of what happens to Slobodan Milosevic, for example, should he be found guilty. The death penalty is illegal according to international law.[28] (At the time of writing, what sentence he might receive remains unclear.[29]) So, while the creation of new courts is an important development, it does not seem that ideas about punishment have been part of this development.

Second, while there are now draft articles on state responsibility, it took more than fifty years to draft those articles. Clearly, more thinking needs to be done on this issue by the international community. It is also clear that punishing a state is highly problematic, especially when its regime is a dictatorship or authoritarian system in which the people have no rights and no role in formulating policy.[30] At the same time, there certainly exist states in which many people support policies that restrict the rights of individuals or minority groups. Democracies that wage war do, in some way, distribute the responsibility for those actions across the population. Should we perhaps begin to make distinctions between different types of states in evaluating whether or not they should be punished? Are democracies more liable to collective punishment than dictatorships? Such questions deserve more consideration than they have so far received, perhaps at the level of theoretical exploration rather than international action.

A final suggestion is to move from punishment to reconciliation. The new and important body of work in this area suggests that, in general, punishment is not an appropriate approach to international affairs. The disastrous consequences of the Treaty of Versailles suggest the problems that can occur when some states seek to punish others, as France and Great Britain did to Germany following the First World War.[31] But although this position has much to be said for it, I remain sceptical. While reconciling past enemies is important, the desire for retribution and return to a just system remains strong. Although those impulses can spiral out of control when military force is used to enact them, I am not sure that ignoring this desire will lead to positive results. Yet my scepticism may ignore the thin line between revenge and retribution. The Bush administration's use of the rhetoric of evil and its argument that the US will create a world order that reflects the rule of law, reminds us of the dangers of power yoked to a morally righteous cause. Interventions undertaken to punish, especially when justified within a larger moral discourse of right and wrong, can quickly turn into acts of revenge. The just war tradition provides us with the means to avoid these dangers, even if it does not tell us what to do instead.[32]

NOTES

1. See Clendenen (1961).
2. Comparative justice can be defined as the assumption that neither side in a conflict can claim absolute right, along with the corollary that no side can be labelled absolutely evil. This is not to be confused with moral relativism; rather, the assumption is that the warfare should never be conducted with absolute moral certainty.
3. See Foucault (1979) for an analysis that traces the historical development of rehabilitation as the moral purpose behind punishment.
4. Rachels (2002).
5. Kant (1991a), p. 155.
6. Henkin et al. (1993), p. 871, quoting a United Nations tribunal.
7. This example is the closest to a reprisal of those that I cite; but the Reagan administration's arguments about combating terrorism and making such actions illegal in the international system suggest a more punitive element.
8. See Lake (1994).
9. Blair (1999).
10. Holzgrefe and Keohane (2002) assume that the air war in Kosovo is an example of a humanitarian intervention.
11. Article 2(4) of the UN Charter states that all members 'shall refrain in their international relations from the threat or use of force'. At the same time, Article 51 recognises an antecedent right of states to act in self-defence. This escape clause in the Charter allows uses of force, especially when states expand the definition of 'self-defence' for a wide range of ends. For a recent critical analysis of self-defence, see Rodin (2002).
12. For the texts of these articles and a narrative of how they were drafted, see Crawford, J. (2002).
13. Johnson (1999), p. 31.
14. Grotius (1925).
15. Ibid., Book II, chapter 20. Some argue that the shift away from a punitive justification for military force occurred when Emmerich de Vattel, in his *The*

Law of Nations (1758), disputed Hugo Grotius' idea that just war principles can justify punishment. See Chesterman (2002), p. 18.

16. Elshtain (2003), p. 61.
17. US Catholic Bishops (1992).
18. Lopez (2002).
19. Boyle (2002), p. 13.
20. See Weigel (1987).
21. Augustine [AD413–26] (2001), pp. 205–27.
22. Some argue that John Locke, a theorist of the state of nature and classical liberalism, believed that individuals in the state of nature *can* punish, even if there is no sovereign. See Simmons (1991).
23. US Catholic Bishops (1992), p. 29.
24. Ramsey (1965), pp. 31–2.
25. Grotius (1925), Book II, Chapter 20, section 3, p. 508.
26. See Walzer (1992), p. 128.
27. Schall (2001).
28. Schabas (1997).
29. No one found guilty so far by the Yugoslav tribunal has been sentenced to more than twenty years. While it is not clear what will happen to Milosevic, this evidence suggests that his sentence will be similar.
30. See Lang (1999).
31. See Minow (1998) and Lu (2002).
32. This chapter has benefited from the feedback of the following people: Mark Evans, Neta Crawford, Brian Orend, Terry Nardin and Toni Erskine. Comments by members at the Just War Theory Revisited conference, November 2003, University of Wales Swansea, were also extremely beneficial.

Chapter 3

IN HUMANITY'S NAME: DEMOCRACY AND THE RIGHT TO WAGE WAR

MARK EVANS

⟨◁▷⟩

INTRODUCTION

The American-led invasion of Iraq in 2003 and its subsequent occupation has been the most controversial event in world politics of recent times. As is abundantly clear from the frequency with which it is invoked in this book, it raises a whole battery of issues for just war theory to address. Indeed, one might think of it as a laboratory in which the theory may be put to the most exacting tests. In this chapter, we consider some questions arising from the controversy as to whether the invading coalition possessed the authority to launch the war: did it have the *institutional* right to do so? For it is a crucial tenet of traditional just war theory that not every organised armed body of people has the right to use those arms, even if they were to do so in a manner that satisfied the theory's other criteria. (This is criterion 1(g), as laid out in the Introduction.) The main reason for this, it may be reasonably conjectured, is that the demands of political order must always restrain the resort to war and, without the insistence on a precisely identified legitimate authority, 'just wars' would lead to a chaotically anarchic world.

In the Introduction, I observed how in modern times just war thinking was instrumental in the shaping of conventions governing warfare in international law. Unsurprisingly, much of the dispute over the Iraq war in this regard centred upon its legality with respect to these established statutes and practices. Complex and heated though the debates are, we might summarise the charge that the US-led coalition faced thus: the United Nations Charter permits war only as a last resort

71

and in self-defence except where Security Council authorisation explicitly permits otherwise – a proviso not in this instance met. The case for the defence marshalled a variety of counter-arguments: one was that the self-defence justification alone sufficed (an argument explored in Chapter 1); another was that previous Security Council resolutions *did* provide adequate legal justification to obviate the need for a further explicit authorisation; a third was based around the claim that NATO's 1999 air war against Serbia over the Kosovo crisis established a precedent for the legitimate circumvention of the Security Council.

I do not propose to enter into legal and institutional technicalities in this chapter, not because they are unimportant (for they are hardly that) but because, in this dispute, they may not be sufficiently fundamental to what is essentially at stake. This thought has been implicitly expressed by Anne-Marie Slaughter's suggestion that the war could be considered as 'illegal but legitimate.'[1] This judgement could mean one of two things here. It might express the idea that the 'legitimate authority' criterion, into which is incorporated the requirement of conformity to existing recognised laws, is in fact dispensable when considering the *moral* legitimacy of the resort to war. Alternatively, and more subtly, it might be intended to mean that the technical illegality of the war does reduce its moral credentials but that on balance that is not enough to fault its *overall* moral justification. One explanation for this judgement could be that there are certain deficiencies in the international legal and institutional order which, at least currently, precludes the legitimate-authority criterion from being as decisive as it intended to be, although these deficiencies are not so great as to justify any comprehensive or permanent waiving of it. A possible justification of the Kosovo war on these lines could run as follows. No Security Council resolution in support of a proposed attack on Serbia would ever have been forthcoming: Russia, one of its permanent members, would inevitably veto any attack on its Serbian ally. But an institutional arrangement that allows a single power and its dubious motivations to be such a decisive obstacle to what morality otherwise permits or even demands should be regarded as too imperfect to constitute a fully adequate 'authority' in this regard: hence the moral permissibility of NATO's action. This exemption, however, holds only so long as the UN is not totally ignored: the conduct and, in particular, the aftermath of the war must somehow acknowledge its *pro tanto* authority.

A scenario such as this vividly illustrates why we have to go beyond the purely legal aspect when thinking about the legitimacy of a war. Not only does the law ultimately matter here only because of the moral precepts it embodies, we should also not assume that the laws we have, and the institutions and practices which operationalise them, are always up to the tasks that morality sets for them. We need to think about how morality might direct us to fill in the gaps and rectify the failings in the way we do things. In this chapter, this task takes us to the very core of the morality with which just war theory is concerned – its account of justice – and which our legal and political institutions should seek to respect in full. Thinking about the latter is an engagement with ideal theory: a working-out of what the ideal world order would look like. This provides us with the yardstick by which we can measure the deficiencies of the arrangements we actually have here and now. I am particularly concerned to identify what it is about the non-ideal world that introduces the kind of indeterminacy about the 'legitimate authority' criterion displayed in the Kosovo example. But the present exercise also isolates two absolutely key moral orientations in just war theory that not only frame the ideal theory which underpins it but which also constitute part of the regulatory considerations governing non-ideal behaviour. These are, firstly, its moral universalism – its concern with *humanity* – and, secondly, its *democratic* bias, which has not been properly analysed before.

Shortage of space means that the accounts of both ideal and non-ideal theory given here (and summarised in the Introduction above) are far from complete. Also, I cannot provide the full defence of them that they may well require to persuade the reader. What the chapter does aim to offer, though, is a set of proposals as to how we might begin fruitfully to approach the issues it raises, a sketch of a perspective from which to think about the problems of the legitimate authority criterion and what morally matters most of all in just war theory.

JUSTICE AND THE IDEA OF GLOBAL CIVIL SOCIETY

What is so special about the state that its defence should have been thought for so long to constitute the main, if not the sole, just cause for war? In a world of nation-states, it is perhaps not surprising if many of us have not even thought of this question let alone formulated an answer to it. It has indeed been widely assumed that the sovereign state just *is* the fundamental political unit and, as a result, worthy of a respect which is denied whenever it is attacked; only if it has itself attacked others (or is imminently likely to do so) does it forfeit this right to respect of its sovereign inviolability, according to this view.

It is not, however, difficult to pinpoint the limitations of this standpoint. States matter morally in this regard only because the people who live in them matter morally. The self-defence justification for war obviously rests on the idea that the people of a state have, *ceteris paribus*, the right not to suffer attack. They have the right to resist not only the attempts to kill or injure them but also to conquer them or otherwise deprive them of certain liberties; it is *their* sovereignty as 'a people' that counts. 'The state', then, is not the irreducible unit of moral concern. But as soon as we start telling this story of people and their rights, pressure is exerted on the claim that the defence of states is what just war theory should posit as 'just cause'. For example, some peoples have fought wars for statehood and *ipso facto* have not fought them as states; these are struggles against other states which claim to have sovereignty over them. And, as has recently become more widely accepted with the development of the idea and practice of humanitarian intervention, wars might be fought on behalf of other peoples who are under attack from their own state. Again, the justification of humanitarian intervention rests upon the claim that the sovereignty of the state has moral significance only in so far as the rights of its citizens matter. Derived from those rights, its sovereignty is not absolute but conditional on its respect for them. And whereas once it seems generally to have been assumed that only the people in question could have the right to oppose their state when it egregiously failed to meet this condition (their right of revolution), now 'humanitarian intervention' asserts the right of other peoples to come to the aid of those whose states, in violating their rights, have consequently forfeited the right of inviolable sovereignty. Indeed, in so far as the latter right is essentially derived from the rights of its citizens, we might say that the rights-violating state deprives *itself* of that right.

The arguments in the rest of this chapter emerge from an elaboration of the basic intuitions in this account. And we should immediately see that the heart of the moral tale being told here is the claim that people have rights which both yield and limit the moral sovereignty of states and, as expressed in the moral possibility of humanitarian intervention, establish moral ties between peoples of different states such that one people could have the moral right, and perhaps even the duty, to come to the aid of another against their own state. The moral theory in which we should house this claim is, therefore, going to be 'trans-statist'.

Now I would like to suggest that a concept which is very congenial in this regard is Mervyn Frost's 'global civil society' posited as an 'ethical ideal'.[2] It should straightaway be stressed that 'global civil society' as a moral concept is just that: it does not refer to any *empirical* manifestation of extra-statist transnational organisations and relationships. We can therefore affirm it without committing ourselves to the view that a global civil society as a set of concrete institutions and relationships already exists.[3] Instead, it refers to the moral society whose existence we *infer* from the claim that all human beings have certain basic – 'human' – rights. My argument, therefore, proceeds from this claim as a given: it can be followed in so far as one is prepared to grant it as a starting-point. Although this is hardly the most controversial of presuppositions, it is not self-evidently valid in the minds of everyone either. The case for it is not one that I shall give here; rather, I invite readers to buy into the assumption that it is valid to see where it might lead us. (In fact, the unfolding of its consequences and corollaries may well constitute the best argument we can give for accepting it.)

In recognising that we all have these rights, we thereby recognise a certain commonality (the same basic moral status) among human beings. Further, it follows from the universal attribution of rights that a certain network of relationships exists between human beings, generated from the respect and the responsibilities entailed on the part of others by the possession of rights and which is mutual and reciprocal. This is the 'society', organised around the civility which arises from rights-based relationships and encompassing all human beings.[4] Hence, the concept of global civil society rejects the claim that a rights-based moral theory such as this has an atomistically non- or anti-social character, which some thinkers are wont to believe.

The point, or function, of global civil society is that it provides the framework within which subsets of humanity associate for specific purposes, or on the basis of shared interests, whilst having none of its own – beyond the establishment of a just and stable peace in which these diverse communities and projects may flourish. So it shares this important characteristic with what Terry Nardin calls 'international society':

The common good of this inclusive community resides not in the ends that some, or at times even most, of its members may wish collectively to pursue but in the values of justice, peace, security and coexistence, which may be enjoyed through participation in a common body of authoritative practices.[5]

Now it is of course crucial to indicate what principles might be found in this morality, and some might immediately expect it to embody nothing other than a purely Western morality entirely unsuitable for the universalist pretensions of global civil society. Indeed, some argue that the very idea of a 'human right', regardless of any specific form of such, is ethnocentric and thus would regard 'global civil society' as a culturally particularistic picturing of the world in a Western liberal image. The evidence for this charge is held to be those cultures and belief-systems that do not share these principles. In response, one should point out that if we affirm any idea of human rights, or any alternative universal moral claim, then we are committed to saying that any culture which rejects it is wrong (for otherwise we have to abandon its universality, its 'humanity'). And while we can accept that many of what have been proposed to be 'human rights' in practice are too ethnocentric plausibly to pass as 'universal' (for example, Article 24 of the Universal Declaration of Human Rights proclaims a right to paid holidays from work, which is surely appropriate only for certain kinds of society), it is much more difficult to deny universal applicability or domain to all conceivable moral beliefs which are not as a matter of fact universally shared or recognised.

'Global civil society' acknowledges the extent of cultural diversity within humanity and will almost certainly not want to embrace all of what people have nominated as 'human rights', but it does not regard diversity as going 'all the way down'. Its morality is a 'thin' universalism, under-determining any particular form of social life in full but specifying in minimal form what kind of society is fit enough for humans to live in: a 'humanitarian morality',[6] if you will. Put differently, it identifies certain fundamental evils that would constitute 'inhumanity' as a universal standard of moral disapprobation that has no truck with attempts to excuse such evils on the basis of 'legitimate' cultural diversity. These evils, certainly when perpetrated deliberately, are what might constitute the familiar category of 'crimes against humanity'. The content of this morality may be flexible over time – humanity may revise its conception of what crosses the threshold into unacceptable inhumanity – and how these principles are instantiated may vary from society to society. And we need not pretend that agreement on the general form of this morality can be straightforwardly reached. But I suspect it is easy enough to begin to piece it together: would we really cede moral justification to a genocidal racism, say, against a universally applicable insistence that it is absolutely evil and wrong, simply because a particular group believes it to be justified?

I will not try to give a complete and authoritative account of humanitarian morality, but we have enough to carry the present argument forward. For we can now say that, although the existence of states continues to have some intrinsic value, their sovereignty is ultimately premised upon their support for, and contribution to, the maintenance of global civil society as a moral society. And the theory of justice on which just war theory rests is drawn from humanitarian morality. Teasing out the claims here: we might grant that one of the principles of global civil society is that sub-sets of humanity, especially but not necessarily exclusively states, have the right to political self-determination. In a world shaped by Westphalia, this primarily translates into the right of state sovereignty. Mutual respect for this right is a cardinal principle of the international order – and thus we have the statist 'self-defence' justification for war. But this principle is nested among, and hence qualified by, certain other principles, a failure to respect which may lead to the justifiable overriding of the sovereignty principle – the 'humanitarian intervention' justification which we have suggested should be added to the concept of 'just cause'.

This general suggestion leaves a lot of room to deliberate the question of when a rights-violation is so severe that war may be justified. Such violations, it might be pointed out, happen all the time in various degrees: war must surely become an option only when global civil society is fundamentally impugned by them. But perhaps the threat to the existence and integrity of global civil society that gives rise to a just war need not be all-consuming in the sense that it could destroy global civil society in its physical entirety: that might be too stringent a condition for war's justifiability. Just war theory, however, is precisely meant to be our guide in this deliberation, asking the questions that focus on when a just cause does indeed justify war.

If we recall that just war theory springs from an ideal-theory account of 'just peace', we can see how the norms of global civil society frame the basic character of that peace. The use of force has no place in a world that has fully respected and instantiated global civil society as a moral framework for the mutually respectful accommodation of diverse human associations. Part of war's tragedy is, of course, that morality's precepts cannot be respected in full. In its non-ideal character, just war theory accepts that it sanctions the violation of what is inviolable at the ideal level. Some of humanitarian morality's precepts – which it is reasonable to assume include some formulation of a right to life – obviously will not be fully respected in war. But their violation is justified by the ultimate aim of restoring, as best one currently can, the norms of global civil society against the attack on them that has yielded the (just) cause for war in the first place. It would be even worse for those norms if war was not initiated (recall the 'lesser of two evils' characterisation introduced in the Introduction). A just war must always be fought with the idea of global civil society as its ultimate orienting and constraining consideration.

Before we move on, another feature of the 'global-civil-society' basis for just war theory needs to be stressed. Having decentred the state, this characterisation allows us to conceptualise just wars fought by, and between, non-state associations and for non-state-based goals, something of which some have believed the theory incapable of handling. Far more than just state-based conflicts, then, are brought into its purview. And by making global civil society its moral basis, the theory makes humanity as a moral category its heart. No *purely* local, transient cause, nothing that does not in some significant way concern us all as human beings, can constitute 'justice' in its eyes. 'Just cause' is humanity's concern: it is that serious. And this, I submit, has crucial cosmopolitan implications for the question of the authority to wage war.

SOME PRINCIPLES OF INSTITUTIONAL ORDER

Historically, the 'legitimate authority' criterion was invoked to prohibit the waging of 'war' by just any group of people (for example, mercenaries). Limiting the permissibility of war to states may indeed help to reduce the scourge of war, but we have adduced some of the numerous reasons why the exclusively statist focus is inadequate. But if we wish to retain the idea that just war theory should give only certain types of armed body the right to wage war, we seem to have a problem. The moral thrust of the argument thus far has taken us in a cosmopolitan direction, but wars – and even 'world' wars – break out among distinctly sub-universal, local or regional groups … with the state stubbornly remaining a central actor. What can a 'cosmopolitanised' legitimate-authority criterion say in this regard?

It is tempting to think that, in order to make headway with this question, we should first work out the institutional configuration of the ideal world, in which the norms of global civil society are fully effective. In fact, it is not obvious how much we need to say in this regard, for if war is a mark of a non-ideal world we would not expect to find provision for it in the ideal world. Though non-ideal theory is oriented by the ideal, it is typically forced to uphold principles and practices that are not mere partial approximations of this ideal but which in fact are radically different, perhaps at least superficially quite contrary, to it. But – it is orientation that we seek, so we at least need some specification of the ideal world's character to guide the inquiry.

Two considerations are relevant here. The first is that a cosmopolitan morality might naturally comport with a proposal for a genuinely cosmopolitan mechanism by which it can be realised. Now it is very familiarly stressed in the liberal-democratic tradition, for example, and following Kant, that a world state is neither necessary nor desirable for the purpose of securing a just and peaceful world order.[7] So I think it is safe to assume that just war theory's ideal world need not be presented as a single global super-state. But it does imply that there is some kind of overarching institution as far as individual states, or regional association of states, are concerned: a global structure to maintain and police the norms of global civil society.

The second consideration brings us to another major theme of this chapter: the democratic bias of just war theory. I hasten to note, what I will stress again later, that this is *only* a bias, a preference, which does not imply that no non-democratic body can ever figure on the side of justice in a just-war scenario. But that bias is evident in the inclusion of a right to self-determination as something whose violation could constitute a just cause for war. This is a right of peoples to choose their own mode of social organisation and governance, and *to that extent* it is a democratic right. Even at the ideal level, beyond the need for war (and to make a point that I will repeat), this may be compatible with a people freely affirming a non-democratically organised way of life for them-selves. However, at the global level on which I will focus for now, it would be odd indeed if an institutional order which embodied the norms of global civil society, and therefore this particular right, was actually organised on lines that were not democratic in some meaningful sense. For it is natural to think that a non-democratic cosmopolitan order would be sub-optimal compared with a democratic alternative in allowing full realisation of this right.

Aficionados of recent international relations theory will here spot the drift in the argument towards the concept of 'cosmopolitan democracy', closely associated with thinkers such as David Held.[8] Some are highly dismissive of it as describing the hopelessly unrealistic prospect of a fully democratised international order, a fantasy indulged in at the expense of any utility in specifying what it is actually possible to achieve. Perhaps those who think it is currently possible are indeed fantasists. But the theory is obviously best posited at the ideal level: a picture of the world as it ought to be which it is still worth painting even if we can see no way of establishing it as such. We can criticise (as many often do) the existing world order for its anti-democratic character. And we can cogently do so only in so far as we have a conception of what ought to be the case instead: a democratised world, which is what ideal theory can here posit. The impossibility, if it is indeed an impossibility, of greater global democracy is due not to any physical or logical impossibility (which would indeed render the idea of cosmopolitan democracy absurd). It is because certain peoples in certain positions won't change their ways, when in fact it is not literally impossible for them to do so. In so far as they *could* do differently, they can be held morally responsible for the world that they create – and morality can criticise them if their creation falls short of what is required.

So it is not nonsensical to entertain elements of the cosmopolitan-democratic theory at the ideal level even if little of it is actually realisable in the relevant sense. Its impact on just war theory, then, should be considered. And I propose that it could influence the non-ideal theory question of legitimate authority in waging war as follows:

[a] The 'cosmopolitan' label suggests that a global body, if one such exists, may invoke some measure of overall jurisdiction with regards to the waging of war wherever it breaks out because it is the norms of global civil society which have thereby broken down. For if a just cause for war is a response to a threat against humanity's fundamental moral order, then some institutional embodiment of the global society which is the ultimate object of

the threat should in some sense have primacy in sanctioning that response.

[b] The 'public justification of war' (criterion 1(h), identified in the Introduction) demands political accountability on the part of just warriors. Again, if a global society is so intimately concerned with a just war, then a global forum should ultimately be where this accountability is to be held.

[c] What democratic procedures do exist in non-ideal institutions should not be lightly flouted, and a just war should not fundamentally challenge democratic norms.

IMPERFECT INSTITUTIONS, IMPERFECT OBLIGATIONS

Not least because it, and its supporters, regard it as such, we can readily nominate the United Nations as the kind of institutional body which could constitute the legitimate authority in the sanctioning of war in the non-ideal world. It is the Security Council (under the terms of Article 51 of the UN Charter) which has the right to authorise military action among member states except in the case of self-defence, and even with regards to the latter it must be kept informed and allowed the opportunity to take 'measures to maintain international peace and security'. So we have, even though only at a very protean level, the basis of an account of transnational *democratic* political legitimacy.

But it is also a truism of world politics today that the UN manifests deep structural flaws that hamper its ability to function, as intended, as a cosmopolitan political authority even within the limits formally laid out. The structure of the Security Council reflects the post-Second World War settlement, which can hardly be said still to reflect the balance of power and the interests of all member-states today. It enables the permanent members in particular extraordinary power to manipulate or stymie UN action in the name of their own self-interest. More generally, the purely state-based representative structure of the UN is not 'democratic' in the sense that it fails equally to represent the interests of members of global civil society.

I will not rehearse further these, or other, familiar complaints against the present structure and behaviour of the UN. We have enough, I think, to run with the claim that the UN as presently constituted falls short of how it should 'ideally' be constituted even with respect to how such a cosmopolitan political authority would address non-ideal-world problems such as the outbreak of war. So we need to appreciate that, even within non-ideal theory there are levels of 'ideality', degrees to which the full-blown ideal are approximated, and the UN as currently constituted is not on the top rung.

Now consider the following. It is an idealisation of the actual event it describes, but I am concerned only to expose a point of principle and not to pass judgement on the historical event in question. NATO's war against Serbia over Kosovo proceeded without authorisation from the Security Council. But this would not have anyway been obtained given the implacable opposition of Russia and China. Here, we might say that Russian and Chinese *realpolitik* considerations, emerging at least in part from what are still overly state-centric (instead of genuinely humanitarian cosmopolitan) interests precluded the possibility of this authority being granted. But let us grant that the intervention was otherwise morally permissible and perhaps mandatory: only the legitimate authority criterion in just war theory was not satisfied. Would it not be justifiable to put this down to an institutional failing – a failure properly to operationalise the norms of global civil society as best one could in the non-ideal world – which does not necessarily deprive the right of other powers to act unilaterally in the stead of this unjustly hampered institution? Put another way: the degree of non-ideality in the structure of our authoritative cosmopolitan institutions preclude the full operation of the legitimate authority criterion in the manner that the theory intends. For it is emphatically not designed to allow narrow state self-interest to act in ways that run wholly counter to the interests and obligations of global civil society. When we do not have such authority, and when the 'authority' we do have acts in opposition to just war theory's other moral requirements, on what moral grounds must we still insist on the absolute decisiveness of the 'authority' criterion?

A further supporting scenario: there is widespread agreement that the failure to intervene in Rwanda in 1994, where 800,000 people were slaughtered in a terrifying outbreak of ethnic genocide, is an egregious indictment of the international community. But let us imagine that an attempt to marshal a full-blown UN-backed military response to the genocide would have met with institutional obstacles similar to those which arose over Kosovo. Would it really be justified for there to be no intervention simply because no formally appropriate institutional authorisation was forthcoming? Could the lives of these people count for less than the legal impropriety of unilateral action?[9]

The animating thought behind these scenarios is that the genocides in question generate obligations among other members of global civil society to rescue and punish. Were our institutions up to scratch in the non-ideal world, a legitimate authority could discharge these obligations effectively. But – and this is crucial – surely the obligations do not disappear if they have not been properly institutionalised. Rather, we should say that they have been left *imperfect*.[10] On my conception, an 'imperfect obligation' is generated when something demands attention – when its non-address would be a definite moral negative – but there is no authoritative allocation of responsibility to pay that attention (as there is in a perfect obligation). Suppose there was no recognised authority or aid body to come to the rescue of a group of people suffering invasion and persecution. Their need for aid is desperate – and hence obligation-generating, certainly in the sense that supererogation cannot properly characterise the moral urgency which is present here (that is, it is too urgent to allow us to say that although it would be good if someone charitably helped, this would be above and beyond the call of duty so there would be no moral 'crime' if nothing was done). But due to an imperfect institutional instantiation of the demands of morality, we cannot pin the blame for the failure to rescue on the part of any particular agent.

So: such a situation may well provide some grounds to justify intervention on the part of *anyone* if they so chose to step into the breach, although I would not want to say that the option can be so liberally taken up. Not every capable military body may be equally entitled to take up the imperfect obligation, and a fully-expounded just war theory should consider whether it can propose further regulatory norms in this regard. Certainly, a just-warring authority must be one that is prepared to submit to the moral authority of global civil society – and has a *pro tanto* reason to defer to its closest institutional approximation. By this, I mean that its first obligation is to submit thus, but on reflection it may be overridden by one that, it transpires, is more powerful. In the above scenarios, this would translate as: give the UN its chance but if it fails, it may be justified for other states or organisations to assume moral responsibility even if there is no international-legal provision for such. What this argument emphatically does not condone is action based on the following line of thought:

> multilateralism is fine in principle. What is not fine is having our interests adversely affected by the inability to gain a sufficient

degree of multilateral support. And what is not fine is subsuming US interests … in some larger notion that, if the only option is unilateral, we should be paralysed. So, multilateralism is preferable, if we can get a consensus. But if the only way you can get a consensus is by abandoning your most fundamental interests, then it is not helpful.[11]

UNILATERALISM AND THE IRAQ WAR, 2003

If there may be times when the legitimate-authority criterion cannot be properly respected, we seem drawn to the following conclusion: the unilateralism of the American-led coalition in the 2003 Iraq war is not *by itself* reason to judge the war unjust. For we do not have an institutional order that is sufficiently well-developed for us to be sure that it is morally reasonable to run with its current conception of legitimate authority in the waging of war. Its imperfections mean that we *may* have to live with imperfect renderings of just war's criteria, at least with respect to the legitimate authority criterion.[12] Put differently: certain degrees of sub-optimality within the realm of the non-ideal may justify the downgrading or suspension of some of just war theory's demands.

Obviously, this particular way of phrasing the issue was not explicitly deployed by President Bush and I am not saying that the unilateralism of the action was justifiable on this basis. The point is that, for the opponents of the war, the argument does not necessarily stop with the lack of prior UN authorisation. But even if the legitimate-authority criterion could be set to one side, the argument does *not* support the suspension of any other just war theory criteria; indeed, it insists that the ideal of legitimate authority continue to act as a regulatory constraint even when it cannot be fully satisfied. Though they may be justified in by-passing what structures of cosmopolitan authority are currently in place, the powers in question remain obligated to do what they practicably can to promote the ideal of cosmopolitan authority. In the Iraq case, this would almost certainly mandate the US-led coalition to involve the UN to a maximal degree, where possible, in the management of the country's post-war affairs – beyond what it is expedient for it to foist upon others.

Further, the moral possibility of unilateralism must always be balanced against the dangers of the precedents it sets (invoking the 'consequences' criterion: 1(b)). Cosmopolitan theory wishes to lift the international order out of the potential Hobbesianism of a purely state-based arrangement. Unilateralism may threaten a reversion to that highly undesirable situation and this strongly suggests that the flouting of what cosmopolitan authority we have now must be an exceptional, rather than normal, affair not undertaken without very careful and sincere consideration of the implications it has for the possibility of effective cosmopolitan order. Domestically, most of us accept that a highly imperfect sovereign is better than the Hobbesian world in which there is none at all, and, *mutatis mutandis,* we can accept the claim that unilateralism runs the risk of reversing the acceptance of the international equivalent of this maxim.

Nevertheless, if this argument has merit a significant consequence is entailed for just war theory: the legitimate-authority criterion does not have equal weight with others in so far as it can be waived without rendering a war unjust. The dropping of this criterion in special circumstances is not without precedent in the theory: witness the supreme emergency exemption, discussed in Chapter 4, which waives the 'discrimination' criterion of *jus in bello.* But this merely reinforces the point that we now have two types of criterion in the theory: one, such as just cause (1(a)), which cannot be waived, and one, such as those just cited, which can be. The consequences this has for just war theorising are discussed in this book's conclusion.

DEMOCRACY AND JUST WAR THEORY

There is one further element to the claim that there is a democratic bias in the theory, which takes us from the international to the 'domestic' level. According to the conception of the post-war just peace, the just warriors may in principle be justified in promoting some form of democratic political order even when there was none before. Now, from one angle this may not appear to be a radical or shocking claim: the democratic reconstructions of (West) Germany and Japan after the Second World War seem hardly controversial. But in more recent times, many have expressed fears that the propagation of representative/liberal-democratic values in non-Western contexts is nothing other than a form of cultural imperialism. Liberal democracy may be fine for the West and perhaps some other contexts, so the argument runs, but it is wrong to think that it is necessarily the best form of government for all societies. This is an argument that we have heard expressed over the 2003 invasion of Iraq, where the desirability (and, indeed, the feasibility) of representative democracy as a model for the post-Saddam polity is fiercely contested by those who resist the coalition's certainty on the matter.

Once again, I am not directly concerned to take sides in any particular instance of the Iraq argument; I merely seek to identify normative possibilities on the basis of the principles we find in just war theory. My point here is simply that the democratic favouritism of – in this instance – the West should not be seen as *necessarily* parochial and illegitimately universalised. This is because I think the democratic bias in just war theory frames its conception of the just peace in *jus post bellum* and it is perfectly understandable, therefore, why the supporters of just war theory exhibit such democratic bias as a point of principle. And recall that theirs is presented as a humanitarian morality: it is in the name of humanity and not a particularistic cultural preference that this demo-cratic bias is on exhibit.[13]

Let me illustrate: the 1991 war against Iraq was waged to liberate Kuwait, which had been an autocratic monarchy. Following the expul-sion of the Iraqi army, the al-Sabah family was restored to power. Many were troubled at what they regarded as the moral paradox of a war fought in the name of the Kuwaiti people's self-determination which resulted in the restoration of a political order that frustrated those people's ability to exercise meaningful self-determination. On my reading, they were right to be so troubled. For a just war theory whose theory of justice is based upon the idea of global civil society, the sovereignty and self-determination of a state only matters morally in so far as the self-determination of its citizens matters morally. Thus there is obviously something paradoxical, or contradictory, or at least incomplete, in the justification of the Kuwait liberation and its domestic political aftermath.

Now I wish only to uphold a *pro tanto* and hence defeasible demo-cratic preference. We still always need instead to argue for it in any one instance. And we might begin by observing that there is good pragmatic reason to think, for example, that, domestically, the processes of, say, forgiveness and reconciliation in *jus post bellum* cannot be properly facilitated without some kind of substantive democratic political repre-sentation. Currently, even those regimes which are in practice not democratic typically claim to be so, acknowledging by default the moral power of the democratic ideal. They are often not slow to invoke the idea on the international stage either. Sometimes, 'self-determination' is used to defend themselves against the actions of others (whilst failing to see the paradox of their denial of political self-determination to their own people), sometimes to demand the right of their interests to be taken into account in determining international policy.

I am not denying the conceptual possibility that a sovereign people could genuinely determine collectively to be ruled by an autocrat, and modern-day autocrats probably feel it necessary very often to claim that they rule by the grace of their people as well as, say, their god. (They may well sincerely believe that to be the case as well.) In practice, however, we would be rightly sceptical of such claims and it is perfectly reasonable to demand that there be in place institutional mechanisms to verify them. Given this, one might wonder whether in fact some sort of institutionalised democracy would not in fact be required after all.

Of course, 'democracy' can take different forms in different contexts and we could obviously debate the veracity of the democratic credentials claimed by existing institutional arrangements which purport to have them.[14] But the democratic ideal is not open-endedly permissive in what institutional forms and practices it can support – and, for supporters of just war theory, it is actually rather mysterious as to why anyone should think this delimiting feature might be unacceptably disrespectful of cultural variety. If it merits airing at all, the argument against the promotion of some kind of democratic system in a *post bellum* situation is best conducted on the basis of a non-ideal pragmatic shortfall with respect to what ideally should be instantiated. And we cannot deny a priori that in certain cases such an argument may be very compelling, and not least for just-war thinkers. The viability of representative democracy in post-Saddam Iraq is sufficiently dubious as to necessitate this debate, for example. But note how, for just war theory, the 'burden of proof' has shifted to the 'non-democracy' side: it is the case for not having democracy that has to be made.

CONCLUSION

As I warned at the start, this chapter has been able only to sketch some basic concepts and claims without the full elaboration and defence they merit. It presents merely the beginning of a complex philosophical reworking of certain aspects of just war theory and much more has to be done to address the obvious questions and problems that readers have

doubtless identified.[15] Two points, however, are evident from the foregoing. First, even genuinely just war-based arguments about the
justifications of particular wars and their aftermaths can be a lot more
complex than just war theory has traditionally acknowledged. This
merely exposes still further the gross inadequacies of many of the
philosophically weaker arguments that are actually conducted about
wars. And second: the need to think through the issues raised here much
more deeply and systematically indicates strongly that just war theorising, far from having exhausted its possibilities, remains as dynamic as the
world it confronts.

NOTES

1. See Slaughter (2003).
2. See Frost (2002). The use of the term 'ethical' by Frost denotes what, in this
   chapter, is called the 'moral'. Frost's preference reflects the Hegelian character
   of his theory. It should be stressed that my borrowing of the 'global civil
   society' idea does not commit me to this Hegelianism or to other aspects of his
   theory; the account I develop here can stand independently of large parts of
   Frost's argument and therefore does not necessarily stand or fall with it.
3. For discussion of 'global civil society' as a more empirical term, see Keane
   (2003).
4. The idea that 'global civil society' encompasses all human beings marks one of
   my points of departure from Frost, but these differences in our specific usages
   of the 'global civil society' idea need not detain us here.
5. Nardin (1983), p. 19. Those familiar with Michael Oakeshott's work will
   recognise this to be an internationalised version of the idea of 'civil association'.
6. This concept is explicated in Evans (2002).
7. See Kant, 'Perpetual Peace: A Philosophical Sketch', in Kant (1991a), pp. 93–
   130.
8. See Held (1995).
9. For a searing indictment of continuous US foreign policy failure to respond to
   the moral imperatives that arise from genocide, see Power (2003).
10. The following argument is presented at greater length in Evans (2002).
11. Perle (2003). Only if there is a coincidence of 'US interests' and cosmopolitan
    morality does the present analysis support Perle's argument.
12. Elsewhere, I have argued that, for similar reasons, the selectivity apparent in
    the 'humanitarian concerns' of the West, and others, cannot *by itself* be
    regarded as evidence of hypocrisy. Again, this is not to say that no hypocrisy is
    present in the actual selectivity displayed in recent history. Instead, the
    argument insists that more argument than the mere identification of selectivity

is required to establish that hypocrisy is present. See Evans (2002).
13. Critics may still challenge the claims to universality; I do not take that argument further here. All I am saying is that just war theory can coherently and consistently deny cultural particularity in holding its democratic preference to be a universal consideration.
14. To show that this is not a crude triumphalist apology for Western liberal-democratic capitalism, I think it is perfectly apposite for a democratically inclined account of *jus post bellum* to reject the acceptability of a post-conflict society such as present-day Iraq effectively losing control of key parts of its economy as Western-owned multinationals take control of its oil industry and the like.
15. I intend to carry forward this project in a monograph entitled *War, Morality and Humanity*.

JUSTICE IN THE CONDUCT OF WAR

Chapter 4

THE CONCEPT OF PROPORTIONALITY: OLD QUESTIONS AND NEW AMBIGUITIES

KATERI CARMOLA

The main problem with the principle of proportionality is not whether or not it exists but what it means and how it is to be applied.[1]

INTRODUCTION

In November 2001, in the first few months of the war on terrorism, US and UK forces in Afghanistan, together with the Northern Alliance, rounded up more than 400 Taliban and suspected al-Qaeda fighters and brought them to the Qala-i-Jangi fortress outside of Mazar-i-Sharif. They neglected to disarm the prisoners completely, and in the midst of some initial interrogation procedures, some of the detainees detonated some grenades, seized weaponry and rioted. In response, airstrikes were called in, and over the next twelve hours they proceeded to bomb the prison relentlessly, eventually killing all 400 prisoners. A few days later, US Secretary of Defense Donald Rumsfeld was asked, during his daily press briefing, whether the response might have been 'disproportionate'. He replied:

> Now, the word 'proportion' – 'proportionate' is interesting. And I don't know that it's appropriate. And I don't know that I could define it. But it might be said – and I wouldn't say it – (laughter) – but it might be said by some that to quickly and aggressively repress a prison riot in one location might help dissuade people in other locations from engaging in prison riots and breaking out of prison and killing more people. I don't know if that's true. It might also persuade the people who are still in there with weapons,

killing each other and killing other people, to stop doing it. It's – ah – your question's too tough for me. I don't know what 'proportionate' would be.[2]

Despite Rumsfeld's confusion, the idea of proportionality is one of the oldest and most central concepts of just war theory, and has long been formalised in both the law of armed conflict and military strategy. Along with the requirement of discrimination between combatants and noncombatants, 'proportionality' attempts to make the violence of war proportionate to the threat it is meant to overcome, and make the unintended mistakes of a war proportionate to their intended benefits.[3] Proportionality figures prominently in judgements about the justice of a war itself, *jus ad bellum*, and the justice of the means employed, *jus in bello*. It is also used in thinking about punishment, including issues of post-conflict justice or *jus post bellum*. Its very ubiquity, in fact, is both a strength and a weakness: although it has operated in just war thinking from the very beginning, and even though it permeates our rhetoric and thinking about both morality, law, and strategy, proportionality remains an ambiguous idea, understood by all and no one at the same time. The concept of proportionality contains all the power and the problems of just war theory: how do we judge something as just or unjust? How do we speak meaningfully about tactics and technologies, victims and soldiers, in ways that respect both enduring commitments and changing realities?

With such concepts it is often easier for analysis to begin with cases where it seems to be lacking – zones of perceived injustices or disproportionality – in order to get a glimpse of what the positive concept might be. Here too, however, difficulties arise. It is not only Rumsfeld who has had a hard time figuring out what might constitute a proportionate or disproportionate act. At a recent Red Cross conference on proportionality and civilian casualties in The Netherlands, a prosecutor for the International Criminal Tribunal for the former Yugoslavia voiced Rumsfeldian confusion. He noted that in contemporary usage the word 'disproportionate' had become so abstract as to be almost meaningless:

You will not find anybody, certainly not myself, trying to give a proper meaningful standard for something that is 'disproportionate.' When you are talking about people, if you have one dead civilian and one dead soldier, is that disproportionate? … Nobody knows. We just have this concept, this word 'disproportionate'.[4]

These endemic ambiguities have been exacerbated and increased by the current global 'war on terror'. The war against al-Qaeda and the Taliban regime in Afghanistan and the 'preemptive' use of force and subsequent occupation in Iraq were both justified as proportionate responses in a war of national self-defence. Tactics that included various new forms of air war, the use of proxy troops, the relaxation of the rules against targeted assassination and torture, the indefinite detention of illegal combatants and 'ghost detainees', have been deemed 'proportionate' to the grave threat of terrorism. And the invasion and subsequent counter-insurgency actions in Iraq have been repeatedly described as displaying a 'measured' show of force. At the same time, terror tactics explicitly aim to undermine the two cardinal rules of just warfare: proportionality and discrimination. Fighting the current war on terror therefore opens up some of the fundamental commitments of just war theory and international humanitarian law, and asks us to rethink their purpose and the standards that guide their use.

At present, the ambiguous but central role of 'proportionality' is threatened on a number of fronts. First, its use is so widespread and its invocation so automatic that it has become almost a cliché. Second, the role of explicit and mass civilian targeting by terrorists, and the classic guerilla and urban warfare uses of civilian populations, have put civilians at the front and centre of postmodern warfare. Third, the very different attitudes towards death found in the Western militaries and in the terrorist forces – marked most obviously by the contrast between casualty aversion and force protection on the one side, and suicide bombing on the other – have highlighted the problem of what Walzer calls 'battlefield equality' in proportionality calculations. At the same time, our judgements of proportionality are currently distanced from crucial notions that formerly provided guidance and boundaries. These guideposts were provided by religion in early just war thinking, and then replaced by a language of rights, in international humanitarian law. A war fought against terror as a tactic, and against terrorists as illegal combatants, is a war fought against those without formal rights according to the law of armed conflict, and a notion of combatant rights is one of the concepts that provide restraint and moderation, or proportionate force, in war. Without it we are thrown back, I would maintain, on vague ideas of proportionality for guidance, and a secular conception of proportionality is easily abused and justifiably suspect.

Strictly speaking, the term 'proportionality' is used to refer to acceptable or justifiable levels of civilian casualties incurred during military operations: it refers to the 'proportionate' level of collateral damage, the unintended killing of civilians justified by the benefit of hitting a specific target. But the term also has a much wider and fluid scope that informs both strategic and tactical decisions on all levels. Weaponry is banned because of its disproportionate effects and the 'unnecessary' suffering it causes to soldiers as well as civilians. Soldiers are attacked using 'overwhelming', disproportionate firepower only (ideally) to make the battle or war shorter and therefore more 'proportionate' in the longer run. So I argue here that, in just war theory, law and strategy, there is a commitment to proportionality with respect to combatants as well as the innocent civilians caught in the crossfire.

In order better to understand some of the current commitments that guide thinking about proportionality, I begin by laying out how it has appeared conventionally, in just war theorising, international law and military targeting. Then I contrast this to the somewhat confusing use of the concept in the war on terror, and speculate as to what might account for some of our judgements. I end with some reflections on torture, risk and reciprocity.

CONVENTIONAL UNDERSTANDINGS OF PROPORTIONALITY

The concept of proportionality is embedded in any serious treatment of both justice and political action. Idealists and realists alike have long advocated the idea that justice involves a shifting notion of proportions, and a weighing or balancing of the costs and benefits of specific situations. In Aristotle's treatment of justice as a proportionate 'mean' in Book V of *The Ethics*, in Thucydides' account of measured justice as being in the interest of the state in the Mytilenean debate, and in Machiavelli's caution as to the dangers of 'excessive' cruelty, the pragmatic discussion of justice always includes proportionality, and such a proportionate response is seen as underlying the practice of politics. As Aristotle puts it:

> The very existence of the state depends on proportionate reciprocity; for men demand that they shall be able to requite evil with evil – if they cannot, they feel they are in the position of slaves – and to repay good with good – failing which, no exchange takes place, and it is *exchange that binds them together*.[5]

Insofar as war and violence have always been seen as enacting justice (especially punitive justice) and not merely asserting power, elements of proportionate restraint and the proportionate application of force have always played a strategic role.

For these theorists and strategists of war and statecraft, however, the necessity of proportionality is rooted in the human tendency towards disproportionate, unmeasured, passionate, and cruel responses. Proportionality is a concept that must be repeatedly invoked because it is so easily abused: as Clausewitz reminds us, war by its very nature tends towards the extreme and 'utmost use of force', and 'an act of violence *which in its application knows no bounds* and wherein any proportionate response to another's power is met by an escalating response and so on'.[6] This propensity for exaggeration and escalation, for overreaction and disproportion, can only be reined in, says Clausewitz, by political calculations and judgement; by wise policy.[7] The present-day manifestations of such calculations and policies can be found in the rules of engagement, use of force continuums, and targeting rules that guide conventional military tactics, and in the political and ethical arguments that justify the act of war in the first place. But in and amongst these more practical applications of the doctrine there is another consistent justification of proportionate action, one that is rooted in the care for the soul (or psychological well-being) of the combatant and the profession of the military. A lack of restraint harms not only wise policy, but also those who perpetuate this policy. More than anything, it was this concern that guided early just war thinkers.

The original Christian just war thinkers repeatedly stressed the necessity of restraint in order to maintain the virtue of the actor, and to mitigate the inner consequences of acts of violence: how could acts of war and violence be justified in advance, and forgiven in retrospect? Among the other requirements for a just war – just cause, proper authority, last resort, and probability of success – proportionality required balancing the future costs and benefits of any particular recourse to violence or war, including those inflicted upon the combatants themselves. For the earliest Christian thinkers such as Augustine, war was especially harmful to those soldiers engaged in an unjust or disproportionate war, so the use of proportionate force was necessary to rein in the real evils of war.[8]

The early developers of the chivalric code and the laws of armed combat also based mandatory conduct in a concern for the well-being of the knight, and the maintenance of the traditional warrior class, with status and honour tied to the appropriate (and restrained) application of violence. It was here that the requirement of discrimination had its origins: warriors could only honourably kill those who were legitimate and immediate threats to them. While Christian just wars often included unrestrained wars against infidels, the chivalric knight could not honourably kill non-combatants in conventional combat and still retain his status as a warrior. The traditional warrior ethos, with its membership requirements, standards of behaviour, and purification rituals, was then conjoined to a Christian concern with the inner soul of the warrior.

The third foundation of just war theory was provided by utilitarian or consequentialist thought. Although similar to the pragmatic concerns of Aristotle and Clausewitz described above, what distinguishes utilitarian thinking is an underlying concern with the overall good of actions, regardless of how it is calculated. The end of an action is not 'merely' state survival, or the maintenance of power, but some kind of additional 'good,' articulated as such. What is weighed, or balanced, is the 'good' of actions, their 'good' consequences (or not), and the 'good' achieved by sometimes 'bad' actions. Here, life itself and peace, rather than pure interest, is almost always seen as the underlying good that can serve as a basis to judge the loss of life among combatants and non-combatants.

Proportionality, in these three origins of just war thinking, balances the costs and benefits of warfare out of a concern for the outer status and inner soul of the combatant, the inherent innocence of the non-combatant, and for the ultimate good of life and peace: the consequences of violence. And this balancing is done as part of the prudent exercise of judgement that underlies any action taken into the future by a group. Again, proportionality shows up in two connected ways; the proportionality of the war itself (will the good of the war outweigh the evil of the harm inflicted?), and the proportionality of the means used (will the tactics employed result in an end that will outweigh the possible, but unintended, harm done to noncombatants and combatants alike?). In making these kinds of judgements, however, we can only judge acceptable levels of collateral damage, or the unintended harms of warfare, if we assume that the war itself, and the specific battle in particular, are just: either that the mistakes made are worth the short-term 'military objective', or the long-term benefit, or, more nefariously, that the other side 'deserves' the harms inflicted upon it, either because they have lost their right of protection, or because they have never had it in the first place.

It is just this latter connection between the justice of the war itself and the justice of the means employed that is so worrying about proportionality calculations. For Walzer, just war thinking begins with a notion of proportionality, a balancing of ends and means, military necessity and the obligation to protect victims.[9] But as he demonstrates in his criticism of Sidgwick and other utilitarians, this can easily lead to a notion of the 'sliding scale', the idea that the very justice of the war itself allows for unjust means to be employed, for a greater end.[10] The balancing of ends and means that is so much a part of proportionate justice carries with it this danger: ends can be exaggerated, or falsified, or simply misstated. Threats can be magnified, and actors demonised, thereby allowing overly harsh or prolonged reactions. The sliding scale, says Walzer, is almost always a recipe for disproportionate and un-measured uses of force. In certain narrow circumstances, however, Walzer seems to allow for a just use of unjust and overwhelming means, disproportionality in a state of 'supreme emergency'. But even here, he qualifies the situation. The rights of those being abused, say by strategic air bombing or, less dramatically, interrogation techniques, are being 'overridden', not 'denied'.[11] That is because for Walzer a theory of proportionality must be backed up by, and grounded in, a theory of human rights, which includes combatant and non-combatant rights, and even the non-derogable rights of terrorists.

The idea of proportionality has long been a staple of the laws of armed combat, applying again to weaponry, actions taken against soldiers, and actions involving civilians. The 1907 Hague Convention stated that 'the right of belligerents to adopt means of injuring the enemy is not unlimited', and went on famously to limit any weaponry calculated to cause 'unnecessary suffering'.[12] Most recently, in response to the unconventional wars of the mid-twentieth century, especially the guerilla warfare amidst civilians in Algeria and Vietnam, the 1977 Additional Protocols to the Geneva Convention explicitly extended the definition of proportionality to the protection of civilians. Civilians had always been shielded by the doctrine of discrimination, but the wording now also prohibited attacks that might cause '*incidental* loss of civilian life, and injury to civilians ... which would be *excessive in relation to the concrete and direct military advantage anticipated.*'[13] So, although non-combatants had always enjoyed some formal protections in the customary codes of war, the idea of proportionality was now used to judge the appropriateness of the acceptable levels of harm that could be unintentionally inflicted. The Additional Protocols then added that the only lawful objects of attack could be those that 'offer a *definite* military advantage', and that no violence or destruction should be 'disproportionate'.[14]

Recent cases in international law have attempted to address some of the ambiguities of this rule. The NATO bombing of Serbia and Kosovo in 1999 gave rise to a number of cases wherein the collateral damage seemed to be disproportionate. The combination of zero casualty rates among NATO forces, an unprecedented amount of precision guided weaponry, some high profile targeting mistakes, and at least 500 civilian casualties in a war promoted as 'humanitarian' resulted in charges of NATO war crimes. Charges of disproportionate and indiscriminate attacks by NATO forces were brought before the International Criminal Tribunal for the former Yugoslavia (ICTY), which then appointed a committee to address the allegations. These were contested by the International Committee of the Red Cross (ICRC), among others, and the argument went to the heart of the proportionality calculus problem: when working out acceptable levels of unintended losses, do you balance the harms against the policies and hoped-for gains of the campaign as a whole, or against the specific action taken? In one of the most notorious examples civilian train passengers died when their train crossed a bridge that was being bombed by a precision-guided missile, dropped from a NATO jet. The bridge was considered to be a military target whose destruction was seen as necessary to halt transportation of military equipment from Serbia to Kosovo, and once the bomb was pro-grammed, it could not be deflected even though the pilot supposedly caught sight of the train approaching the bridge, with a little time to spare.[15] The proportionality calculus would have demanded the balan-cing of the deaths of these innocent civilians with the good intended, but here the 'good' is hard to specify. Was it the destruction of the bridge itself, and its dual use for civilian and military transportation? Or was it the campaign for the human rights of Kosovar Albanians? Or the eradication of a legally elected, though bellicose, Serbian government? The law was unclear on this point, and legal scholars have long noted that those calling something disproportionate will point to the smaller action taken (the necessity of bombing the bridge), while those arguing for the proportionate action will see the act in a much larger picture (the protection of human rights, the need to rescue NATO from its earlier inaction in Bosnia, etc.). In this case, the Committee argued that, despite perceptions of disproportionate actions taken, no war crimes had been intentionally committed. It admitted, however, that 'the law is not sufficiently clear' in questions of proportionality. In a strongly worded critique, an ICRC lawyer asserted that the Report had adopted too 'broad a rule' of proportionality.[16]

Although these questions have become the critical lacunae of international law, they are also present in both the minute-by-minute judgements and the long-term strategies of military doctrine. The doctrine of proportionality, as used from within the military, guides the tactically minded rules of engagement and the 'use of force continuum', the choice of weaponry on the battlefield, and targets in bombing campaigns. It also guides the deployment and posture of soldiers themselves, especially their exposure to risk. Finally, and in line with *jus ad bellum* concerns, calculations of proportionality surround the rhetoric used to characterise a campaign: the language of threat, retaliation and justification. And at times, the *language* of precision and proportionate responses hides the very real disproportionate effects of the new technology.

In order adequately to understand how the military presently employs the doctrine of proportionality it is necessary first to take into account the effects of the two kinds of wars that occupied the military during the Cold War period: the fantasies and fears of nuclear confrontation and the strategy of deterrence on the one hand and protracted, unconventional, and asymmetric guerilla wars, most especially Vietnam. The frustrations of Vietnam are manifested in a variety of ways: the oft-mentioned Weinberger-Powell battlefield doctrine of 'overwhelming force'; the suspicions about 'operations other than war' (the use of the military for such 'soft' and incremental actions as peacekeeping, humanitarian intervention, nation building); and the resistance to the new focus on the increase in use of Special Operations Forces and to counter-insurgency in general. All of these doctrines and suspicions have transformed the ways in which we calculate proportionality, but all are related to another post-Vietnam syndrome: the aversion to casualties that has marked the use of force in the engagements of the last decade.[17]

The best example of the present-day military usage of proportionality is in the various computer-modelling programs that assess probable targets in an air campaign. The military readily admits that in the 'new wars' of the last decade or so, the ability precisely to guide weaponry and minimise civilian casualties is extremely important. 'Virtual war', or war in which munitions are often targeted and fired from a safe distance, is at the same time combined with an up-close-and-personal view of civilian suffering, and it requires a great deal of care to minimise not just the fact, but also the negative consequences of civilian casualties. Even though the military repeatedly points out that the laws of armed combat do not forbid civilian casualties, they admit that the perception of recklessness in wartime can be an effective political tool. 'For democracies waging modern war, [the law of armed combat] is indispensable for military success … Adversaries will use the fact or perception of Law of Armed Conflict (LOAC) violations to shatter the public's confidence in a war.'[18] Strategically, proportionality is necessary to maintain both the justice of the tactics employed, and the will to continue to employ them. 'A perception of poor conduct by a belligerent erodes the just cause of the war and undermines its legitimacy because causing unnecessary deaths or damage is seen as counter to inter-national norms and customs. In modern coalition warfare, attention to the law of war is a strategic imperative.'[19] So proportionality here is almost a marketing imperative, helping above all to sell the campaign to a sceptical public who can see the very real effects of bombs gone awry.

On the one hand this is in keeping with the ways in which the military should, in fact, see the need for restraint: from a realist per-spective. Unrestrained and disproportionate conduct will have strategic and political repercussions: it will not pay off over the long run, and part of the duty of law and just war theory is to provide both useful and moral guidance in difficult situations. On the other hand the current combin-ation of casualty aversion, precision-guided technology, and urban guerilla insurgencies, has resulted in a situation where what is deemed proportionate blurs some of the boundaries of Western military practice.

Prior to the war in Iraq, with its mounting daily casualties of soldiers, contractors, and Iraqi police forces, the military had been accused of disproportionate force protection, at the expense of civilian victims. Casualty aversion affects the calculations of proportionality in the following ways.[20] First, as I have argued, calculations of acceptable risk and loss among soldiers always, if not optimally, take into account the necessity of the war and its 'justice': operations that are not seen to be military and politically just and necessary by both civilian and military leaders alike are marked by a lower level of risk undertaken by soldiers.

Second, the remoteness of such operations is often staggering, wherein bombs are launched from thousands of miles away, with no risk at all to soldiers (except the important way in which distant, 'virtual', warfare results in an increase in overall animosity towards the posture of the USA). In fact, one could argue that terrorists see themselves as enacting a notion of reprisal, acting outside the bounds of war in protest over perceived injustices in the customs of remote air warfare. In Iraq, the remote bombing that marked the campaign in Afghanistan has been replaced by much more conventional urban combat. Nevertheless, air war in general, whether by helicopter gunship or remote aircraft carrier, tends to give the impression of disproportionality and indiscrimination, whether in Gaza, Baghdad, or Mogadishu. And asymmetric conflict like that in Iraq has always been marked by just such a notion of 'allowable illegality' in response to, or in reprisal for, injustice.

A final, more subtle way in which the proportionality calculus shows up within the military is in response to the economic costs of combat, both in terms of weaponry risked, and in the economic cost of training a professional soldier. Acceptable levels of risks nowadays take into account the cost of loss in human, economic and even psychological terms. Highly trained professional soldiers are 'assets' that should not be squandered in unclear conflicts for unclear ends, and in attacks that require an inordinate amount of risk. When war against terrorists is factored in, the danger of skewed calculations increases.

PROPORTIONALITY AND THE WAR ON TERROR

The most important work of the 1977 Additional Protocols was the classification of belligerents: what kinds of combatants should receive the protections of the laws of war? Although the 1949 Geneva Conventions were originally seen to apply only to combatants in state-to-state conflicts, the Additional Protocols applied the obligations and protections of the laws of war to those belligerents in intra-state conflicts, civil wars, and wars of liberation that met certain minimum requirements: centralised command and control, open display of weapons, and some sort of identifying insignia.[21] But terrorists, unlike guerilla warriors, never openly identify themselves as combatants. And terrorism has always been a tactic that is seen as outside the laws of war: those who employ it are illegal combatants, and not entitled to the rights and protections afforded to those who respect the principles that guide these laws. As the Bush administration and many legal experts have argued, the war on terrorism thus lies outside the scope of both the Geneva Conventions and the Additional Protocols, and complicates their usage and applicability.[22]

There are two ways in which this war stretches the boundaries of the laws of armed conflict. First, terrorists are by definition outside of the legal definition of a combatant, and so are formally unprotected. Extending the legal protection of combatant rights to those who do not, by definition, respond to a notion of reciprocity carries with it the significant danger of legitimising a delegitimised and abhorrent tactic. Secondly, the judgement of a proportionate response requires a knowledge of the 'end' of combat in two significant ways: the literal end, in time, wherein peace will be resumed, and an overall goal or strategy that is do-able, an end that justifies the means and the injustices of some of those means. The eradication of a form of evil, wherever it may be, might be a laudable but hardly realistic goal. Certainly, the 'end' of a war on terror and terrorists, seems to offer no definite guidelines for judging those means. How many civilian casualties should be balanced against ridding the world of weapons of mass destruction and the terrorists who use them? For how long must this threat be combated? The deaths of Taliban, al-Qaeda, and Northern Alliance prisoners at Qala-i-Jangi prison constitute a perfect example: falling between the cracks of the legal definitions of combatants, with unclear prisoner-of-war status, the response to their uprising could only be criticised on the grounds that it was vaguely disproportionate.

AFGHANISTAN AND IRAQ: VARIATIONS IN PROPORTIONALITY JUDGEMENTS

The war against al-Qaeda and the toppling of the Taliban regime in Afghanistan in late 2001 was widely seen as a justified response to the attacks of September 11th. Political commentators, scholars and ethicists saw some sort of military response as warranted and even as fulfilling most of the requirements of a just war.[23] There were some, however, who pointed out the need to continue to see acts of terrorism as constituting criminal acts, or 'emergencies', rather than acts of war: was it possible to have a war against a global non-state actor?[24] In Afghanistan, because of Taliban support for al-Qaeda, the case seemed relatively simple: there could be a limited war in Afghanistan, to topple a regime accused of harbouring a terrorist group. But could the war be pursued to Pakistan and Saudi Arabia, to Indonesia or Sudan? Aside from a limited well-publicised remote attack over Yemen, there has been little open war in other states.[25]

With Afghanistan, in addition, there was a vague sense of a need for a kind of swift reprisal: that the deaths of innocents on September 11th allowed for a kind of limited impunity in attacking Afghanistan. This is not to say that targets weren't chosen carefully, or that there weren't attempts to limit collateral damage. Plenty of evidence exists to show the opposite. But the character of the campaign in Afghanistan was marked by a sense of justified reprisal, not the 'measured show of force' so often invoked in Iraq, but a need to demonstrate 'overwhelming firepower' to our enemies. The tally of civilian deaths, as a result, was disproportionately high, especially when compared to the risk taken and lives lost among American and British troops. The proportionality calculus, so to speak, was skewed to allow for a more acceptable level of civilian casualties, in this case because the threat was so extreme and the need for retaliation urgent. Interestingly, the ratio of combatant casualties to civilian casualties in the campaign 'over' Kosovo had a similarly skewed number, but was for the entirely opposite reason: the lives of our soldiers and the loss of their equipment were not deemed worth the lives or the human rights of the Kosovar Albanians.

Despite praise for the fact that large numbers of Marines supported the Special Operations Forces 'boots on the ground' in Afghanistan, evidence of continued risk aversion gave rise to criticism on a number of fronts. The overuse of proxy Northern Alliance troops often resulted in ineffective campaigns, corruption and numerous allegations of prisoner-of-war and detainee abuse. The high-pressure need for quick intelligence clearly contributed to the bending of the rules for interrogation, first in Afghanistan, and then more notoriously, in Iraq. The overuse of air power led to the most blatant mistakes and civilian casualties, most of which have now been catalogued and analysed by numerous organisations.[26] The war in Afghanistan was seen as justified, as *jus ad bellum*, but its methods and means opened it up to criticism as relatively indiscriminate and ineffective.

In contrast, the invasion of Iraq is now widely seen as a disproportionate and illegal response to an unclear threat. The justifications for war – the arguments for its justice and its necessity – spanned a number of fronts. First, it was argued that this would be a war of preemptive self-defence in the face of the supposed presence of weapons of mass destruction. At other times, it was argued that this was a war of law enforcement, since Iraq had repeatedly denied weapons inspectors full access, and had flouted UN resolutions. Finally, it was argued that this was a war of humanitarian intervention against a brutal pariah regime, a war of Iraqi liberation from dictatorship and regime change. These arguments received criticism on many fronts: was this kind of war the proportionate response? Despite this, once the war began, and throughout the occupation, there has been little criticism of disproportionality. Even though many civilians died during the initial battle in Baghdad, and the toll since has amounted to at least ten times the numbers of coalition soldiers killed (the number of which at the time of writing had just past one thousand). Despite counter-insurgency campaigns, air strikes, and pitched battles, the civilian death toll has received far less press than the scandal involving humiliation and torture at Abu Ghraib and the kidnapping and murder of Western hostages. Why might this be so? The following simple chart (one employed all too often by political scientists) lays out the contrast.

Table 4.1: Proportionality in the Afghanistan and Iraq Wars

	Afghanistan	Iraq
Jus ad bellum Just strategy?	Proportionate: • Last resort • Self-defence	Disproportionate: • No weapons of mass destruction • No relationship to war on terror
Jus in bello Just tactics?	Disproportionate: • Too many civilian casualties • Not enough ground force	Proportionate: • Soldiers at risk

What might account for these different assessments of proportionality in the areas of *jus ad bellum* and *jus in bello*? I suspect that a large role is played, perhaps unconsciously, by the proportionate risk taken by our own soldiers. Civilian casualties are seen as acceptable mistakes if there are risks taken by those who seek to avoid such mistakes. Despite the relative coherence of the campaign as a whole, despite the 'necessity' of the war itself, collateral damage is harder to justify if it is not matched, or at least acknowledged, by risk taken on the ground. This means that the demand for proportionate justice in warfare is not simply a balance of ends and means: 'is the "end" or aim of the war (or battle) just enough to allow, or excuse, mistakes and excesses in the neighbourhood, or in the jail?' The demand for proportionality also balances the exposure of perpetrator and victim to violence and risk.[27] Just as in domestic law, the 'punishment' has to fit the crime, and we excuse certain mistakes or disproportionate results (capital punishment, for example) if sufficient care was taken to prevent them, or if the crime is seen to be so heinous as to 'warrant' a kind of over-reaction. Perhaps the first 'combat' death of the war, that of the CIA interrogator Johnny Spann, at the Qala-i-Jangi prison uprising in November 2001, gave rise to the kind of chaotic and disproportionate response (the destruction of the entire prison and all of those in it) that so stumped Rumsfeld above. In other words, violence can only be proportionate (just, legitimate, understood) if there is actual vulnerability exposed and risks taken.

One way of testing this argument is to look at the extreme case, that of torture: the infliction of extreme suffering by one who takes no risk. When there is an extreme asymmetry in power, we do not see the exercise of that power as proportionate or just, and it strikes us so: we call it 'cruel and unusual', 'unnecessary suffering', and we call the human right abused 'non-derogable'. Part of why this is so, I argue, is due to the asymmetry of risk: the torturer is safe, and the victim is completely powerless. It does not matter, here, whether the victim is innocent or guilty, combatant or non-combatant. We now judge torture to be a disproportionate response to danger. And although there has been widespread debate, especially since September 11th in the USA, as to what exactly constitutes torture, and what kinds of circumstances may warrant what kinds of interrogation methods, there is an underlying consensus that sheds useful light as we try to clarify the boundaries of proportionality. The consensus which claims that torture is wrong rests on a number of assumptions: that the intelligence gathered is not necessarily reliable, that there is a fundamental human right being abused, and that the consequences of condoning torture often lead to an exacerbation of conflict. But there are two assumptions, often less articulated, that share some elements of early just war thinking on the reasons for acting proportionately. First, it harms the victimisers, and by extension the society that condones their actions. And this harm – political, cultural or psychological – rests at least in part on the disproportionality of the risk taken and harm inflicted. We do not condone the application of overwhelming force to those that are completely in our power. By extension, what strikes us as disproportionate in warfare are those kinds of actions that do not carry any risk, and inflict, at the same time, large-scale destruction. Partly, I am arguing, this is because it reminds us of torture. And in fact, this is what much of modern air war and 'psycho-ops' theory attempts to do: to apply mental pressure to civilian populations instead of wholesale killing. But we deem these kinds of actions disproportionate if they are done with impunity, or with little risk to those who strike. And in wars which are fought in the media as well as on the battlefield or in the neighbourhood, perceptions of disproportionality and overwhelming, riskless, force, incur the same kind of resentment that torture has always done among insurgents and the populations who support them.

The second risk of both disproportionate action and torture are the costs to the perpetrators, which again, was stressed in early just war thinking. Restraint and proportionality in both aims and means protected the soul of the combatant – or the politician – from the dangers of excess, from the lust of violence for its own sake. I suggest that at the intersection of military strategy and just war thinking, this same concern with the well-being of the combatant, his mental health as well as his physical survival, contributes to the calculation of proportionality.

HOW TO THINK ABOUT PROPORTIONALITY NOW?

In a moving essay on the problem of proportionality, Blaise Pascal wondered how it might be possible for human beings ever to understand themselves in proportion to the vastness of the universe, and the minuteness of a mite.[28] What are the natural boundaries for our own self-conception? New kinds of warfare and new kinds of combatants, weaponry and threats, can often result in a sense that the old boundaries and old rules, should no longer apply. Our ability to wage war justly often seems to be at odds with the ability to wage war successfully, and never more so than when we do battle against 'terror', or 'evil', in general. But the rules and guidelines for restraint in warfare and for care in target selection ask that one must always balance harm done, intentionally or unintentionally, to combatant or non-combatant, or quasi-combatant, with the consequences of that harm, and most specifically the 'success' of the mission. Military commanders and legal experts will always argue whether the 'good' which balances the harm done is the ultimate good of the entire campaign or war, and its articulated goal (the liberation of the Iraqi people, or the stabilisation of the Middle East, for instance), or the good of the specific battle or air strike. As Rumsfeld noted in the quotation which began this chapter, there are ways in which an airstrike, or a seemingly disproportionate act at a prison (or in an interrogation room), could have the deterrent effect of stopping other riots (or making other inmates more fearful). This more amorphous and hard-to-characterise balancing act begs the question, it seems to me, since strategies and threats can always be magnified to allow for any kind of action or excuse any kind of mistake. Proportionality, as Walzer reminds us, must be guided by a sense that those who are the victims of our violence have rights that were 'overridden', not 'denied'. In addition to the careful target selection that we try to use, the victims and kin of those who suffer collateral damage deserve our apologies, and some kind of swift reparation.

Finally, there is the difficult notion of how those with more military power should behave, relative to those who may have less power but be more willing to fight indiscriminately, and using the kinds of terror tactics we have witnessed recently in Russia and Spain, and on September 11th. Why should states continue to abide by human rights rules and the law of armed combat, while fighting back against terrorists? Here, statesmen of old, even realists like Machiavelli and Thucydides, would argue for the prudential use of restraint, and early religious thinkers would remind us of the inner cost of a loss of restraint, or disproportionate behaviour, for ourselves and those soldiers who act in our name.

As formal human rights law has expanded, the laws of armed conflict have become more and more codified, and as military lawyers exercise influence over targeting, actual state practice – that all-important basis for customary international law – is being rewritten. For both international law and just war theory, this is a time of uncertainty, and one that calls for careful consideration of our standards of evaluation, as we exercise the judgement, protest the decisions, condemn or approve of the actions, and question the rhetoric of those who justify war and its means.

Table 4.2: The Main Argument

Proportionality Calculations	Type(s) of War	Respect for Proportionality Evident in (examples):
in traditional/ classical codes of conduct	traditional (e.g. Homeric)	chivalric codes
in just war theories	conventional	• *Jus ad bellum* • *Jus in bello* • *Jus post bellum*
in international humanitarian law codes and conventions	• conventional: regulated by Hague, Geneva Conventions • unconventional: regulated by Additional Protocols	legal prohibition of • 'Unnecessary' suffering • Excessive force • Civilian harm
in conventional modern military strategy	• air war • ground war	• 'Collateral damage' calculations • Rules of engagement
in the 'war against terrorism'	unconventional: • counter-insurgency • 'proxy' • covert	unclear that the enemy ('terrorists') deemed to be morally subject to proportionality constraints

Concern with Proportionality Focused on (examples):	Means to Secure Proportionality (examples):
ethical status of warriors	• desire to embody ethical virtues • reciprocity of combatant behaviour
• 'innocence' (moral responsibility and liability of combatants and non-combatants) • 'corruption' – protecting souls from evil resulting from unjust violence	control of military activity by: political/military authorities
• types of weaponry • combatant behaviour • civilian protections and exemptions	• national and international legal sanctions • monitoring by international NGOs
• professional responsibilities of combatants	reciprocity of combatant behaviour
concern is manifest only in so far as war's perceived popular legitimacy still regarded as partly dependent on it: potentially highly diminished when 'terrorists' are the opponents	no formal means recognised beyond whatever indirectly results from strategic considerations and 'casualty phobia'

Table 4.3: Individual Cases

Cases	Victim Status	Risks taken	Proportionate or Disproportionate?
Torture: Abu Ghraib	Combatants	None	Disproportionate
Torture: Guantanamo Bay	Combatants civilians	None	Disproportionate
Bombing of Qala-i-Jangi prison	Combatants/ POWs	None	Disproportionate
Deaths in Afghan village	Civilians	Very few	Disproportionate

NOTES

1. This comes from paragraph 48 of the Final Report to the Prosecutor (of the International Criminal Tribunal for the Former Yugoslavia) by the Committee Established to Review the NATO Bombing Campaign Against the Federal Republic of Yugoslavia, 16 June 2000. The document is available at http:www.un.org/icty/pressreal/nato061300.htm.
2. See www.defenselink.mil.news/Nov2001/t11302001_1130sd.html.
3. Basic texts summarising the concept of proportionality include Coates (1997), Johnson (1999), Lackey (1989), Norman (1995) and Walzer (1992).
4. William Fenwick, quoted in Netherlands Red Cross (2001), p. 84.
5. Aristotle [c. 350 BC] (1955), Book V.v, 1133a, p. 281.
6. Clausewitz (1976), Book 1, chapter 5.
7. Ibid., chapters 23–4.
8. See Augustine [413–26 AD] (1991), Book XIX, chapter 7. This is not just for Christians: almost all cultures have rituals of purification to restore the combatant to health after engaging in violence.
9. Walzer (1992), p. 129.
10. Ibid, pp. 130–3.
11. Ibid., p. 259.
12. 1907 Hague Convention IV, Articles 22 and 23e. See also the earlier Declaration of St Petersburg (1868), and the Hague Declaration IV, 3 (1899), on the use of expanding bullets. See finally the 1980 Convention on Prohibitions or Restrictions on the Use of Certain Conventional Weapons Which May Be

Deemed to be Excessively Injurious or to Have Indiscriminate Effects. See Roberts and Guelf (eds) (2000).

13. 1977 Additional Protocol I to the 1949 Geneva Conventions, Articles 51 and 57. See Roberts and Guelf (eds) (2000).
14. Ibid.
15. This comes from General Wesley Clark's account of the incident, given at a press conference at NATO Headquarters, Brussels, on 15 April 1999.
16. Ronzitti (2000).
17. See Carmola (2004).
18. Denny (2003).
19. Ibid.
20. For an excellent account of the political and military reality of casualty aversion, see especially Larson (1996). I discuss casualty phobia in recent conflicts in Carmola (2004).
21. See 1949 Geneva Convention IV, articles 1–3, and 1977 Additional Protocol 1, article 44. See Roberts and Guelf (eds) (2000).
22. See, for instance, Aldrich (2002) and Roberts (2002).
23. Among others, see most prominently Elshtain (2003).
24. See Howard (2002).
25. Covert 'police actions' are not counted here, and in general do not come under the just war theory provisions, as their covertness undermines the role of citizens in assuring themselves that wars undertaken in their name are just and reasonable. This is a problem that I address in Carmola (2004).
26. See especially Conetta (2004).
27. This even occurs in soldier-to-soldier battlefield judgements, usually made by outsiders. Witness here the criticism, in the 1991 Gulf War, of certain 'discriminate' but 'disproportionate' battlefield tactics such as bulldozing Iraqi troops in their sand trenches, the use of Fuel Air Explosives, and the disproportionate attack approved by General Barry McCaffrey on the 'highway of death'.
28. Pascal [1660] (1961), no. 84, pp. 51–6.

Chapter 5

JUST WAR? JUST CHILDREN?

HELEN BROCKLEHURST

—◁▷—

Despite the enormous shifts that have taken place in the conduct of warfare over the past centuries, theories of just war have had a remarkably continuous currency: largely the same nomenclature and considerations run through the tradition's history. Indeed, few concepts have had such enduring resonance as the very idea of a just war, shaping even the otherwise guileless rhetoric of contemporary US presidents, for example. This volume, a critical *re*appraisal of just war tenets, itself illustrates and explores that appeal in the context of a new and particularly challenging security environment. However, in terms of just war theorising's application to children, this is but a first meeting: just war theory *appraised* – and it is not an easy introduction. Childhood is an ambiguous life-stage, war and security are contested concepts; contested, too, is the relationship between humanitarian and international human rights law and the status of child victims and child perpetrators. Neither is this an introduction that can or should be made comfortably. For many children who have been present or engaged in war, it is made posthumously. For all children it is necessarily made on their behalf, an issue of participation which will be addressed later.

Children's unqualified conceptual absence from just war theorising itself suggests an assumption of children's status as comparable to (adult) civilians or innocents. This implicit judgement will be challenged theoretically and empirically. It will be shown that just war theory has a more complex arena of application than has previously been recognised, and it will be argued that it should recourse to children additionally and separately. Children are vulnerable in different ways from adults, and war is also fought directly by children. Children's participation in war

114

fundamentally challenges the traditional conception of *jus in bello*, its many tensions exacerbated by the ambiguity surrounding the very application of the concept of 'childhood'. More significantly, it will be suggested how, in its present form, the doctrine of just war theory might ultimately bind children and indeed all persons into the very frameworks and evils from which it attempts to free them.

First, the chapter will turn to the conceptions of the child that may be informing or be able to inform just war theory.

CHILDREN

Children's experiences (and specifically here their experiences in war) are shaped both by their underdevelopment as persons and by assumptions and concomitant expectations about childhood that are bestowed individually, collectively, simultaneously, arbitrarily and even contradictorily. Central to this chapter then, is the significance of the variegation in the conceptions of the child. We may each hold a basic idea of what a child is. As Archard explains, such a '*concept* of children requires that children be distinguishable from adults in respect of some unspecified set of attributes'. But 'a *conception* of childhood is a specification of those attributes'.[1] There is no single definition or conception of the child in use for all children worldwide, even based on age, a fact which matters a great deal when we are trying to articulate what it is about children that might make us consider them as referents for just war theory, for example as being never liable for death or as a group whose security should be prioritised. Debates over conceptions of children are extremely complex above and beyond the evident differences in conceptions held across different cultures and jurisdictions. For example, if one turns to international common law, and the United Nations' Convention on the Rights of the Child (ratified by all but two states) a child is defined as 'every human being below the age of 18 years, unless under the law applicable to the child, majority is attained earlier'.[2] A simple definition such as this, of a primary life span, does not however illustrate how or why half of the world's human beings who are under the age of eighteen[3] are potentially receiving or deserving of different treatment compared to adults.

It is clear, though, that childhood appears to have seemingly incontestable, natural and self-evident qualities. Certainly, maturation is both a distinguishing feature of children and also one that importantly affords them different or extra needs to adults. But physical development, though in many ways a defining characteristic of childhood, continues into adulthood, finally stopping near the age of twenty-five. Perhaps, then, there could be specified a certain degree of underdevelopment which defines 'childhood'. Implying that this degree indicates a lack of self-sufficiency in crucial respects, Ruddick suggests, 'when you see children as demanding care, the reality of their vulnerability and the necessity of a caring response seem unshakeable'. Yet how we see children does not necessarily dictate how we react to them. 'The presence of a child does not guarantee its care.'[4] Children's care or protection may, however, be prioritised as, unlike other persons, they have yet to realise the full potential concomitant with experience and growth. This may be central as to why, if they are killed or maimed, their loss is deemed to be in some ways so qualitatively different to – often worse than – that of an adult. As with other aspects of children's uniqueness, this is a normative assessment, and its duration may be contested. When has a person realised their potential? When is a life not wasted? It is certainly an easier judgement to make the younger the children in question happen to be, but it may not help us much in demarcating the boundary we seek.

The most common marker of the boundary of childhood is the 'age of majority', which is not *directly* a physical quality so much as a social, religious, cultural or legal device by which societies officially establish the transition to adulthood. Biological or mental issues of underdevelopment are not absent from this identification, of course. As the 'minority' of a community, children are most frequently deemed to lack the capacities necessary for running their lives as full members of it, comparable to the cohort of mentally impaired adults. The age at which a child is allowed to vote in effect also marks the age at which a community formally acknowledges mature intellectual capabilities and in most of the world's sovereign states this is set at eighteen years.[5] Yet interestingly, in terms of both moral and cognitive development, children reach levels comparable with adults between the ages of twelve and fourteen. As already mentioned, physical growth occurs throughout childhood and into adulthood: cell renewal and growth continues throughout both periods. However it is only during a certain span of early childhood that the physical appearance and development of particular vital organs, including the brain, takes place. This fact is significant in itself, pinpointing one of the very few characteristics of children that are not shared by other dependent persons. Concomitant with this threshold of 'vital' development are risks. Before the age of five, for example, a child's undeveloped body will absorb more toxins than they will in the rest of their entire adult lifetime. Their brains are also rapidly developing, leading to less tangible risks inherent in their immaturity, and common in war:

> While an adult may be severely affected by a traumatic experience and as a result suffer some personality alteration, a child's personality, in the absence of pre-existing development, may not be altered, but actually developed by a traumatic event. Any or all of a child's cognitive development may not only be altered but actually developed.[6]

Despite huge variations in the span of childhood experienced worldwide, then, such factors help to explain why a majority of cultures do hold a conception of a very young child as an 'infant' and the majority deem a prepubescent person, that is up to the age of about twelve, to be unquestionably a 'child'. This span, barely more than a decade, in which a conception of childhood is bestowed, and bodies and minds are perhaps uniquely vulnerable to harm, does then offer a starting point for a possible universal category of 'childhood'. Though narrow compared to typical Western and rights-based spans of childhood, these years may be thought of as a lowest-case denominator where for all children the attributes of adulthood are not totally granted or attained. But there is admittedly also a sliding scale of vulnerability even within this age-span and, in moving beyond it, a transition is taking place whose form, duration and timing may vary widely in children, and also vary between female children, for example, with regard to the onset of menses.

The recent work of Boyden and Levison is worth citing in full here to capture the diversity of 'childhood':

> Many different kinds of criteria – although seldom age – are used to demarcate childhood. These criteria include the commencement of work, end of schooling, onset of menarche, betrothal, and marriage amongst others … Further, children in different social classes within the same society may reach adulthood at different ages, depending on their social and economic roles.[7]

Several processes of majority may unfold sequentially and simultaneously. Cadet soldiers in the UK may marry with parental consent at
sixteen, make life at sixteen, risk life and take life at seventeen, but not
legally watch a violent or pornographic movie under any circumstance
for another year. As Boyden and Levison note, 'because they raise
children's social and economic status and constitute public affirmation
of community membership, such transitions far outweigh the universal
age-based threshold in their significance for children'.[8]

Childhood and its end-point may, then, be *essentially* a cultural
construction. Attempts to locate universal patterns in childhood
encounter significant evidence of both genetic and cultural variation. A
society's priorities may also quite explicitly force a change in the
parameters of childhood. 'Childhood' is clearly a concept which can be
manipulated to suit needs: it can be made and unmade, especially in
war. Through Military Orders imposed by Israel on the occupied
territories, for example, Palestinians have been reclassified as adults
from the ages of sixteen. Their Israeli counterparts are deemed to be
children until eighteen.[9] The former are thus liable for adult crimes and
adult punishment. In many conflicts, deliberately premature adulthood
is bestowed upon children through militarised initiation rites so that
they may participate more fully in the fighting. Even without formal
rites, intentional participation in conflict can be interpreted by boys and
their peers as a gateway to adult or youth status.

CHILDREN AND WAR

Throughout history, children have knowingly and unknowingly participated in armed conflict. From total war to low-level civil war, they have
featured significantly in both intra- and inter-state practices of security,
as threats, models, investments, resources and icons.[10] Their use is not
new – but contemporary recognition of this has been hard-earned
indeed. Periods of military intensification, secession or disintegration
give rise to intensified practices of nationalisation and militarisation;
practices which involve appropriation of the child and familial sphere
and are often in place prior to the actual outbreak of conflict. Notably,
children can acquire or volunteer political and military agency before,
during and even after political violence. Terrorism, civil war and total
war are dependent to varying degrees on the manipulation of children,
and they share similar rationales. Children and their guardians are a

form of security themselves and are clearly treated as such. Battles which use children's bodies and minds as effective weapons have so far taken place without being recorded in the pages of security textbooks, remaining outside the knowledge of those who accept the typically presented parameters and ontology of security. Women and children are still fought *for*, as if they are 'safely inside' and away from the politics that will be acted out for them. But through the incorporation of children and the family into militarised practices and the logical corollary of this, the targeting of the (enemy) 'civilian' sphere, concepts that just war theory relies upon – war and peace, victim and perpetrator, military and domestic – are disturbed.

Children's use or their presence may also render *them* as protectors just as it may also render them *un*protected. According to Peterson:

> the dichotomies of protector – protected, direct – indirect violence, war and peace are inter-woven. Denying them as oppositional dichotomies means recognising the complexity of (inter)dependence, the interrelationship of oppressions and the uncertainty of security.[11]

To substantiate this point, consider the example of child soldiers. In spite of the international legal norm that a child is a person under the age of eighteen, the international age limit for soldiers' voluntary recruitment and use is currently set at fifteen and many are much younger than this. Over forty-five states use approximately 300,000 child soldiers.[12] (Their lives are highly expendable and, as such, the total figure almost certainly runs far higher.) It is estimated that the majority are active in government armed forces and the youngest are to be found in armed groups.[13] They may constitute ten per cent of current combatants.[14] An outline of their use and abuse in this capacity, then, can help to frame some issues regarding the potential for just war theory's different treatment of children.

The changing character of warfare in the latter half of the twentieth century markedly altered the tasks with which children are now charged. Lighter weaponry coupled with extreme poverty, Western training techniques and educational indoctrination for example, have considerably advanced the capacity of the child soldiers and young resistance fighters and with this also created new opportunities for children's abuse. Guerrilla war and very light weaponry alone[15] make it possible for children to fight and kill from as young as six years. The list below (which is not exhaustive) is of typical roles adopted or assumed by children and currently recognised and addressed by advocates of children's rights:

- uniformed government troops with weaponry and varying degrees of competence
- uniformed and non-uniformed combatants in armed groups with weaponry and varying degrees of competence
- unarmed messengers or distracters on the front line
- recruiters and trainers of other children
- commanders of units of children
- informants
- prisoners or detainees
- human shields detained in strategic locations
- minesweepers
- 'non-participants' avoiding capture or action

These roles do not assume that the child's status is shared or agreed by all parties concerned. These children may be solely in adult company, with other children, under the direction of adults, or even under the command of older children. They may be active agents with varying degrees of self-awareness. They may or may not be willing combatants. In today's conflicts the distinction between voluntary and enforced recruitment is often blurred, given the fact that militias may offer far more to children than just a life of combat. The more unstable a country is, the more the military may even resemble a safe harbour in some senses. Children may be motivated to enlist as perhaps the only way to ward off poverty and insecurity, attracted by the familial-style environment and the provision of food and clothing. Orphaned and traumatised children may 'simply' receive food or treats in return for using guns.[16] Their role may primarily be a means of survival in the face of other threats: starvation, isolation, or abduction to name but a few. Children may therefore join to *live* – not to kill or be killed. Conversely, child soldiering may be experienced as a well-founded and complex site of development and apprenticeship, particularly in longstanding guerrilla campaigns. Groups such as the Tamil Tigers of Sri Lanka have been known to provide education integrated with military experience, tutoring boys from the age of nine in the importance of discipline, honesty and respect for the rights of ordinary citizens.[17] Here, child soldiers may be allowed to imitate adults in combat but only in specific positions that do not exceed their strengths or place them at risk of physical harm, 'apprentices' behind the frontline. They are also free to leave.

Children's roles as soldiers may overlap with those of adults and some children may clearly relish taking control. Other roles may be specially designed for them based on pejorative assumptions about their physical and mental underdevelopment and opportunities found within. In Colombia child soldiers are 'nicknamed "little bells" by the military, which uses them as expendable sentries, and "little bees" by the guerrillas, because they "sting" their enemies before they know they are under attack'.[18]

A significant change in child soldiering, thought to have been actually promoted by agencies from the West during the bitter proxy wars of the Cold War, is the deliberate use of children as combatants precisely because of their perceived limitations or weaknesses. Children can be employed to do what their adult counterparts do not want to do or think that children can do better. They have thus become both deadlier and more likely to die. Some children have been encouraged to think of war as only a game, or have been drugged so that they will have no inhibitions. In this way children have been manipulated differently from adults and experience different consequences. Mimicking adults whilst high on drugs or 'playing the game' in Sierra Leone, such children have been perceived as being treated as neither child nor adult, neither victims nor aggressors – but both.[19] Young children are more vulnerable to harm than other soldiers by virtue of their susceptibility to terror and less developed faculties, though older children may be no less vulnerable than some adults and perhaps some are more resilient.

The roles, circumstances and responses outlined above illustrate the ambiguities of children's status as combatants. The dominant representation of child soldiers however is unambiguously of persons who have attained premature adulthood despite inhabiting a child's body.

UN-POLITICAL CHILDREN

A crucial theme which needs to be explored at this point is the dominant and arguably generally held perception that the 'political child' is an oxymoron. This is integral to so much of our thinking about politics, war and justice. We do not commonly regard the child as a political child, least of all as an actor in the international system, yet children's politicisation is enabled precisely because it is also being simultaneously underplayed. As the author has explored elsewhere,[20] the conceptual separation of political experiences and childhood is symptomatic of three related ways in which the relationship between children and the political is enacted.

Firstly concepts of the political and of the child can be demonstrated to be antithetical or contained: a mutual exclusivity, which can also be traced back through their respective originating disciplines of thought. Children have been typically defined from the standpoint of adults and therefore perceived as their opposite, a conception that both privileges adult qualities and separates children from these qualities:

> The ideal adult is equipped with certain cognitive capacities, rational, physically independent, autonomous, has a sense of identity and is conscious of its beliefs and desires, and thus able to make informed free choices for which it can be held personally responsible. Childhood is defined as that which lacks the capacities, skills and powers of adulthood. If childhood has virtues they are such only because of their very inappropriateness to adult life.[21]

Writers such as Farson argue that a modern-day conception of child-hood is actually invented, and forcibly so, through a desire to distin-guish between adult and infantile qualities which in turn give adults greater powers.[22] Mutually informing but exclusionary concepts of childhood and politics, then, contort and court as 'political anomalies' the visible examples that disturb their polarisation.

Such examples of 'contained' or un-political childhood, and its corollary – politics as a sphere which impacts on children but shares little with them – are ubiquitous, and arguably prevent significant political recognition of children's actual daily and low-profile interdepen-dence with the political world. In addition, explicit or sensationalised representation of particular child soldiers or hostages, fosters the illusion that they are not prior members of the political sphere but are exceptionally and temporarily drawn into it. The less sensational but no less political roles played by children are obscured. This third mechanism is termed *infant power*, describing the strategic harnessing of very young and/or female children, to embody particular and universal qualities of weakness for political ends, which are invoked in the emotive raison d'être of security and frequently featured in war propaganda for example. The gilding of such children with notably feminine associations, particularly in heavily mediated environments, further legitimises their paternalistic protection, however futile that might be. That children's politicisation is simultaneously underplayed in this way actually guarantees their prolific and undisturbed (ab)use in security practices. In turn, an adult-generated silence about children's political and military presence in these respective disciplines merely sustains children's representation as consequences and not causes, victims and not agents, temporary refugees and not key referents. These modalities are echoed in the media's global and only characterisation of children in war zones as 'premature adults' through having lost their innocence, their childhood. Children's fate is not only sealed on the battlefield, but also in distant minds and on pages such as these.

This conceptual separation of political experiences and childhood becomes particularly prevalent in times of conflict. In apartheid South Africa, children and youth acted as social and political agents and defenders of communities, yet in their subsequent portrayal their enemies exaggerated their ages, or switched to the term 'youth', and used criminal descriptors such as 'rioters' as if also to render them politically impotent. After the struggle their political contribution has had little recognition. Their new-found political agency has become wasted. Ironically, if recalled or repeated, it redefined them as 'problematic elements' and isolated them from the very community they helped to bring about.[23] Similarly very young Palestinian children of the *intifada* are labelled first as Arabs or terrorists in Israeli media and indifference is shown to their age.[24] Unlike South Africa, of course, this conflict continues and with it comes their politicisation. As one social worker in Palestine has noted, 'the community doesn't allow child prisoners to be children as they are considered heroes and political prisoners'.[25] Not surprisingly, this perception adds to the many barriers in reintegration and healing which are aimed at children.

JUST WAR?

The fragility of just war theory is often illustrated through questions. What is meant by war and who defines war? In other words, when has war started and when and for how long do we apply just war theory? What is known or understood of justice by combatants? As shown, the political world is constitutive of children's roles and presence and not separated from them or simply impacting on them. In terms of children, then, the questions may be harder still. When one considers the nature and extent of children's involvement in conflict can we say that just war theory has been conceptualised with children properly in mind? If we are only just beginning to understand children's agency then perhaps we can only just begin to know the extent to which responsibility for them and responsibilities also held by them are being met. The following three points which validate a separate consideration of children as subjects of just war theory are adjoined by questions that are consequently urged upon us:

In war, children are vulnerable in different ways to adults.

Children may experience physical, mental and emotional harm differently from adults and they may be specifically maltreated with this intention. The unique vulnerabilities of very young children may make them first in the queue for protection.

- Is war that harms or targets children ever just?
- Might risk to children limit or guide just cause and conduct more so than other referents?
- Of what understanding of justice might such children be conscious?

Children are disproportionately vulnerable in war.

In the multitude of ways that war is harmful, it is typically more so for children. Civilian children along with women form ninety percent of casualties in ongoing conflicts.[26]

- How can just conduct reflect this disproportionality?
- Should we for example also secure (young) children's immediate guardians in order to best secure them?

Warfare is exercised directly by children.

Child soldiers, increasing in number, create potential dilemmas of just combat for their adversaries and leave post-conflict challenges of personal and societal restoration in their wake.

- Does harm or potential harm of children warrant greater urgency for intervention?
- Is 'a child' ever rightly regarded as 'a combatant'? If so, does children's bellicose participation warrant a different proportional response? What are such children's understandings of justice? Are child combatants also subject to just-war responsibilities?
- Might children's permitted roles in war also necessitate parallel criminal culpability in peacetime?

Just war is supposed to be fought in a way that distinguishes combatants from non-combatants. For child soldiers this distinction is presently complicated in three further ways.

- Current different standards in international law provide contradictory interpretations of children's legal status as combatants. Soldiers of sixteen or seventeen years, for example, may be treated as victims in international law and yet also be permitted to become child soldiers under international humanitarian law.
- We cannot always easily distinguish child soldiers from adults. In the fog of war and in uniform there are few discerning characteristics of combatants between fifteen and eighteen. Children may play roles that are not easily ascertainable as combative or threatening, particularly if they are not in uniform. This fact might ostensibly provide a defence for unintentional military engagement with them as adults. Information on the possibility or prevalence of child soldiers, however, can be well ascertained and it should not be difficult to establish suspicion of their use. Restricting soldiers to the age of eighteen and above would certainly make identification of most child combatants possible.
- It is more likely that a child soldier is not a willing combatant. Again there is a sliding scale here. True, the less developed you are, the less able you are to comprehend and assimilate terror and risk, but young children are far more likely to be abused during their 'enlistment' and might consequently have had far less choice or control over their position than adults.

In practice, however, child soldiers can be engaged with in non-lethal ways which also assist in their escape and later safe refuge. But as Singer notes, there is as yet no doctrine for engagement with child soldiers used by mission planners or deployed units.[27] Perhaps there cannot be as this is both illegal and also commonly understood to be incongruous. One perspective might hold that just war theory need only specify that states not recruit child soldiers. Its business is arguably not the detection or protection of (what it tells us to treat as illegal) child soldiers recruited against this directive. In this scenario, children's prior unjust involvement in conflict constitutes a violation of their human rights and a war crime in contravention of the Geneva and Hague Conventions. It is therefore in the domain of the international criminal courts.

Literature on just war theory does not currently differentiate clearly between adults and children. As it stands, children are most likely to be embodied in categorisations: as civilian, non-combatants, and innocent. In a classic contemporary text such as Walzer's *Just and Unjust Wars*, for example, they rarely feature in historical illustrations. They are not entirely absent, however. When Walzer equates barbarism with 'killing women and children',[28] perhaps tellingly these referent victims have become synonymous with 'civilians'. Enloe points out that the running-together of these two words by broadcasters and writers to denote victimhood also renders both of them 'child-like' in a pejorative sense.[29] In his case study of the rules of engagement formed during the Vietnam War, Walzer considers how civilians were held responsible for their overtly non-military decisions. He notes that 'the fact that ten-year-old children threw hand grenades at American soldiers, blurs the nature of this responsibility'.[30] He doesn't say how. Neither does he consider if these children were anything other than 'civilians'. As participants in many conflicts children can be perpetrators and victims simultaneously, presenting unique problems for their liability. In common with some adults, older children may contribute indirectly but still knowingly to conflict. Unlike adults, young children might contribute directly yet unknowingly. Perhaps this ambiguity is still a significant rationale for non-combatant immunity and/or the efforts made to limit further risk to them during a military response or intervention.

'CONSCIENTIOUS CHILDREN' AND ETHICAL PARTNERSHIPS

In order to pin down or establish a new common norm of protection for children, a new category of 'young child' premised on vulnerability to harm and non-combatant status may first be needed. These children, perhaps newborn infants up to six years old, most certainly would be discernible. Physically unable to use retaliatory or conventional force they can also clearly be deemed innocent. Similar divisions of childhood can be found in the Geneva Convention. Soldiers would be obliged to help these particular child 'civilians' leave the scene of battle, perhaps with their primary carers in order to guarantee their care. This is not a scenario without precedent. Corridors of peace for the evacuation or inoculation of children under five years are one of the few examples of a policy successfully applied during conflict. The fact that young children's physical survival may also be encoded in the psychologically reassuring proximity of older primary carers, however, provides a sobering and highly challenging caveat in any attempts to isolate or rescue just children. Enforcing this measure for only the youngest children is not a perfect solution, of course, but it is a start – and it definitely proves intention not to kill. But it would leave a 'grey area' of children at middle childhood, and older children. Older children, like all persons, could retain the right to be non-combatants and to be so protected, and rightfully declare their child status as 'conscientious children'. How then can we make sure that children's voices are heard? Do we even know where and when these conversations could begin, where and when genuine ethical partnerships with childen could be forged such that their experience of war is fully acknowledged?

What we understand by and of 'war' determines the parameters of just war theory. In evidence of the limitations of our understanding, and incredibly, there is no reliable data or survey of children's roles in conflict worldwide, nor any way of even establishing the numbers involved.[31] The will and the funding for the necessary research have not been forthcoming from states. Yet, notwithstanding this, children are nearly always invited to help secure a transition from violence and towards peace. However, their political agency or labour during a conflict is rarely *fully* acknowledged after it, with implications for their rehabilitation and continued maturation and their society.[32] Children have too often become newly aware of a political rather than personal concept of security,[33] yet too often as well their 'rehabilitation' seeks effectively to depoliticise them. As Boyden and Levison have established, children engage actively with the conditions of war[34] and its aftermath should be perceived as the chance for a rebuilding of civil society which is sensitive to the moral deficiencies of past and present. In this regard, children need an integrated acknowledgement of what they have experienced, with restoration of their childhood through appropriate reparation, rehabilitation, and reconstruction. Indeed, as society's future is invested in them, children may well warrant priority in *post bellum* considerations. But at precisely what point do requirements of *jus post bellum*, and its implicit goals of stability in the interests of all, begin or cease for children and how might they be levied? An additional problem is the typical increase in gendered violence in the period following a ceasefire. Women and girls, many of whom are also caring for children, have experienced only continuous misery, violence and exploitation and rightfully question the boundaries of war.[35] Again, for example, child soldiers pose a significant problem in many intrastate conflicts as their illegal use by state and militia is often not acknow-ledged for fear of reprisals or raising tensions. Conversely, researchers have recently drawn attention to the fact that children who perceive themselves to be neither victims or combatants are significant in number yet rarely traced or consulted in post-conflict reconciliation and integration programmes.[36] Their agency remains unknown – but such an incomplete scenario is not at all surprising given the present scope and capacity of the policy area.

In a practical sense should children themselves, then, also *directly* inform how just war theory should be understood and applied? Until recently it has been assumed that children are less capable of making judgements, particularly moral and political judgements, than adults.[37] Clearly, however, children everywhere have made many deeply political judgements. The most radical development in the legal concept of the child has been the realisation that the children have a degree of self-determination and autonomy, and can be assisted in making choices rather than being solely the passive object of concern.[38] When American school children were taught 'to equate emotional maturity with an attitude of calm acceptance toward nuclear war',[39] did war also almost actually begin in the minds of children? Did the concept of justice ever arise for them when millions of plastic atomic-bomb 'toys' spilled out of children's breakfast cereal packets across America? In the context of such deliberate practices of 'dissociation' – a 'justice gap' in the experiences of children – was ethical debate with these children really not possible? Catholic bishops advocated that educational institutions, from primary schools to colleges, be directed towards peacemaking in the face of nuclear war.[40] Unheeded by cereal makers, this may have been the first time that children might have been better advised to skip the first meal of the day.

How, then, are these concerns illustrated in the current writing about children as ethical beings? Mainstream texts on ethical issues are exclusively about adults and for adults.[41] Children, it may be noted, are frequently missing from them; typically they receive only scant attention at best, despite what should now be clearly seen as the interconnectedness of the child's world and adult's world. Why in fact segregate children's consideration of ethical issues at all when children's experiences are also lived with those of adults? Pages dedicated to adults' dilemmas *about* children dwarf the references to how children can, do and could impact on ethical issues. Even in introductory ethics texts designed for children or beginners, the puzzle of animals' rights for example, is considered whereas children's different status or potential readership is not.[42] This is not to deny that there are deep pockets of rich research on children to be found in education and development sciences. New research suggests that children's level of moral reasoning and inclusive moral engagement is more advanced than we have mostly given them credit for. Children are now suspected of being able to reason morally during the period of middle childhood, from seven upwards[43] – and particularly so during war, with implications for child soldiers and indeed all children who think about (child) soldiers.

Peacetime un-preoccupation with children's perception of war is surely just as challenging and intimately related as indifference to their moral capacity during war. Even the drafting of Bills and Conventions of rights for children is no guarantee of their consultation, as the United Nations Convention on the Rights of the Child proved.[44] Does this neglect of our responsibilities towards them also disable society's full understanding of itself? Without encouraging participation[45] can we ensure the 'deep reflection by Everyman and Everywoman' demanded by Jean Bethke Elshtain?[46] Should this also read 'Everychild'? That children themselves are not as able to assert political influence strengthens the argument for bestowing them with separate, non-'adult-based' rights. And this fact should not obscure questioning of why they do not get to contribute alongside adults in the first place. Elshtain summarises well the unusual position of children in our conceptual frameworks:

Perhaps we can find ways to sustain childhood, not as a time of innocence, but as a time of apprenticeship that occupies a border in between private and public in a sphere or zone that adults bear the heaviest responsibility for sheltering and sustaining, not to protect children from politics but to prepare them, for all the responsibilities for adult life.[47]

In a situation where we cannot distinguish between war and peace, actors, civilians, innocents, perpetrators and victims, do we have any more to lose by not engaging with children? I would hope, for example, that within Walzer's suggestion that society should be able to engage and remove a dictator collectively there is space for consultation with children – perhaps particularly children over the age of twelve who have reached an equitable level of moral development if not control over their lives. Can we really say that they are any more or less able to make choices over risk to their life than adults? Responsibility in all spheres of politics and human rights requires a new recognition of children and the role they have played and can play in informing our conception of the political.

The complexity that children's presence in war raises does not itself explain why they have been absent from debates within just war theory. This lack of engagement is however also mirrored in the practices of the international community. Whilst many organisations have been formed to raise the profile of children in armed conflicts it was only the very recent ending of the Cold War that released the political will, or perhaps the incentives, for an international agenda for children's rights to be formed. War, the bloodiest testing ground of children's rights, now yields higher numbers of child casualties in ever more complex and damaging ways. Children are acknowledged as one of the 'new' factors challenging the principles and practices of humanitarian intervention.[48] Perhaps correspondingly, children and war have become a policy area in government organisations. In 1999, and notably for the first time, the United Nations Security Council passed a resolution on 'Children and Armed Conflict'. Since then it has produced another three. In December 2003 the European Union Political and Security Committee also agreed to guidelines, and the esteemed American Social Science Research Council (SSRC) developed a new international research network. The United States could be an important site of agitation here, given its security reach and influence, and with policy change there yielding potentially the greatest impact for children worldwide (notably, the US was one of only two countries which did not ratify the United Nations Convention on the Rights of the Child). However, such interest in children and war cedes almost complete deference to children's roles in warfare and their broader multifaceted political capital. Traditional approaches do not recognise and cannot explain the relationship between children, the state and war, leaving threat construction by the state largely unexplored. Critical Security theorists, feminists and post-modernists have questioned and problematised 'secure' concepts in the discipline of International Relations, yet perceived only as a special interest category, and a singular category at that, children do not even disturb the frameworks of power that subjugate them. Children's roles in war are sustained through their roles in non-war. Unlike other social groups however, children cannot yet easily negotiate their own concep-tualisation, participation, representation and partnership in the crucial matters of security.

CONCLUSION

The traditional doctrine of just war is based on a simple dynamic that assumes the non-combatant status of children and necessarily prevents recognition of children in the capacities of which they are capable. All signatories to just war theory shape perceptions of children's appro-priate roles and responses to conflict. As a tradition it also fails to distinguish the most vulnerable children on which war increasingly impacts. An ethic of care based on their rights to life and freedom from harm should be characterised first and foremost by close attention to the relative and essential characteristics of childhood. Without equal moral partnership, individual children will not be guaranteed this, especially as they age. Facilitation of young children's protection or desire for protection is our duty towards them until they indicate otherwise. It may then increasingly become their duty to determine their relationship to conflict, as perpetrators or as non-participants. But until then it is ours, as we have shaped the conditions that have now led to their victimhood and their disenfranchisement.

War is part of a 24/7 global complex. As warfare spills out of battle-fields, and civilians are increasingly targeted, just war theory may need to be stretched, temporally, spatially and conceptually. The examples of children's political presence in this chapter aptly illustrate the continuum between preparation for war and acts of war, and our unpreparedness for children's political and military enfranchisement in the aftermath of war. Children are what wars make of them, and war is also what children make of it. The examples in this chapter show that it is not sufficient to apply just war theory's moral considerations only in wartime. Just war's antithesis is presumably unjust war, though in the examples illustrated here the question of 'just peace' is also equally relevant and arguably serves as the basis for formulating 'just war'. For children however there is as yet no just peace. The absence of constant and culturally specific engagement with children arguably undermines justice *per se* however we define war or peace. Protection of persons in their early stages of childhood, and ethical partnerships beginning in middle childhood, are, then, possible beginnings for the formulation of future children's 'just wars'.[49]

NOTES

1. Archard (1993), p. 22.
2. UNICEF (1989), p. 2.
3. Carlsson (1989), p. 21.
4. Ruddick (1990), p. 18.
5. Goodwin-Gill and Cohn (1994), p. 7.
6. Van Bueren (1998), p. 60.
7. Boyden and Levison (2000), p. 28.
8. Ibid.
9. Cook, Hanieh, Kay (2004).
10. Brocklehurst (2003).
11. Peterson (1992), p. 32.
12. Halsan (2001), p. 342.
13. Harvey (2003).
14. Singer (2001).
15. Schafer (2001).
16. Bellamy (1999), p. 33; Human Rights Watch Africa (1995), p. 28.
17. Goodwin-Gill and Cohn (1994), pp. 29, 97.
18. Singer (2001).
19. See McGreal (1995), p. 7.
20. See Brocklehurst (2005).
21. Archard (1993), pp. 29–30.
22. Farson (1974), p. 31.
23. See Marks (2001).
24. Cook, Hanieh, Kay (2004), p. 149.
25. Ibid., p. 135.
26. Ottunu (1999), p. 6; Carlton-Ford, Hamill, Houston (2000), p. 401.
27. Singer (2001).

28. Walzer (1992), p. 180.
29. Enloe (1993), p. 166.
30. Walzer (1992), p. 189.
31. Otunnu (2000), p. 2.
32. Brocklehurst (2003), Knight (2004).
33. Cairns (1996), p. 186; Dodge and Raundalen (1991).
34. Boyden and Levison (2000); Boyden (2003).
35. Meintjes, Pillay and Turshen (2002), pp. 3–4.
36. Peters, Richards, Vlassenroot (2003).
37. Freeman (1983).
38. Freeman (1996).
39. Brown (1988), p. 90.
40. US Catholic Bishops (1992), p. 135.
41. See, for example, Dower (1998).
42. Nuttall (1993).
43. Matthews (1984); Costello (2000); Boyden (2003).
44. Boyden (1990), p. 222.
45. Hart (1992); Cockburn (2000).
46. Elshtain (1992), p. 325.
47. Elshtain (1996), p. 26.
48. Murphy and Weiss (2000), p. 116.
49. I would like to thank Mark Evans for his invaluable guidance and support.

Chapter 6

IS THERE A SUPREME EMERGENCY EXEMPTION?

BRIAN OREND

—◁▷—

'We have a right, indeed are bound in duty, to abrogate for a space some of the conventions of the very laws we seek to consolidate and reaffirm.'

Winston Churchill[1]

The supreme emergency exemption is a doctrine which pushes to the very limits the relationship between *jus ad bellum* (the justice of resorting to war)[2] and *jus in bello* (the justice of conduct in war).[3] It has high profile support, including such luminaries as Winston Churchill, John Rawls and Michael Walzer. But it is Walzer who is fundamentally responsible for the structure of this exemption: Churchill merely inspires it, and Rawls merely apes it.

As Walzer defines it, the supreme emergency exemption allows a country victimised by aggression[4] to set aside the rules of *jus in bello* and fight however it wants, provided: (1) there is public proof the aggressor is just about to defeat the victim militarily; and (2) there is similar proof that, once it does so, the aggressor will not simply crush the political sovereignty of the victim community but, moreover, institute a brutal policy of widespread massacre and enslavement against the individual members of that community. His favourite, and only, example of such an aggressor is Nazi Germany.[5] (More on that example shortly.) Let's push our definitions, and sense of the stakes, toward greater clarity.

For convenience, we can speak of three general rules[6] of *jus in bello* which just war theory endorses: (1) noncombatant immunity from direct and intentional attack; (2) the use of proportionate means only against legitimate military targets; (3) no use of means *mala in se*, 'evil in themselves', such as using poisonous weapons or forcing captured soldiers to fight against their own side. What Walzer is saying is that, under supreme emergency conditions, the country with *jus ad bellum* on its side (the victim of aggression) may set aside all three *jus in bello* rules and fight *however it wants to* – without restraint – to stave off the threat. In particular, the victim country may wilfully violate noncombatant immunity, and do such things as deliberately attack enemy civilians with lethal force. Traditionally, such transgression has counted as the clearest violation of *jus in bello* rules, and been seen as one of the very worst war crimes. Indeed, one of the grandfathers of just war theory, Hugo Grotius, once said that noncombatant immunity is a rule so powerful and morally resonant that it 'cannot be changed, even by God'.[7] So, what we have in the supreme emergency exemption is probably the most controversial, and consequential, amendment to just war theory ever proposed. The stakes regarding its acceptance into just war theory are enormous, and disturbingly relevant to an era hardly unacquainted with genocide and weapons of mass destruction.

WHAT CASES COUNT AS SUPREME EMERGENCIES?

Churchill, Walzer and Rawls concur that Britain experienced a supreme emergency in the early 1940s. By 1940, Nazi Germany stood triumphant in Western and Central Europe, and Scandinavia too, following its shattering success during the Blitzkrieg. Neither the USA nor the USSR were, at this point, in the war to drain the pressure off Britain. Hitler had plans to invade the UK, and was 'softening up' the target with *Luftwaffe* bombing raids, especially on London itself. Churchill, who coined the phrase 'supreme emergency' in this regard, argued that he had to authorise exceptional measures under such conditions. He suggested that the British were 'fighting to re-establish the reign of law and to protect the liberties of small countries. Our defeat would mean an age of barbaric violence and would be fatal, not only to ourselves, but to the independent life of every small country in Europe.' He declared, 'it would not be right that the aggressive power should gain one set of advantages by tearing up all laws, and another set by sheltering behind the innate respect for law of its opponent. Humanity, rather than legality, must be our guide.' He concluded, 'we have a right, indeed are bound in duty, to abrogate for a space some of the conventions of the very laws we seek to consolidate and reaffirm'.[8] And so Churchill authorised the Royal Air Force to begin bombing raids on German cities, knowing full well – even intending – that German civilians would be killed. This was partly in retaliation, or reprisal,[9] for Hitler's own original bombings of London, but it was also designed to deter any conquest of Britain. The German people, delirious with the Blitzkrieg's success, had to be made to feel the sting of war lest their approval drive Hitler's armed ambitions even further. Air power was the only tool at Churchill's disposal in this regard, and he employed it to the full during this period, which culminated in the Battle of Britain. The fact that Hitler gave up his invasion plans, and turned his murderous attention towards the Russian border, was cited by Churchill as evidence that his supreme emergency strategy had worked.[10]

Walzer and Rawls agree with all of this, yet are even more permissive than Churchill himself regarding the time during which Britain experienced a supreme emergency. After all, Britain 'stood alone' against the Nazis in the West until America entered the theatre in substance, in 1942. Even then the Allies didn't experience much success until the campaigns in North Africa and Italy in 1943. In the East, the Soviets only became embroiled in 1941 and initially suffered terrible set-backs. So both American thinkers are inclined to think Britain's supreme emergency lasted from 1940 until well into 1943, and thus all RAF bombing of German residential centres during this time was permissible. Walzer puts the moral issue in stark terms: 'can one do *anything* [his italics], violating the rights of the innocent, in order to defeat Nazism?' He answers yes, and justifies himself thus:

> Nazism was an ultimate threat to everything decent in our lives, an ideology and a practice of domination so murderous, so degrading even to those who might survive, that the consequences of its final victory were literally beyond calculation, immeasurably awful. We see it – and I don't use the phrase lightly – as evil objectified in the world.[11]

When supreme emergency conditions evaporate, however, the justification for deliberate civilian targeting dissolves. And so Walzer and Rawls argue that continued Allied bombing of German cities – and emphatically the fire-bombing and razing of Dresden in 1945 – was unjust. Indeed, Churchill himself grew to regret the later bombings, admitting they were motivated more by bloodlust, the passions of war-fighting and, above all, by a desire for revenge for the London bombings, than by any plausible moral or even strategic concern.[12]

Rawls, in his writings on supreme emergency,[13] is mostly concerned with using the doctrine as a tool for criticising America's use of the atomic bomb on Japan in 1945. He suggests that perhaps the only thing which could justify the use of nuclear weapons – which of course are wildly destructive and completely indiscriminate – is the experience of a supreme emergency. But America in August 1945 was not in a supreme emergency at all; on the contrary, it had just triumphed in Europe and had Japan on the brink of defeat. In fact, America was clearly one of the most powerful and privileged societies on Earth at that time. So the moral case for its using weapons of mass destruction (WMD) was nil. In Rawls's view, Truman's decision to do so was a cynical piece of *realpolitik* designed to show Japan and the world just how powerful America had become. It was not done to stave off devastating loss but to secure whatever terms of Japan's surrender America wanted, as well as to impress potential future rivals like the Soviets and Chinese with American capability.

What is interesting in Rawls's reflections is that they are not merely backward-looking, designed to render correct judgement regarding historical cases. They are also forward-looking in that they provide conditions for future use of controversial wartime measures. It is a clear inference from his reflections here that a country suffering from a supreme emergency might be justified in using nuclear weapons, and perhaps other WMD, to prevail against an aggressor.

Which leads me to speculate whether Walzer himself might also have forward-looking cases in mind.[14] For Walzer, apart from being American, is very proudly Jewish, and is deeply concerned about the fate of Israel. Israel, of course, occupies a precarious position in the Middle East: very small geographically, surrounded by hostile (or, at best, cool) neighbours, the only democracy amidst a sea of authoritarian regimes, each of which it has encountered in war in the past sixty years. The concentration of population in its few major cities makes Israel an easy target, compared to most others, for utterly devastating widespread destruction. The continuing controversy over the Palestinians, moreover, fuels an almost constant state of security crisis in Israel, and remains a *cause célèbre* amongst many Arabs, fuelling rage and terrorism. Might we imagine a dystopian future unfolding, according to which Israel finds itself in a condition of supreme emergency at the hands of its neighbours and/or domestically located terrorists? If so, what may Israel permissibly do at that moment, especially in connection with its nuclear arsenal? Could it contemplate launching nuclear strikes against Tehran, Riyadh, or Damascus? More bitingly, what about its own West Bank, or Gaza Strip, holdings?

This horrible hypothetical underlines the continuing relevance of the proposed supreme emergency exemption: it is not just an outdated device for assessing 'Churchill versus the Nazis'. In fact, in the era of terrorism and WMD, it is every bit as relevant as when Hitler's evil darkened the world. So it is worthwhile to contemplate how so-called 'asymmetric threats', like terrorism, configure in the supreme emergency debate. Symmetric threats come from other states; symmetrical warfare is classic inter-state armed conflict, and perhaps intra-state civil war as well. Asymmetric threats come from non-state actors; asymmetric warfare is when a state engages in armed conflict with such non-state actors as al-Qaeda, a diffuse terrorist network united by ideology with cells spread across many states. Other non-state actors might include mercenaries, Mafia and even drug cartels.

Some, such as Davida Kellogg, and, from time to time, officials from the Bush junior Administration itself, sound as if they believe America is in a supreme emergency following the September 11th attacks on New York, Washington DC and Pennsylvania.[15] This is, however, hard to see: while America was victimised by aggression that day, there is little to show that America's military defeat, then or now, was close or imminent, which Walzer demands in his criteria. Indeed, America has since gone on the military offensive, quite decisively taking down two regimes in countries on the other side of the world. America faces security threats of varying severity, yes, but not a supreme emergency. It is difficult to imagine any state actor, or combination of such, putting America in such a position, much less a non-state actor.[16] The only way I could conceive of such a scenario would be in connection with WMD: if a group could somehow detonate enough WMD to truly devastate America – a very big, massively populated, resourceful and diverse country – then that would fulfil the three supreme emergency requirements of victimisation by aggression, military collapse and widespread massacre. This indeed gives America, and other developed countries, strong reason to be very vigilant regarding the spread and control of WMD. (After all, it is often said that terrorists don't want such weapons for deterrent purposes, since they aren't states with territorial interests to protect. Terrorists want WMD for either blackmail or actual use, and in that sense can, in some circumstances, be even more dangerous than enemy states, even though they have fewer resources. This is true, and underlines the seriousness of contemporary terrorist threats and ambitions, and the need for *gravitas* in confronting them.) But it does not as yet give Western nations reason to deliberately attack civilians in the ongoing and otherwise legitimate war on terrorism. The September 11th attacks were outrageous and shocking acts of aggression, and they justified the return strike on the Taliban in Afghanistan. But they manifestly did not put America in a condition of supreme emergency, with all the permissiveness and laxity in targeting which Walzer has it imply. When it comes to genuine victims of supreme emergency, we are much more likely to find them at the other end of the power spectrum – the small, weak and vulnerable communities and countries which are decidedly unlike the one and only 'hyper-power' which the United States has become.

Consider, for instance, communities targeted with, or victimised by, genocide, such as Turkish Armenians during the First World War, European Jews in the early 1940s, Rwandan Tutsis in the mid-1990s and perhaps Albanian Kosovars in the late 1990s. If any community experiences a genuine supreme emergency, it is those confronted with genocide. Examples more distantly rooted in history might include Native Americans at the hands of the conquistadors, or Black Africans on the eve of the armed slave trade.[17] Reference to all these cases is done to underline the reality and urgency of the supreme emergency debate – to illustrate that it's not just about the Nazis or science fiction scenarios sketching out nuclear wars. Supreme emergencies – thank goodness – are not everyday occurrences, even in war. But they seem actually to have happened several times in history and, if the history of warfare teaches us anything, it is not to be surprised at the depth and breadth of violent atrocity of which humanity is capable. As responsible just war thinkers, we must confront this exemption and consider its nature.

OPTIONS REGARDING 'SUPREME EMERGENCY'

There seem to be five major – insightful, influential and logical – options for considering how to conceive of the supreme emergency doctrine.[18] Let us examine each of them in turn.

[A] *There is No Such Thing*

This perspective asserts that there really is no such thing as a supreme emergency, and that Walzer's proposal is a bastardisation of just war theory. The objection here is rooted both conceptually and historically. In the conceptual sense, the supreme emergency conditions are too vague and subject to interpretive disagreement to be useful and (relatively) immune from gratuitous, self-serving abuse. Consider the vagueness of Walzer's conditions. First, they require that there be a clear victim and perpetrator of 'aggression'. Just war theorists are quite familiar with disputes regarding what exactly counts as aggression (for example, is it a purely empirical or partly normative concept?) and 'defence' against it (is it purely defensive or can some anticipatory attack be consistent with the idea?) Second, there must be 'public proof' of imminent military defeat and subsequent massacre or enslavement. Such 'proof', though, can be hard indeed to come by. They say, after all, that truth is the first casualty of war. Discerning the future tides of war-fighting can be very difficult, especially amidst the heat of battle. We know that, in war, people overestimate the risks they face. We have also recently witnessed, in connection with America's 2003 Iraq war, the apparent failure of even the best-funded intelligence agencies to come up with plausible and well-grounded conclusions, in this case regarding Iraq's possession of WMD before the attack. Thirdly, there is the issue of what counts as an imminent 'military defeat'. Is it simply a big, crushing loss in a high-profile battle? Is it loss of one's political capital to the enemy? Or is it, as I would suggest, something more like the total collapse of an effective armed forces capability? Next, there is vagueness regarding what 'close and imminent' means? Are we talking weeks, days, or hours? Are we agreeing, with Oliver Wendell Holmes, that the threat of supreme emergency must merely be 'a clear and present danger'? Or are we saying something more stringent, as I would be inclined to believe, such as you have imminency when, unless you switch to exceptional measures, you'll lose and then be massacred. Finally, the criteria require that, after the military defeat, you know you will be subjected to 'widespread massacre and/or enslavement'. Massacre and enslavement are fairly straight-forward, but widespread is not. How much is widespread: 5 per cent, 10 per cent, 50 per cent, or more of your population? A distinctive sub-set of your population – such as a visible or especially powerful minority group – even if, overall, it doesn't add up to many numbers or a large percentage?

This sceptical perspective might also wonder whether the one example that these theorists all seem to agree on, namely Britain in 1940, really was a supreme emergency. After all, while Nazi *invasion* was clearly imminent, Britain's *military collapse* was not, or at least it is not a clear causal connection to go *from* suffering invasion *to* suffering total military collapse. We also cannot forget Churchill's political self-interest in exaggerating the threat that Britain faced: doing so would drive the British people to greater efforts, and it would also serve as a strong rhetorical and moral tug on the United States to join the war on the Allied side. Moreover, Walzer and Rawls surely err when they talk of Britain 'standing alone' against the Nazis at this time. For Britain had all of its colonies and ex-colonies fighting alongside it from the first days in 1939, including Australia, Canada, India, New Zealand and the Caribbean island nations. This is to say that Britain had far greater resources to draw on than any of the Continental countries that fell to the Nazis during the Blitzkrieg, and that includes France. In fact, Britain probably had more to draw on than all those countries put together, and to boot had the advantage of geography. To what extent, then, did it actually face a supreme emergency as Walzer defines it? Drawing on these considerations of conceptual vagueness, and questionable historical application, the sceptical perspective might well conclude that the supreme emergency exemption is a big, bad, dangerous moral loophole in just war theory, and we're better off without it.

While I do think that this perspective adds some very healthy precautions and scepticisms regarding the supreme emergency exemption, in the end I believe it fails to persuade. While far too many just war theorists accept the exemption uncritically, and apparently on Walzer's authority, it really does seem as though supreme emergencies can be real. Witness the examples of genocide offered above. Also, from the fact that supreme emergencies can be hard to define conceptually, it does not follow that we should get rid of, or dismiss, the very idea itself. There is a whole roster of vitally important ideas in moral and political philosophy – such as freedom, equality, human rights, justice and democracy – that we should have to throw out as well if that were the case. The conceptual difficulty just means that our jobs aren't easy. The same holds for the objection regarding the liability of the concept to self-serving abuse. We know full well that, subjectively, *all* belligerents in *every* war will try to claim for their side *any* concept which justifies their actions. But, as I believe Daniel Webster first said in this connection, 'even the devil can quote Scripture'. Just because people or countries claim that their actions are justified does not make them so. The task for them is to show that their subjective beliefs correspond to objectively defensible standards and inter-subjectively plausible evidence. This is an absolutely vital point, not just for supreme emergency but for all of just war theory, and it seems it cannot be made or stressed too strongly or often.[19]

[B] *Churchill's (Jus ad Bellum) Consequentialism*

This perspective states that, when in supreme emergency, only *jus ad bellum* matters: therefore the rules of *jus in bello* may be set aside. Churchill clearly believed this, and Walzer partially believes it. (More on Walzer's nuanced view to follow.) Other exemplars of this view may be Generals Grant and Sherman during the US Civil War. Both believed that the South was the aggressor, and that its social system of slavery was so unjust that it could not, under any conditions, be allowed to win. Thus, they both took a very permissive view regarding what the North was entitled to do to bring about victory. Note, for example Sherman's notorious 'scorched earth' policy against the state of Georgia.[20]

The strength of this view is that it offers a morally coherent response to the supreme emergency dilemma. And if you're a consequentialist in terms of your stance on ethics, it may offer you complete satisfaction on this issue. Upon reflection, though, I think this perspective has four fatal flaws to it.

The first flaw is precisely that it violates the human rights of enemy civilians, universally understood to be noncombatants. As such, it violates our core commitment not to punish the innocent. As Thomas Nagel eloquently puts it, 'hostile treatment of any person must be justified in terms of something *about that person* [his italics] which makes the treatment appropriate'. We distinguish combatants from noncombatants 'on the basis of their immediate threat or harmfulness', and our response to such threats and harms must be governed by relations of directness and relevance.[21] It is not the enemy civilians who are threatening us but their military machine, and so it is impermissible to deliberately strike out at the civilians, because even in a supreme emergency it is not they who are the direct and active agents of the brutal force.[22]

Churchill's consequentialism, like any consequentialism, also runs afoul of the problem that it endorses the proposition that 'the ends justify the means'. We all know the flaws in this proposition, notably the one that it violates the compelling Kantian norm never to treat persons as mere subjects to be sacrificed, against their will, or for the sake of some glorified social project. Individuals all have autonomy unless they themselves forfeit it, and this ties back in nicely to the previous claim about the human rights of enemy civilians, and how they do nothing to forfeit them. Believing and acting on this proposition is also morally corrupting, in the following sense: isn't civilian murder the very thing feared at the hands of the aggressor? If so, what entitles you to commit the very same action?

Thirdly, why have *jus in bello* at all if *jus ad bellum* is all that ultimately matters? Now some people, apparently Grant and Sherman, believe this: 'war is hell', whether just or unjust, so at least let's make sure that the just side wins. This attitude, however, ignores the compelling reason we have in favour of separate-standing *jus in bello* rules: they prevent escalation into indiscriminate slaughter and total, no-holds-barred warfare. And if just war theory stands for anything, it is that total warfare must be avoided. The very essence of just war theory is to insist on restraints in the reasons for fighting, and in the means used in fighting.

Finally, Churchill's consequentialism is at odds with our moral convictions in an analogous inter-personal case of supreme emergency. Suppose that aggressor person A murderously attacks victim B, and B drags in innocent bystander C, to serve as a shield between him and A. How should we evaluate B's actions during his own supreme emergency? I suggest that none of us, upon reflection, would argue that B's actions are morally justified. Indeed, the immediate reaction, normally, is that B is behaving like a selfish and despicable coward, endangering an innocent person's life instead of confronting his own danger like a man. Upon consideration, though, it is compelling to understand that this immediate response may be too judgemental, since it is offered by we who are in comfortable reflection upon a fellow person's desperate choices amidst terrifying danger. (We like to comfort ourselves by supposing we would make better choices under such conditions. But until we experience similar extraordinary pressure and fear, we might want to climb down from our tower of condemnation.) It seems equally erroneous, however, to pretend there's nothing wrong with B doing whatever he wants – including sacrificing C – to save his own life. Yet that is precisely what Churchill's consequentialism would here imply. Clearly, B has no right to violate C's rights in this case: C has done nothing wrong, nothing that would render her rights forfeit. She is an innocent bystander that B, in completely un-Kantian fashion, decides to use as a mere tool in service of his own end of survival. B utterly disregards C's humanity in this instance; he treats her like a prop, not a person. In my view, he is almost as culpable for her death as A, should she succumb to her injuries sustained while serving as a shield between the two.

The most complete and accurate judgement of this inter-personal analogy seems to be this: B has no right to drag C into the situation, and if he does so he commits a severe moral wrongdoing. However, we might be willing to excuse B's actions, on grounds that the terrible duress and mortal fear operative on him in the situation drove him to make the terrible choice he did. Like any animal filled with mortal terror, he desperately reached out for any means necessary to stave off death. This doesn't make his choice *right* or morally justifiable; it makes it *understandable* and, depending on the exact circumstances, *excusable* from criticism or punishment. It will be excusable if we determine that the pressure, in the case, was so extreme that B acted more out of animal instinct than out of a morally culpable decision-making capacity. We would say, under such conditions, that *he was forced to do something terribly wrong*. This case, and this distinction between having moral justification for doing x, and being excused for doing x, are vital in my mind to a proper understanding of a supreme emergency.

[C] Strict Respect for Jus in Bello

This perspective says that even in supreme emergency conditions, one must still scrupulously respect the rules of *jus in bello*. Colloquially, this is the view that 'let justice be done, though the heavens fall'. Kant is probably an exemplar of this view,[23] and Walzer and the international laws of armed conflict themselves are partly so.[24] Nowhere, in any piece of international law, does it say that military necessity is a valid reason for setting aside the rules of armed conflict. In fact, in several places it is said quite clearly that, since the rules have been framed in the first place with military necessity already in mind, no appeal to necessity can over-ride the need to respect the rules.[25]

This view has considerable strengths from the moral point of view. Notably, it avoids each of the four problems detailed with Churchill's consequentialism. Unlike that perspective, this one respects the human rights of enemy civilians; it does not endorse the proposition that 'the ends justify the means'. It keeps *jus in bello* separate and inviolate, and it can be brought into accord with our considered judgement in the inter-personal case.[26] It is also a consistent and coherent response to the supreme emergency dilemma, and if one has deontological moral leanings, it may offer total satisfaction in this regard. Yet this view, in spite of its moral power and seductiveness, also sports flaws.

The first flaw with this view is that it seems quite unrealistic. Strict respect for *jus in bello*, in this case, might result not just in victory for the aggressor, but the kind of horrible slaughter we have previously detailed. Realistically, who is going to follow the advice of this option? Respecting *jus in bello* is, to an extent, agreeing to fight with one arm tied behind one's back. Now, this might be fine so long as one can still win, or at least if one loses, it is simply a 'run-of-the-mill' military defeat. But that is not what we're talking about with supreme emergency: we are talking not just about defeat but about slaughter, slavery and total catastrophe. In the face of such a threat, who in their right mind is still going to fight with one arm tied behind their back? Andrew Fiala says that Kant will still agree, but only because he has a philosophy of history which guarantees the eventual, complete victory of liberal democracy. So Kant can relax about the occasional supreme emergency, and insist on respect for *jus in bello*, since in the end rights-respecting democracies are destined to triumph and brutal, rights-violating aggressors will disappear from the face of the Earth.[27] While that is an accurate description of Kant's philosophy of history, I don't believe that it is why Kant would still insist on respecting *jus in bello*. For Kant, elsewhere, says there is no guarantee that doing the right thing will improve the world, or even serve your self-interests. Here in supreme emergency we perhaps discern the full strength and import of Kant's commitment to morality: you are to adhere to moral demands even if it costs you your life. Morality is thus revealed to be the single most important thing in life for Kant: the very thing that shows humanity at its very best.[28] Critics of Kant, and we can hear them baying at this point, alternatively suggest that first you have to survive, and then you can be moral. Existence precedes ethics, so to speak.

The second weakness with this option is that, in Walzer's eyes, it is

fundamentally irresponsible on the part of the victim country's government, which has a foremost duty to protect its country's citizens from
massacre and enslavement. There is a vital moral duty which the
government owes its own people to do anything to stave off the horrifying
suffering and death which are part-and-parcel of the supreme emergency condition. Walzer actually says that, if the state has any moral
value at all, it is precisely to defend those whom it represents. Failure to
provide such defence – much less deliberate standing-down in the face
of holocaust – is an abdication of office and it dissolves the social
contract which formerly united rulers and ruled, the people and their
state.[29]

[D] Walzer's Paradoxical Dirty Hands

As previously mentioned, part of Walzer endorses Churchill's consequentialism, while another part of him supports Kant's deontology. He
thinks that being politically realistic in supreme emergencies drives one
towards the former, while being morally sensitive inclines one towards
the latter. We have, on the one hand, his previously quoted remark that
one can, in fact, do anything to defeat Nazis. Similar to it is his recom-
mendation, during a supreme emergency, to 'wager this determinate
crime (the killing of innocent people) against that immeasurable evil (a
Nazi triumph)'.[30] On the other hand, Walzer tells us that civilians are
not in any material sense 'dangerous men'. Thus, 'they have done
nothing, and are doing nothing, that entails the loss of their rights.' So
they may not be made the direct and intentional objects of military
attack.[31] He declares, moreover, that 'the destruction of the innocent,
whatever its purposes, is a kind of blasphemy against our deepest moral
commitments'.[32]

Accordingly, Walzer describes his position on supreme emergency as
paradoxical. The victim community may set aside *jus in bello* rules, so as
to protect its people and defend itself from slaughter, yet doing so is still
morally wrong in that it will involve the murder of enemy civilians.
Walzer says that when the very existence of a community may be at
stake 'the restraint on utilitarian [or consequentialist] calculation must
be lifted. Even if we are inclined to lift it, however, we cannot forget that
the rights violated for the sake of victory are genuine rights, deeply
founded and in principle inviolable.'[33] The deliberate killing of innocents,
though it is murder of a kind, can nevertheless be justified in a supreme

emergency: it is simultaneously right and wrong. At the same time, with respect to the same action, we say 'yes and no'. Bomb the residential areas deliberately – murder those civilians – but do so only because you are 'a nation fighting a just war [which] is desperate and survival itself is at risk'. Walzer concludes:

> in supreme emergencies our judgements are doubled, reflecting the dualist character of the theory of war and the deeper complexities of our moral realism; we say yes *and* no, right *and* wrong [his italics]. That dualism makes us uneasy; the world is not a fully comprehensible, let alone a morally satisfactory place.[34]

Walzer's position underlines the sheer difficulty of the supreme emergency dilemma, whereas the other positions might seem simplistic and one-sided by contrast. His reconstruction of contemporary just war theory possesses great authority, and is aimed in this specific regard at balancing the insights of the two extreme positions of consequentialism and deontology. Yet we might wonder about the coherence of this doctrine, as well as its action-guiding properties. The upshot of just war theory, after all, is precisely to devise coherent rules that statesmen and soldiers can refer to as they make choices under heated wartime conditions. With Churchill's consequentialism, the nature of the advice is – in spite of its substantive problems – quite clear: disregard *jus in bello*, and do whatever you can to stave off supreme emergency. Kant's deontology, despite its limitations, likewise provides coherent guidance: you must still adhere to *jus in bello* even in the teeth of a supreme emergency. Where, we might ask, is the coherent advice in Walzer's position of paradox?[35] He seems, after all, to stress that the various options in a supreme emergency are *both* right and wrong. It is in response to this pointed query that we see Walzer's position is, ultimately, not so evenly balanced between consequentialism and deontology as his self-reference to paradox would have us believe.

In the final analysis, Walzer leans a little bit towards consequentialism, and this allows him at least to offer coherent advice, but it comes at the cost of some of the moral controversy attaching to that attitude. Walzer's advice to statesmen and soldiers in a supreme emergency is this: you must set aside *jus in bello* and do what you can to stop the supreme emergency, even though this will involve horrible wrongdoing. You actually have a duty to do this – to get your hands dirty, to shoulder personally the burden of this crime – because the function of your office is to defend your people. This is coherent advice, but still somewhat paradoxical: you have an important moral duty to violate another important moral duty; you have the right to do something that is not right. Even though Walzer urges this 'dirty hands' policy upon statesmen and soldiers, he says they should not face war crimes trials after the war ends. They should, at most, be criticised and shamed after the war. Walzer cites approvingly here the British policy to withhold highest honours to RAF Commander Arthur ('Bomber') Harris, humili- ated as the only senior British military officer denied such honours after the Second World War.[36]

[E] Moral Tragedy, Prudential Strategy

The point of this section is to present an alternative way of thinking about supreme emergency which, on balance, is superior to all the previously discussed rivals.[37] The entry point of this option reminds us that we can look at a person, or action, from at least two different perspectives. Consider, for example, Kant's thoughts on the nature of a human being. Famously, Kant argued that humanity is a composite of 'animal instinctuality' and 'free rationality'. Considering the human being as *phenomenon*, we see a quite limited, corporeal entity, subject to all the physical laws of nature, hard-wired to seek its own survival and satisfaction. Considering the human being as *noumenon*, we see not so much finite body as expansive mind: we discern moral freedom instead of physical necessity, and we witness commitment to reason and justice even at the cost of our own happiness, and perhaps even life. It is the exact same object – the human person – yet seen as possessing radically different properties depending on the perspective chosen. While Kant clearly sided with the noumenal self, he knew the phenomenal self to be in some sense inescapable, and in fact viewed much of life as a struggle between the two for primacy.[38] I propose that much can be gained from viewing supreme emergency analogously under two different perspec- tives: the moral and the prudential. Morally, a supreme emergency is a terrible tragedy. Prudentially, it is a struggle for survival.

From the moral point of view, a supreme emergency is a moral tragedy. A moral tragedy occurs when, all things considered, each viable option you face involves a severe moral violation. It is a moral blind alley: there is no way to turn and still be morally justified. Colloquially, in a supreme emergency, 'you're damned if you do, and damned if you don't'. You're damned if you do, so to speak, because if you 'do', you violate *jus in bello* and commit widespread civilian murder. You're damned if you don't, on the other hand, because if you 'don't', you fail to protect your own civilians from widespread murder. On this understanding, there is no supreme emergency exemption, where such is conceived as a *moral* exemption, permission or loophole. The whole thing is a wretched moral tragedy. This option differs from Walzer's in two important respects. First, it captures and highlights not merely the difficulty of the dilemma but its full-blown tragedy. I think reflection upon war's tragedy is something which just war theory can benefit from, and which has hitherto been ignored. Not everything in war can be morally justified – in supreme emergency we hit a wall where we see that, morally, we run out of permissible options. Yet still we must choose and act. Second, this option retains no aspect of paradox, as Walzer's still does. Walzer suggests that, in a supreme emergency, you have the right to do wrong, and/or a duty to violate duty, whereas no such claims are here made, resulting in a more coherent understanding. You don't have the right to do wrong, or a duty to violate duty: if you do wrong, you do wrong, even under the pressure of supreme emergency conditions.

From the prudential point of view, a supreme emergency is a desperate, Hobbesian struggle for survival, and as a matter of fact any country subjected to it will do whatever it can to prevail. The animal instincts are going to kick in, just as in our inter-personal analogy involving A, B and C. Yet these instincts can still be channelled by rules of rational choice – you want your self-saving actions to be efficacious, after all. Which rules would here help? First, make sure resort to supreme emergency measures are, in fact, a *last resort*. Wartime can create an overheated crisis atmosphere, in which people discern 'emergencies' which aren't, in fact, there. There are a great many options, permissible according to standard just war theory, to be tried prior to actions which violate the rules. As the war goes badly, perhaps things like conscription or assassination should be tried. Perhaps, as the Russians have sometimes done, the thing to do is pull back from one's borders, moving one's people and maybe strategically despoiling some territory, so as to put distance between oneself and the aggressor. We have to make sure supreme emergency measures aren't taken hastily, out of a failure of imagination surrounding standard tactics.

A second rule of prudence is *publicly to declare* what one intends to do. This ties into 'last resort': it gives the aggressor pause, articulating the extreme measures to be taken if he, in fact, persists to push one into a condition of supreme emergency.

The public declaration should also serve as an *appeal to the international community*. The international community clearly has a moral duty, of humanitarian intervention, to aid a country in supreme emergency and do everything reasonable to stop the aggressor. The victim has every self-interest in appealing for such intervention, just as individuals in personal supreme emergencies should yell 'help!', 'police!' or 'fire!' to bring in such outside support. At the same time, the reaction of the international community has, sadly, been known to be inefficacious, half-hearted or absent altogether and so, pending the imminency of the supreme emergency, the victim must always act of its own accord and not pin inflated hopes on the historically fickle replies of the international community.[39]

Fourthly, one must, to the extent possible, keep one's mind clear of other temptations, such as the passions of revenge, or bloodlust, or just an inclination to destroy, to take others down with you, so to speak. This is to say there should be a *right intention*: not one of moral purity, but one of prudential effectiveness, namely, that the purpose of one's actions is survival.

Any supreme emergency measures, above all, must have a *reasonable probability of success*. This fifth rule is absolutely vital: are the extreme measures contemplated going to make a difference? This is particularly important in connection with civilian targeting: if it's the aggressor's military machine which is pushing one into supreme emergency, how is killing his civilians actually going to help? To be blunt – if it came down to this – why not employ a tactical WMD against the aggressor's front line, instead of unleashing civilian slaughter? Now, Churchill argued that his policy of civilian bombing worked, because Hitler gave up his UK invasion plans. True, but the bombing didn't actually beat Hitler – what did was sustained standard tactics, aimed at his military machine and industrial supply, for several years after that. We should note that probability of success is relevant on several levels: not just 'will our first strike stave off supreme emergency?' but 'how is the aggressor likely to respond to that first strike?', 'can we withstand his response and formulate a forceful second strike?' and so on.[40] These questions are, of course, very difficult to address under the crush of these conditions, yet some consideration simply must be given to them since the ultimate goal remains one's survival.

CONCLUSION

Having this twofold perspective on supreme emergency is very advantageous. It raises the issue of moral tragedy, and it contains more detailed, practical rules of thumb for soldiers and statesmen than any of the other approaches. I suppose the final question is this: which perspective is more important, the moral or the prudential?[41] I view this as a loaded and misleading question. Both perspectives are vital to a complete analysis: victims of supreme emergency are going to fight to survive, and they need rules of thumb to help them achieve that goal. At the same time, supreme emergency measures, while (hopefully) pruden-tially useful, remain morally wrong in so far as they involve *jus in bello* violations. I view the scenario as directly analogous to the inter-personal case: the victim was forced to do wrong. Owing to the severe duress of the supreme emergency condition, the victim resorted to immoral measures to stave off disaster and death. We can excuse the victim's actions, but never justify them. And I think the excuse from punishment should be extended to everyone involved in the extreme measures. Picking out one official, like 'Bomber' Harris, for public shaming seems both *pro forma*, and unfair. *Pro forma*, because it's purely symbolic, and unfair because in Harris's case many others – including Churchill himself – were involved in the bombing, but only he was singled out.

I do believe that the victim country, supposing its supreme emer-gency measures to succeed, owes its citizens and the international community a full public accounting, after the war, for what it did and why it did it. But that's all – no war crimes trials, no shaming, no symbolic hand-wringing. It was forced to do terrible things in order to survive.[42]

NOTES

1. Churchill, quoted in Walzer (1992), p. 245.
2. For more on *jus ad bellum*, see ibid., pp. 3–33 and 51–125; Luban (1980), pp. 160–81 and Orend (2000a), chapter 4.
3. For more on *jus in bello*, see Walzer (1992), pp. 34–50 and 127–224; Nagel (1972), pp. 123–45; Fullinwider (1975), pp. 90–7; and Orend (2000a), chapter 5.
4. Aggression is commonly understood to involve the use of armed force to

violate either the territorial integrity or political sovereignty of a country commonly acknowledged to be an independent nation by the international community. The simplest example of aggression is country A launching an armed invasion of country B, for instance to gain more territory.

5. Walzer (1992), pp. 251–68.
6. These, of course, are intended to be seen as the broadest moral rules, within which dozens, if not hundreds, of more specific rules regarding the use of armed force can logically be located. For more, see Orend (2000a), pp. 110–35.
7. Grotius quoted in Christopher (1994), p. 109.
8. Churchill, quoted in Walzer (1992), p. 245.
9. For more on reprisal, see ibid., pp. 207–24, and Orend (2000a), pp. 125–7.
10. Churchill discusses aspects of bombing policy at Churchill (1986a), pp. 34–50 and Churchill (1986b), pp. 34–50, 399–411 and 463–80.
11. Walzer (1992), p. 253 and Walzer (1971), pp. 3–21.
12. See n. 10.
13. Rawls (1999a), pp. 98–105; Rawls (1999b).
14. I stress the following is pure speculation on my part.
15. Kellogg (2002). In terms of the Bush Administration, the pronouncements especially of Donald Rumsfeld and even the President himself can incline in this direction.
16. In terms of state actors, we could imagine a grisly scenario involving war between the USA and say, Russia and/or China. The latter two probably do have enough WMD to put America into a supreme emergency.
17. Thanks to Neta Crawford for these examples. On the history of genocide, see Chalk and Jonassohn (1990); Totten (1997).
18. We should note how the Doctrine of Double Effect (DDE) – often called upon by just war theory to solve difficult dilemmas – is *not* a viable option when dealing with supreme emergencies because the DDE, among other things, only lets you perform actions which are otherwise permissible, and in which the unintended bad effects are *not* the means to producing the intended good ones. But in supreme emergencies, the actions contemplated are *not* otherwise permissible (for example, deliberately killing civilians), and the bad effects *are* the means to producing the good (for example, hoping the civilian casualties will, somehow, quell the aggressor's military effectiveness). For more on the DDE, see Walzer (1992); Orend (2000a), pp. 110–35. Thanks to Alex Moseley for discussions on this.
19. See also Orend (2000b).
20. Walzer (1992), pp. 29–34.
21. Ibid., pp. 146, 219; Nagel (1972), pp. 133–41.
22. For more on the connection between innocence and noncombatancy, see Orend (2000a), pp. 111–21.
23. See Orend (2000b).

24. Again, see the following remarks for Walzer's complex view.
25. See Reisman and Antoniou (1994); Roberts and Guelff (2000); Bailey (1972); Best (1994); I. Brownlie, (1963); Detter Delupis (1987); Dinstein (1995); Howard (1994).
26. This would be the sense in which Walzer agrees with this view.
27. Fiala (2002). See also Doyle (1983a and b) and Doyle (1997); Brown (1996).
28. Orend (2000b).
29. Walzer (1992), pp. 251–68; Orend (2000a), pp. 86–134.
30. Walzer (1992), pp. 231, 259.
31. Ibid., pp. 146–51.
32. Ibid., pp. 262–8.
33. Ibid., pp. 195, 228.
34. Ibid., pp. 251–68, 325–8.
35. I develop more fully the paradoxicality of Walzer's position here, with extensive reference to quotes, in Orend (2000a), pp. 127–34.
36. Walzer (1992), pp. 251–68; Walzer (1973).
37. I wish especially to thank Danny Statman, of the University of Haifa, and Toni Erskine, of the University of Wales Aberystwyth, for stimulating and sharpening my thoughts regarding what follows.
38. Orend (2000b), chapter 1; Orend (1999).
39. See Prunier (1995); Rieff (1995); and Dallaire (2003). See also the chapter by Lang in this volume.
40. Thanks to Neta Crawford for emphasising this.
41. Toni Erskine has urged this question, and choice, upon me. But I don't think I have to choose, for the reasons explained.
42. Thanks so much to everyone at the Gregynog conference on 'Just War Theory Reappraised', especially Mark Evans.

JUSTICE AND THE END OF WAR

Chapter 7

SECURITY BEYOND THE STATE: COSMOPOLITANISM, PEACE AND THE ROLE OF JUST WAR THEORY

PATRICK HAYDEN

The lessons learnt from international politics in the post-Cold War era and the nature of global conflict today compel us to accept an important fact: it is impossible to protect and enhance human freedom and well-being exclusively through the traditional paradigm of state security. The security of the individual human being must also be taken into consideration. Political theory and practice must come to accept this global reality, since all too often the best laid plans for achieving state security have come at the cost of an increase in human suffering, fear and deprivation. What is required is a new global outlook: a cosmopolitan approach that recognises the highly interdependent nature of human life across political and territorial boundaries and the growing irrelevance of the traditional conception of state sovereignty as an end in itself. This new global outlook may be best represented by the human security paradigm. For cosmopolitans as well as for human security advocates, the traditional realist claims to sovereignty and non-intervention on the part of states are being supplanted in international relations by a norm of humanitarian assistance driven by the human rights and security interests of individuals.[1] According to cosmopolitanism, state sovereignty in itself provides no reason not to intervene when necessary, for example, to prevent humanitarian disasters and gross human rights violations. Thus cosmopolitans have advanced various arguments intended to contest realism and its apparent insensitivity to the causes and effects of humanitarian injustices in which states are often complicit.

This chapter first reviews the emergence of the concept of human security and its meaning and implications for challenging the dominant realist paradigm of state security and that paradigm's rationale for the state's monopoly on violence. The chapter goes on to support the idea of a human right to peace, this right serving as a core component of an adequate formulation of human security. Finally, it explores how a robust formulation of just war theory can provide us with reasonable criteria for thinking about how we ought to respond to some of the most severe threats to human security, while doing justice to the human right to peace.

FROM STATE SECURITY TO HUMAN SECURITY

The modern theory and practice of international relations has been dominated by political realism, an approach that is committed to a unified view of power and national security as defining of the political world. My concern is with the basic way in which realism, as embodied in conjunction with the Westphalian inheritance of state sovereignty, has shaped the contemporary security paradigm of world politics. This paradigm assimilates several of the following basic premises of realism: states are the primary actors in the world's political system; states seek power as a means and as an end to ensure their survival in an anarchical world; power is defined in terms of the possession of resources and military might; states are rational, egoistic actors in so far as they pursue what is in their best interests; and state interests are driven primarily by the necessity of national survival.

Realism reflects a belief in the anarchy of the Hobbesian state of nature. While domestic anarchy can be restrained by establishment of the sovereign state, the relations between states still occur in an 'anarchical society' due to the absence of an international hierarchical political authority.[2] The international order, it is thought by realists, necessarily consists of a system of independent, self-interested states, each assuming the worst about the others and seeking to ensure its survival in a dangerous, 'self-help' world. In a realist international system, states are concerned only to further their own interests and interstate cooperation is carried out only prudentially. In such a system relatively weak international institutions are the result of governmental practices based on the current distribution of power and states' attempts to maintain or improve their relative ranking. International politics thus constitutes a competition over the balance of power and a continual effort to achieve national security in a world that is conceived as being inherently insecure.[3] Somewhat paradoxically, war and other forms of state-organised violence are regarded as the most effective instruments with which to assure national survival.

Realists reject the possibility of any positive conception of long-lasting peace in the circumstances of international relations conceived as anarchic. The best that can be hoped for is a tenuous preservation of an 'ordered' society of states brought about through the incessant contestation of opposing forces in world politics. In this system sovereign states continually find themselves in a perpetual 'security dilemma'. In the search for protection from other states' potential aggression, each state seeks to enhance its power either through its own means or with the limited assistance of allies and coalitions. Yet by doing so, other states then perceive themselves to be threatened and consequently strive to enhance their own power further. The result is a vicious circle in which security and insecurity are locked together in a self-perpetuating loop.[4] Each state is simultaneously thought to be a guardian of security and a threat to security, and an atmosphere of mistrust clouds world politics.

Because traditional security politics takes as its referent the state, the scope of security is limited primarily to threats of a military nature from other states. The aim of national security is to secure the welfare of the state as such, that is, its sovereignty, territorial integrity, political independence, and domestic order. If the state is territorially secure, realists contend, then the individuals living in that state necessarily are secure as well. The desired balance of power is struck when the potential or actual violence and coercion embodied in each state is capable of being met by the retaliatory force of other states. In this way, however, violence is structured into the very functioning of the inter-national system. Given the realist paradigm of international politics as a struggle for power, it can be argued that the traditional national security paradigm is inherently deficient as a means actually to obtain the desired end of security. In a world structured around the dictates of political realism, an international system based on the relative distribution of military and economic strength is better characterised not in terms of security, but in terms of global insecurity. The world of the realists' making is marked by the instability of power struggles, the casual resort to military force, the pursuit of narrow self-interests, the hyper-production of weaponry, and callous indifference towards the interests of persons beyond (and perhaps even within) the borders of each state.

The limitations of the traditional view of security have become a central concern since the end of the Cold War. In 1991 the Stockholm Initiative on Global Security and Governance issued a report that recognised 'challenges to security other than political rivalry and armaments' and called for a 'wider concept of security'.[5] Three years later this wider concept of security was described as 'human security' in the United Nations *Human Development Report 1994*. According to this report, human security includes 'safety from chronic threats such as hunger, disease, and repression', as well as 'protection from sudden and harmful disruptions in the patterns of daily life'.[6] In 1995 the new concept of human security assumed a prominent role in the report of the Commission on Global Governance, which stressed that the concept of global security 'must be broadened from its traditional focus on the security of states to include the security of people and the planet'.[7] More recently the independent Commission on Human Security, co-chaired by Sadako Ogata and Amartya Sen, stressed that 'attention must now shift from the security of the state to the security of the people' so as to 'protect the vital core of all human lives in ways that enhance human freedoms and human fulfilment'.[8]

The human security perspective represents a radically different approach to security from that offered by the traditional realist paradigm. The fundamental difference in orientation between the two approaches is that for the traditional paradigm security means the protection and welfare of the state per se, whereas for the new formulation security means the protection and welfare of the individual human being. While the classical paradigm is clearly realist in that it is narrowly preoccupied with the state and national security interests, the human security paradigm is cosmopolitan in that it adopts a more comprehensive approach concerned in the first instance with persons and threats to their existence and dignity. It should be noted that the human security paradigm does not suggest that national security becomes irrelevant; rather it becomes embedded within a wider framework of interests that takes the quality of life of the individual human being and the justice of fundamental social institutions as primary components of security viewed holistically.

Former Canadian Foreign Minister Lloyd Axworthy depicted the cosmopolitan character of human security when he observed that threats to human security are those that 'strike directly home to the individual' and 'largely ignore state boundaries'. Such threats are often violent and systemic in nature, and require 'action and cooperation at different levels – global, regional and local – if they are to be tackled effectively'.[9] Human security concerns transcend the traditional statist confines of national security, and tend to focus on elimination or prevention of the causes of threats to human security. The types of threats identified with the human security concept include armed conflict, ethnocultural violence, genocide, terrorism, violent crime, slavery, government repression, discrimination, environmental degradation, deprivation of basic needs, underdevelopment, and the spread of small arms and weapons of mass destruction. In sum, for the human security concept, the core threats are those that present a clear and consistent danger to human life and dignity. Another way of putting these last points is that human security 'recognises that an individual's personal protection and preservation comes not just from the safeguarding of the state as a political unit, but also from access to individual welfare and the quality of life'.[10]

Consequently, the human security approach is concerned with both direct and indirect violence, or organised and 'structural' violence, none of the forms of which can be understood in exclusively national or territorial terms and many of which are exacerbated by the statist biases of conventional international politics. In addition to the commonly recognised forms of direct violence (such as international and domestic war, genocide and ethnic cleansing) other forms of direct violence (including slavery, physical abuse, crime and terrorism) along with forms of structural violence (such as political repression, discrimination and the lack of food, water and basic health care) are all identified as critical threats to personal safety, well-being and dignity.

Because the new security paradigm places the individual's well-being and dignity within the context of humanity rather than the sovereign state, the normative focus of realism gives way to that of cosmopolitanism. The security referent is no longer the citizen of a particular sovereign state, but all persons understood as 'members of a transcendent human community with common global concerns'.[11] Security is not the domain of a privileged few, but the entitlement of all human beings. Neither is the goal of security simply the preservation of the state; rather it is the preservation of human well-being. The normative focus also shifts from that of power struggles and unilateral militarism as the means by which to obtain national security, towards recognition that genuine security can only be ensured through multilateral efforts aimed at evading or curtailing war and other forms of direct and indirect violence, protecting human rights, and providing the social and environmental resources needed for a safe and dignified human life. In short, human security is inseparable from conditions of peace and justice.

HUMAN SECURITY AND THE HUMAN RIGHT TO PEACE

Given the transformation of the security paradigm, it is necessary to identify new concepts that will help to provide content to the human security approach, and introduce a basis from which to develop a deeper understanding of specific threats to human security and ways to realise its goals. In this section the argument is made that a human right to peace is a justifiable and necessary cornerstone to the further elaboration of the human security framework.

Adopting a human rights approach to human security is useful for several reasons. First, human rights are fundamental moral norms that aim to protect people from severe and pervasive threats to their well-being, such as oppression, domination and exploitation. Second, human rights are also internationally recognised legal norms and thus provide specific and enforceable protections of individuals' important interests, liberties or powers. Third, human rights are universal, in the sense that all persons possess human rights simply because they are human beings. Consequently, given their cosmopolitan character and the fact that they function to prevent or minimise many of the critical threats to personal safety, well-being and dignity, human rights provide a normatively and pragmatically appropriate basis from which to advance claims to human security.

One of the more promising attempts to link human rights and security is that developed by Henry Shue.[12] Shue bases his argument on the concept of basic rights. For Shue there are three 'basic rights', namely, universal rights to liberty, subsistence, and security. These rights are basic, Shue contends, because 'the enjoyment of them is essential to the enjoyment of all other rights'.[13] Shue grounds his concept of basic rights on a critique of the distinction between negative and positive rights, a distinction often appealed to in order to suggest that civil and political but not economic rights are genuine human rights. Shue argues, however, that human rights are functionally interdependent and that the negative–positive dichotomy is 'intellectually bankrupt'.[14] This can be seen when considering the right to security in its most primary sense.

The right to security requires both forbearance and positive action in order to be implemented effectively. Governments are required not only to refrain from direct and indirect violence against the individual but also to take measures actively to protect individual liberty and well-being from such threats. As Shue points out, 'A demand for physical security is not normally a demand simply to be left alone, but a demand to be protected against harm. It is a demand for positive action ... a demand for social guarantees against at least the standard threats'.[15]

Shue makes a strong case for the high priority of security rights – along with subsistence and liberty rights – based on the argument that such rights must be effectively implemented in order for the exercise of other rights to be possible. By this Shue means that the implementation of basic rights supports our enjoyment of other human rights by making violations of those other rights less likely. The right to freedom of expression, for instance, cannot be effectively exercised without the right to be protected from arbitrary arrest, that is, a fundamental right to personal security. Because 'threats to physical security are among the most serious and – in much of the world – the most widespread hindrances to the enjoyment' of other rights, it follows that 'everyone is entitled to the removal of the most serious and general conditions that would prevent or severely interfere with the exercise of whatever rights the person has'.[16]

Basic human rights may be defined, then, as paramount moral claims that every person has to an indispensable minimum level of treatment – including various freedoms, protections, and benefits – needed for the viability and security of human life and to which all human beings are entitled. The claims of right-holders impose correlative duties, such that human rights are violated when duty-bearers fail to fulfil their correlative duties without good cause. As Shue points out the duties correlative to basic rights are both negative and positive. Indeed the duties correlative to human rights are actually of three kinds, although each kind manifests negative or positive attributes which attach to different duty-bearers in varying circumstances: (1) negative duties to avoid depriving right-holders of the objects of their rights; (2) positive duties to protect right-holders from being deprived of the objects of their rights; and (3) positive duties to aid right-holders when avoidance and protection have failed.[17] Thus the correlative duties associated with security rights include a duty to avoid harm, a duty to protect from harm, and a duty to aid those threatened with harm.

From the basic rights perspective it is possible to argue for the right to the highest attainable standards of peace for all. Embedding human rights – and the right to peace in particular – within a broader discourse of human security is necessary for dealing with some of the most serious consequences of war, conflict and other violent and pervasive threats to human existence. Indeed, the human right to peace can prove to be a valuable normative asset in trying to resolve human security crises and in justifying and guiding a wide range of security principles and programmes. With the adoption of the Universal Declaration of Human Rights in 1948, a moral and political vision was articulated which claimed that 'the equal and inalienable rights of all members of the human family is the foundation of freedom, justice and peace in the world'. Central to this vision is the idea that human rights are crucial to human freedom, social justice, and security of the person. The human right to peace was formally affirmed in the 1984 UN Declaration on the Right of Peoples to Peace. In four points, the Declaration stipulates (1) that the peoples of our planet have a right to peace; (2) that the preservation of the right of peoples to peace and the promotion of its implementation constitute a fundamental obligation of each state; (3) that ensuring the exercise of the right to peace demands that the policies of states be directed towards the elimination of the threat of war and the renunciation of the use of force in international relations; and (4) that all states adopt appropriate measures at both the national and international level to implement the right to peace.

The concept of the right to peace suggests the right of persons to conditions of peace and security is indispensable to living a fully human life. It is my contention that the human right to peace is best defined as a right to a secure and non-violent world, meaning a world that is not destructive of the central human capabilities characteristic of a safe and secure existence. Research on peace often distinguishes between 'negative' peace, which denotes the absence of direct violence such as during a cessation of hostilities, and 'positive' peace, which denotes the elimination of indirect forms of violence and the construction of just social institutions that guarantee equal opportunity, a fair distribution of power and resources, equal protection and impartial enforcement of law. Proponents of the concept of positive peace – in much the same fashion as advocates of human security – point out that mere absence of the direct violence of war does not preclude the presence of various forms of indirect or structural violence within society.[18] What we might call the *comprehensive conception of peace* integrates both its negative and positive characteristics, and thus focuses on both minimising the occurrence and effects of conflict and developing a just basic structure of society in order to diminish violent conflict's underlying causes.[19] We can describe the normative condition of comprehensive peace as 'not the mere absence of fighting, but peace-with-rights, a condition of liberty and security that can exist only in the absence of aggression itself'.[20]

Because both direct and indirect violence are the cause of many threats to a safe and secure human existence, the human right to peace is concerned most fundamentally with security from armed conflict, whether domestic or international, and the structural violence associated with political oppression, domination, exploitation, and state terrorism. Given this, peace can be equated with the absence – *to the highest attainable standard* – of direct and structural violence. Crucially, then, the human right to peace is not to be equated with absolute pacifism in so far as there are, under some strict conditions, limited and justifiable uses of force for purposes of protecting the human rights of individuals against gross injustice. I will return to this issue in the following section.

As with the broader human security paradigm, direct and structural threats to human well-being and dignity are the primary focus of the human right to peace because the most severe effects of political violence are death, dislocation, harm to physical and mental health, and loss of freedom. Severe threats to human well-being – such as chemical and biological weapons, landmines and torture – not only kill, but maim, disfigure, shorten a person's life, cause permanent physical and emotional disabilities, and lead to temporary or recurring illness. Violent threats to human security also extend beyond the traditional limits of physical health and affect aspects of what Amartya Sen and Martha Nussbaum call the 'central human capabilities'. These capabilities are functions characteristically performed by human beings and 'are so central that they seem definitive of a life that is truly human'.[21] While Nussbaum and Sen present somewhat different sets of human capabilities, the core capabilities that each identifies include the capability to survive and live a healthy life; to be knowledgeable; to enjoy a decent standard of living; to participate in the life of the community and shape one's social, political and economic environment; to exercise civil and political freedoms; and to be secure from violence.[22] The capabilities approach crystallises many of the norms of human security and the comprehensive conception of peace.

The capabilities point to some basic aspects of human security critical to the human right to peace, namely, those that pertain to avoiding unnecessary harm and to securing the possibility of a minimally good human life for all persons. A minimally good human life means that all people should have at least their basic capabilities protected from direct and indirect violent harm, whatever else they have and pursue. For example, having to live without access to adequate educational facilities, without the opportunity freely to express one's opinions, or without the possibility of participating in political governance might not destroy one's physical health, but each deprivation would seriously harm critical aspects of human functioning, cause humiliation and assault one's dignity. Accordingly, the human right to peace seeks the progressive elimination of forms of direct and indirect violence that create significant risks of killing people or depriving them of the possibility of a minimally good, secure, and peaceful life defined in terms of the central human capabilities. The human right to peace thus articulates the basis of protections against, and the removal of, conditions of unjust violence that individuals should be entitled to claim of the state.

While alternative forms of protection (the laws of war) and other currently recognised rights (the rights to life and non-discrimination) address a number of the problems associated with human security, they do so only in piecemeal fashion and fail to provide an integrated and comprehensive defence of the claim to peace *per se*. However, without a guarantee of the protection of the right to peace, understood holistically as possessing both negative and positive components, a fully human life of dignity is virtually impossible given the generalised, pervasive insecurity created by the traditionally realist organisation of the state system and the militaristic values it promotes. With the emergence of the human security paradigm there is growing recognition that the fundamentally realist nature of the security system of states has negative consequences for the quality of life which reach well beyond the battlefield casualties of war. The promotion of military interests at the expense of peoples' interests erodes the social conditions needed for cultivating the central human capabilities, and generates structural threats to personal dignity and security.[23]

Consequently, the human right to peace aims to protect people against direct and structural violence and their consequences as systemic problems and not merely as isolated instances of otherwise acceptable domestic and international activities. The history of the security system of states demonstrates that the traditional conception of security has been consistently prioritised over the comprehensive conception of peace. For this reason it is no longer adequate to employ an obsolete security discourse that renders peace invisible as an afterthought to militarism, or marginalises it as the merely contingent outcome of the pursuit of militaristic policies. The explicit inclusion of a human right to peace is a necessary requirement for the human security paradigm to be realised. As with other human rights, the human right to peace can be codified in international and domestic law with established mechanisms of enforcement. Thus the human right to peace must be taken much more seriously in our globalised world because the pervasiveness of violence in daily life 'is a major source of insecurity today for people everywhere around the globe'.[24] The logic of violence entrenched in the international system has direct consequences that reach across all borders and affect all persons. In order to promote security throughout the world and protect the right of all persons to a secure and peaceful existence, several principles should be adopted to guide future political and legal developments:[25]

(a) The primary goals of global security policy should be to prevent conflict and war and to maintain the integrity of the planet's life-support systems by removing the economic, social, environmental, political and military conditions that generate threats to the security of people and the planet, and by anticipating and managing crises before they escalate into armed conflicts.

(b) Military force is not a legitimate political instrument, except in self-defence or under multilateral, collective security measures taken for humanitarian purposes.

(c) The development of military capabilities beyond that required for national defence and humanitarian action is a potential threat to the security of people.

(d) Weapons of mass destruction are not legitimate political or military instruments.

(e) The production and trade in arms should be controlled by the international community.

RESPONDING TO HUMAN SECURITY THREATS: THE ROLE OF JUST WAR THEORY

What can just war theory contribute to the goals of human security and the human right to peace? Given the mutually supportive aims of human security and the human right to peace, it may seem paradoxical to appeal to just war theory at this point. How can a theory that provides any degree of legitimacy to warfare be in any way compatible with human peace and security? I suggested above that the argument in support of the human right to peace was not to be equated with pacifism, in so far as there are certain very limited instances in which it is morally justifiable to resort to force. I think the most useful approach to identifying when the employment of military force is justified *as a last resort* is that of just war theory. While the application of just war criteria in practice cannot be considered unproblematic, the criteria nevertheless provide us with a reasonable framework for discriminating between just and unjust uses of political violence. In traditional just war theory there are two basic categories of norms: *jus ad bellum*, the justice of the cause of resorting to war to begin with, and *jus in bello*, the justice of the means or conduct of war once it has begun. Recent work in just war theory points to the need to consider a third category, *jus post bellum*, the justice of the cessation of hostilities and the subsequent transition from war to peace.[26] The criteria of a robust version of just war theory are as follows:

1. *Jus ad bellum*
    (a) Just cause: the war must be fought in a just cause.
    (b) Right intention: states must have the right reason and proper motivation for going to war, which excludes war for personal or national gain, or for some other hidden purpose.
    (c) Legitimate authority: the war must be declared publicly and waged exclusively by the competent authority having the right to do so.
    (d) Last resort: recourse to war must be a last resort.
    (e) Likelihood of success: those engaging in war must have a reasonable hope of success.
    (f) Proportionality of the ends of war: the damage and harm that the war ultimately entails must be judged proportionate to the injustice which occasions it.

2. *Jus in bello*
    (g) Discrimination: combatants must distinguish between military targets and civilian populations, and non-combatants must be immune from attack.
    (h) Proportionality of the means of war: all military actions taken in war must be reasonably expected to produce benefits that outweigh the expected harms or costs.

3. *Jus post bellum*
    (i) Proportionality and Publicity: a just peace settlement should be measured and reasonable, as well as publicly proclaimed.
    (j) Rights Vindication: the aim of the peace settlement should be to secure those basic rights whose violations triggered the justified war.
    (k) Discrimination: distinction ought to be made between the leaders, soldiers, and civilians of a country when setting the terms of a peace settlement, to avoid the application of unfair and punitive measures against the civilian population.
    (l) Punishment: leaders and soldiers – on all sides of the conflict – responsible for rights-violating aggression, crimes against humanity, and war crimes should be held accountable and be subject to fair trials and proportionate punishment.
    (m) Compensation and Rehabilitation: financial restitution may be mandated, subject to proportionality and discrimination, and the reform and reconstruction of an aggressive, rights-violating regime may be permissible.

The structure of comprehensive just war theory indicates that while a war may be justly begun it is conceivable that it will be unjustly fought or unjustly terminated. The justness of any given war therefore must be determined in light of the complete set of norms, and the failure to satisfy one set of norms may preclude judging the war as a whole to be just. Furthermore, it should be kept in mind that no single principle by itself offers sufficient justification for the use of military force. Rather the criteria are taken as individually necessary and jointly sufficient for a war to count as just. For instance, while a just cause is a necessary condition for the resort to war, it is not itself a sufficient condition. A state may rightly go to war only when all the remaining *jus ad bellum* conditions are met as well. Nevertheless, even if sufficient justification exists, the criteria ought to be understood most fundamentally as imposing negative constraints on the use of military force. This proviso means the decision to go to war does not become mandatory simply because all *jus ad bellum* conditions are met; it means only that going to war is a permissible last resort. The purpose of the criteria is not to justify war in the sense of fostering or promoting it but only in the sense of defending morally what would otherwise be prohibited.

The significance of the *in bello* principles is that they require continual adherence to the norms of just war theory. While a state may be justified in initiating war by satisfying the *ad bellum* criteria, it is quite possible that the same state could violate the norms of *jus in bello* during the course of war. If a state were to conduct war in violation of the *in bello* criteria, its claim to be prosecuting a just war would be discredited. The purposes of *jus post bellum* criteria are to ensure the integrity and continuity of the norms of just and legitimate war, and to cement and consolidate the conditions upon which to (re)build a just and stable peace. Parties to the conflict must take responsibility both for their roles in the events leading up to the conflict and for their necessary contributions in the aftermath, in order to construct a more secure and just environment for the exercise of basic human rights. The measures implied by the *jus post bellum* criteria are consistent with the goals of human security, and include establishing a legitimate rule of law, retraining the police and judiciary, demilitarising the armed forces, holding accountable perpetrators of mass atrocities, rebuilding damaged societal infrastructure, and contributing to the formation of mechanisms for rehabilitation and reconciliation.[27]

Turning now to the nature of war itself, it should first be noted that war is a social institution. War may be defined as the controlled and organised use of force, undertaken by political authorities and other organised groups exhibiting a functioning chain of command. War must be understood therefore not simply as the outcome of 'natural' or 'spontaneous' aggression, but as a socially defined form of mass killing.[28] It is a 'complex collective activity' involving two or more actors and directed by a consciously organised social power for the purpose of destroying 'the power of an enemy and its will to resist'.[29] As a complex social institution, war requires the recruiting and training of soldiers, the development and production of weaponry, the devising of strategy, tactics and command structures, the deployment and direction of armed forces, and the specification of targets and objectives, all carried out within an intricate web of rules, norms, and beliefs that distinguish war as a legitimate social practice from other illegitimate forms of killing. In short, war 'is premeditated violence, precisely the kind that is most illegitimate in non-war social relations'.[30]

These last points imply another significant feature of war, namely, that its general legitimacy actually rests upon deeper, yet less settled grounds of justification. This is because the forms of mass killing characteristic of war have come to be regarded as legitimate only in so far as they satisfy a justifiable exception to more fundamental prohibitions against killing. Most, if not all, moral and legal codes reflect the belief that killing is reprehensible and wrong, except in special cases of exception to widely held prohibitions. Such exceptions may include the classic case of self-defence, judicial execution, and revolt or rebellion against despotic rule. What is significant is that any case of killing that claims to meet one of these exceptions must be justified. For purposes of this discussion, the point to take from this is that any *particular* resort to force, including its aims and methods, requires justification if it is to be regarded as legitimate by the wider public. This has become especially true given the extensive development of the laws of war, international humanitarian law, and human rights law during the twentieth century. Following the massive destruction of the First and Second World Wars, and the revelation of such atrocities as the Holocaust and subsequent genocides, the international community has increasingly questioned the legitimacy of war and placed progressively greater legal and moral constraints around the justifiable resort to force and conduct of war.

It is here that we face an inescapable tension that confronts just war theory – a tension between the dual ambition to, on the one hand, *limit* war and, on the other hand, *legitimate* war. Yet this tension does not arise from the theory itself, rather it arises from the larger social context in which killing is both a proscribed and justifiable activity. Just war theory merely reflects humanity's struggle between its awareness that war embodies what is otherwise senseless, repugnant slaughter and destruction, and its recognition that at times the violence of war may be justified on the basis of reasonably necessary exceptions to the norms against killing. As remarked above, the justification of war on the basis of just war criteria is not intended to foster or promote war but only to defend morally what would otherwise be prohibited. Thus the tension faced by just war theory derives from the fact that the justification of any particular war expresses both deep reservations about the use of political violence, and the emerging consensus that human security is frequently more threatened than protected by military force. Therefore even a just war is not to be regarded as a good thing *per se* but as the lesser of two evils. These reservations are reflected in the continued reduction of permissible exceptions to the proscription of war under international law. For this reason it is becoming increasingly difficult to mount satisfactory justifications for war, and just war theory is perhaps the most stringent justificatory framework currently available for defending the exceptional necessity of war given specific, human security-threatening circumstances.

The exceptions to the general prohibitions against the use of armed force are of primary concern here, in particular the need to respond to serious, existing or imminent threats to peace and security, such as unjustified aggression, genocide and ethnic cleansing, and mass atrocities including extreme, rights-violating political violence and state terrorism. To permit such threats to go unmet is to allow an even greater injustice than the sometimes necessary evil of war to triumph over the rights of persons to peace and security. If we understand pacifism to be a thorough rejection of all war, then it will not accept the possibility that any war can be just.[31] One of the central pacifist criticisms of war, including those that conform to just war criteria, is that it inevitably involves the killing of innocent persons, and the killing of innocents is presumptively wrong.[32] It may well be the case that all war does result in the killing of innocents – and history would seem to support this conclusion – yet it does not necessarily follow that killing innocents thereby undermines the case for the justice of any particular war.

More specifically, the pacifist argument fails sufficiently to account for the prospect that there may be some circumstances in which the possibility or actuality of killing innocents is outweighed by the realisation of a greater good. The types of threats to human security previously mentioned arguably constitute greater evils than the use of properly constrained military force in response to them, and to fail to resist or prevent them would therefore perpetuate injustice through an act of omission. Moreover, there is a relevant moral distinction to be made between the intentional killing of innocents, which is prohibited by just war theory, and the unintended and regrettable deaths that result from a just war viewed as the least worst option. Just war theory is not oblivious to the tragic moral costs associated with the killing of innocents; but it would counter that pacifism, by failing to take forceful action when necessary against the most extreme forms of injustice, would itself be unjustifiably complicit in the harm or deaths of innocent victims. Just war theory proposes neither a categorical sanction of military force nor a categorical condemnation of it. Rather, it suggests that the demands of justice – which include protecting vital human rights and security interests – must be met in certain unfortunate circumstances by the properly measured and constrained use of armed force.

The complete and permanent elimination of violent conflict is not only highly unlikely; the idea of such also disregards the continued presence of persistent and serious threats to human security which can only be resolved, at least in part, through the appropriate use of force. Therefore, the argument I have offered in support of human security and the right to peace is grounded in a conception of 'just peace' rather than pacifism. Just peace is a stringently normative position, which requires the presence of basic social and political institutions committed to principles of justice such as fairness, equality, respect, tolerance, opportunity and the protection of human rights. While just peace maintains a preference for non-violent mediation, negotiation, arbitration and resolution of disputes it also recognises, unlike pacifism, the legitimate use of force in certain limited cases where violence must be used to resist and abolish extreme instances of injustice, such as genocide and other gross violations of human rights. Crucially, the appeal to a strictly defined just war framework contributes to further limiting the scope for legitimate military activity, while recognising the responsibility to protect other persons from unjustified cruelties, harms and serious threats to their security. This responsibility to protect can be encapsulated in the basic duties to avoid harm and to protect and aid those whose security rights are threatened.[33]

Therefore, what is suggested here is that any legitimate military action can only be justified from a cosmopolitan perspective that integrates human security and the right to peace, with just war theory. Contrary to realist assumptions, such a perspective regards war as *generally illegitimate*, and requires strong justification for particular instances of warfare as genuinely *humanitarian exceptions* to an otherwise comprehensive interdiction of the use of military force.[34] As a humanitarian exception, armed conflict should only be recognised as legitimate in so far as it is undertaken not for the purpose of enhancing a state's power or furthering its 'national interests', but to vindicate the rights of fellow human beings and restore a secure and peaceful social order. The resort to armed force ought only to be contemplated and undertaken in the name of humanity – as the community of all persons conceived as equal rights-holders – and not of states as such. Just as we can acknowledge the wrongness of crimes *against* humanity, so too can we admit the rightness of acting *on behalf of* humanity.

CONCLUSION

The explicit articulation of a cosmopolitan conception of human security and a corresponding right to peace is a positive development in global politics, inasmuch as it decentres the state in our understanding of security and delegitimises organised violence as the generally accepted means for the 'continuation' of realist politics. I have argued that just war theory, when defined in suitably narrow fashion, helps to contribute to our thinking on issues of human security in several ways. First, it provides a stringent normative framework for a reasonable humanitarian justification of the resort to force. Secondly, it enables us to conceptualise significant moral and legal constraints on war and thus on the powers of states to wage war, thereby displacing the use of force from the statist paradigm of security. Thirdly, it contributes to the delegitimation of unjust wars, that is, military actions undertaken for any purposes other than human security. Fourthly, in so far as it provides a justificatory basis for the increasing demilitarisation of society, it may influence the progressive and just pacification of global politics.

As long as the types of human wrongs that present the gravest threats to human security continue to haunt the global community, there remains a need to be able to respond effectively so as to protect the rights and well-being of individuals. This need poses a genuine dilemma for humanitarian morality and politics, in so far as many of the military capabilities required to defend and to aid vulnerable persons can also be the source of threats to human life and welfare. Yet the existence of this dilemma need not lead us either to apathy or to cynicism. The nexus of human security, the right to peace, and just war theory offers a path out of the traditional security dilemma by challenging the realist rationale for aggressive militarism, and by supporting the emergence of global security structures and processes guided by the humanitarian norms of just peace. In the final analysis, the prospect of achieving a genuinely secure world rises or falls with the possibility of replacing the realist state-based security paradigm with a cosmopolitan person-based paradigm.

NOTES

1. Cosmopolitanism, which claims that we owe duties of justice to all the persons of the world and thus that world politics should focus first on the interests or welfare of persons rather than of states, is increasingly debated in political and moral theory. For representative discussions of cosmopolitanism and global justice see Jones (1999), Moellendorf (2002) and Pogge (2002).
2. Bull (1977).
3. See Morgenthau (1954).
4. Herz (1951).
5. Stockholm Initiative (1991), pp. 17–18.
6. United Nations (1994), p. 23.
7. Commission on Global Governance (1995), p. 78.
8. Commission on Human Security (2003), p. 2 and p. 4.
9. Department of Foreign Affairs and International Trade (1998).
10. MacLean (1998).
11. Falk (1995), p. 40.
12. Shue (1996).
13. Ibid., p. 19.
14. Ibid., p. 6.
15. Ibid., pp. 38–9.
16. Ibid., pp. 21–2.
17. Ibid., pp. 51–64.
18. Galtung (1996).
19. The basic structure of society is, according to John Rawls, the complex consisting of the major political, social and economic institutions of society and the state. See Rawls (1972), chapter 1.
20. Walzer (1992), p. 51.
21. Nussbaum (1999), p. 39.
22. Amartya Sen's work on the concept of human capabilities has been particularly significant in the creation of a new, 'people-centred' paradigm of human development, providing the conceptual foundation of the United Nations Development Programme's *Human Development Reports* since the early 1990s. See Sen (1999), and also Nussbaum and Sen (1993).
23. A clear example of the supremacy accorded to military interests is the United States government's recent approval of a record defence budget totalling more than US$400 billion for 2004.
24. Commission on Global Governance (1995), p. 131.
25. Ibid., pp. 84–5.
26. See Orend (2002b) and the Introduction to the present volume.
27. Ibid., pp. 55–6.
28. Shaw (2003), p. 16.

29. Ibid., pp. 18–19.
30. Ibid., p. 21.
31. There are, of course, different kinds of pacifism and assorted justifications for them. The point here, though, is that pacifism is in general opposed to any use of military force and thus to the idea of just war. For more on this issue see Teichman (1986).
32. See Holmes (1989), p. 189. An even more strict form of pacifism might argue that intentionally killing *any* human being, whether innocent or guilty, is morally impermissible.
33. The Commission on Global Governance argued 'the international community has an obligation to take action in situations where the security of people is imperilled'. That action may include the use of force as a last resort, 'justified on the basis of the violation of the security of people'. See Commission on Global Governance (1995), pp. 85–93. The notion of an 'obligation to take action' has been more recently and expansively explored by the International Commission on Intervention and State Sovereignty in its report (2001). The Commission suggests that the concept of the 'responsibility to protect' is a legitimate, evolving norm in international relations, which should supplant the 'right to intervene' approach to security crises.
34. It should be mentioned that there are relevant and significant forms of *non-military* intervention for humanitarian purposes that can go a long way towards alleviating many sources of human insecurity. The context of this chapter, however, concerns the justification of military force.

Chapter 8

FORGIVENESS AND RECONCILIATION IN *JUS POST BELLUM*

ANDREW RIGBY

In this chapter I want to argue that:

[i]   A necessary feature of any just peace, particularly in post-civil war situations, is that it is a durable one.

[ii] A particularly significant factor contributing to the durability of a peace settlement is that key publics, communities and opinion leaders believe that the peace is sufficiently 'just' as to merit their commitment.

[iii] A necessary element in facilitating the belief that a peace is 'just enough' is that the socio-cultural scars left by the war are addressed in a manner such that the pains of the past cease to dominate the present and open up the possibility of future co-existence between former enemies.

[iv] The manner in which such 'memory' or 'forgiveness work' is carried out will vary from case to case, depending on a number of significant factors, including the balance of power during the post-peace settlement period.

JUSTIFYING THE EVIL OF WAR BY ANTICIPATING A JUST PEACE

In any discussion of the history and the variety of just war thinking it is very important not to lose sight of the core issue which has driven this tradition. War is evil. A particularly strong and clear statement of this view was made by the German writer W. G. Sebald in a discussion of Sir Arthur Harris, commander-in-chief of Bomber Command during the Second World War. Harris, he suggested, liked destruction for its own sake, 'and was thus in perfect sympathy with the innermost principle of every war, which is to aim for as wholesale an annihilation of the enemy with his dwellings, his history and his natural environment as can possibly be achieved.' Sebald then went on to cite Elaine Scarry's view that 'the victims of war are not sacrifices made as the means to an end of any kind, but in the most precise sense are both the means and the end in themselves'.[1] A few pages later Sebald describes the effect of an allied bombing raid on Hamburg.[2]

> Residential districts with a street length of 200 kilometres in all were utterly destroyed. Horribly disfigured corpses lay everywhere. Bluish little phosphorous flames still flickered around many of them; others had been roasted brown or purple and reduced to a third of their normal size. They lay doubled up in pools of their own melted fat, which had sometimes already congealed … Elsewhere, clumps of flesh and bone or whole heaps of bodies had cooked in the water gushing from bursting boilers. Other victims had been so badly charred and reduced to ashes by the heat, which had risen to 1,000 degrees or more, that the remains of families consisting of several people could be carried away in a single laundry basket.

How can one ever justify engaging in such horror? This is the question that drives the just war debate. Even if people on the basis of some moral calculus decide that the evil of going to war is less than that of leaving a particular situation unaddressed, there is still the terrible moral dilemma of attempting to judge how much and what type of 'necessary evil' is justified in the pursuance of a desirable goal.

As a pacifist I can acknowledge that there are just causes, issues and situations which are so brutal and damaging that they cannot be left unaddressed. What pacifists cannot accept, however, is that it is possible to try to remove or overcome an evil by means that embody what might be considered the greatest evil of all – the waging of war and all that entails in terms of the killing, maiming and brutalising of other human beings. As Paul Oestreicher has expressed it, 'In war, however just the cause, no one emerges with clean hands.'[3]

The debate about just war principles is not one that has been confined to moral philosophers. At the time of writing there is still considerable discussion about the legitimacy and the legality of the British government's decision to follow the Bush administration and wage war on Iraq in March 2003. In their attempts to legitimise their actions President Bush and his ally Prime Minister Blair sought to change the terms of the debate. Having argued prior to the invasion that the war was just because the regime of Saddam Hussein possessed weapons of mass destruction that constituted a clear and present danger to the rest of the world, one of the subsequent arguments has been that whilst no weapons of mass destruction might have been found, the war was still just in so far as it liberated the Iraqi people from a terrible tyrant and his barbaric regime. In other words, the evil was justified by reference to the quality of the peace that was anticipated after the war – a new democratic Iraq where people might enjoy their basic human rights and live at peace with their domestic and international neighbours. This has been the type of argument that has been used to justify 'humanitarian wars' such as the bombing campaign against Serbian targets in Kosovo and Serbia proper in the spring of 1999: the evil of war is legitimated as a necessary means of bringing about a desirable and just peace.

The features of such a peace can be portrayed somewhat negatively in terms of the removal of a particularly evil regime and the neutralisation of those guilty of carrying out crimes against humanity, or they can be delineated in more positive terms with regard to the strengthening of human rights, the establishment of a democratic regime and the socioeconomic reconstruction necessary for people to live full and productive lives in harmony with their fellow citizens. Whatever the emphasis, the tradition of justifying the evil of war by reference to the just peace that can thereby be achieved remains as strong as ever.

CIVIL WARS AND THE CHALLENGE OF PEACE-MAKING

One of the limitations of much of the literature relating to the principles underpinning theories of just war is that most refer to either inter-state wars or cross-border interventions by third parties. Whilst the invasions of Afghanistan and Iraq should remind us that inter-state wars continue to represent a threat to peace in the world, it has to be acknowledged that over the last ten to fifteen years intra-state wars have been a more common occurrence.[4] Particular features of these conflicts have included the phenomenon of war-lordism, with different armed factions (frequently sponsored by one or more 'third parties') targeting and preying off the civilian populations. This has reflected a weakened distinction between combatants and civilians and a disregard for the various

Geneva Conventions ruling the conduct of war. This in turn has resulted in a significant increase in the proportion of civilian war-related deaths, burgeoning numbers of displaced and refugees, and the widespread destruction of social capital.[5]

To outside observers it can be very difficult to identify anything resembling a 'just cause' driving the violence in some of these cases. For example, in the conflict in northern Uganda the Lords Resistance Army has never been very explicit about its demands or its terms for a peace settlement. Indeed there has been a growing body of work that has identified 'greed' rather than 'grievance' as the main factor perpetuating many cases of armed conflict. What this means is that many of the key participants in the violence have a vested economic and material interest in its continuation; war for them is the pursuit of economic activity by other means.[6] Thus, anyone trying to unravel the causal threads of the terrible war that has blighted the Democratic Republic of the Congo for so many years would have to take account of the vested interests of key actors in exploiting the mineral wealth of the country under the cover of war.[7]

The challenges facing peacemakers in such conflicts are awesome. As Roy Licklider has phrased it, 'How do you make peace and agree to live in the same state with people who have killed your friends and family? How do you live with these people for the rest of your life? How do you trust them enough to work with them economically and socially to create a functioning political system?'[8] In fact, the research of Licklider and others indicates that negotiated settlements of civil wars are far more likely to collapse than those brought to an end by military victory.[9]

That so many negotiated settlements collapse is indicative to some degree of the seriousness of the challenges facing those seeking to bring an end to the collective violence. If one was to list the characteristics of an ideal-typical post-war society, we could include: economic infrastructure destroyed, weak or collapsed state structures with serious law and order problems, social fragmentation and absence of mutual trust within and between communities, and a widespread culture of violence and impunity.

It follows from this that any durable peace settlement should possess at least some of the following characteristics:

(a) *Inclusiveness*. For settlements to be effective it is vital that they are supported by all the major players, particularly those with the resources to sabotage the process.

(b) *Security.* One of the most tangible features of any settlement must be the ending of large-scale violence and a corresponding increase in physical and psychological security. This can be facilitated in part by the provision of credible security guarantees to parties to the agreement, a role that can often be played effectively by third parties.[10] It also entails the disarming, demobilisation and re-integration of combatants.

(c) *Strengthening of the state.* One of the major challenges facing post-war societies is the establishment of a working government that enjoys the legitimacy and the resources to begin to institutionalise non-violent ways of managing conflict whilst developing its capacity to provide security and other key services for its citizens.

(d) *Economic reconstruction.* To the extent that people experience tangible peace dividends, the likelihood of the settlement enduring is increased. Amongst the most important fruits of peace is the creation of employment and other economic opportunities.

(e) *Socio-cultural repair work.* War, particularly civil war, tears apart the social fabric of societies and leaves deep personal and collective wounds amongst victims and survivors. Unless the traumas caused by the horrors of war are addressed in a constructive manner, then the destructive memories from the past and associated cultures of violence and impunity will continue to be reproduced, with new generations determined to 'get even' and avenge the humiliation and the suffering, thereby undermining any efforts to repair relationships in the post-war society.

A PEACE THAT IS 'JUST ENOUGH'

One can see from the above that the durability of a peace process depends to a significant degree upon the implementation of certain structural and institutional changes in the post-war society. However, whilst such reforms are necessary dimensions of a durable peace, they are not sufficient in themselves to ensure the resilience of a post-settlement peace process. The crucial factor in this is the perception of significant publics, communities, opinion-leaders and other stakeholders that the unfolding peace process is sufficiently just for them to continue to lend it their commitment and resist whatever urge there might be to return to violence. A necessary element in facilitating the belief that a peace is 'just enough' is that the socio-cultural scars left by the war are addressed in a manner such that the pains of the past cease to dominate the present and open up the possibility of restoring some kind of constructive relationships between former enemies. Some insight into the nature of what might be called 'memory work', but which I prefer to characterise as 'forgiveness work', for reasons which should become clearer, can be obtained by exploring how people in general come to terms with painful memories of loss and suffering.

DEALING WITH THE PAST

How do people 'put the past behind them'? How do they 'move on' in the sense of seeking to create a future which is not over-determined by particular traumatic experiences from their past?

The first point that needs to be made is that some people choose not to forget the pains of the past, but appear almost to embrace them – they remain 'pickled in their own history' as an informant described some of the communities in Kosovo during a research visit I made there in 2003. We also need to acknowledge that there is no single method of 'dealing with the past'. Some people seem able to forget, or exclude from the foreground of their consciousness, that which they do not want to remember. Thus, commenting on the manner in which the German survivors of the allied bombing raids sought to resume social life, W. G. Sebald observed,

> People's ability to forget what they do not want to know, to overlook what is before their eyes, was seldom put to the test better than in Germany at that time. The population decided – out of sheer panic at first – to carry on as if nothing had happened.[11]

By contrast, some people are unable or unwilling to let go of the past. They can use the memory as a motivating force leading them to campaign for truth and justice. An example that comes to mind from my own experience is a veteran of the Gulf War of 1990–1 who, after his return to Britain, began to suffer all the symptoms of what became known as 'Gulf War syndrome'. He firmly believed that his chronic ill-health was attributable to a cocktail of vaccinations he had been given by the medical staff of the British army prior to going into the war-zone. This became one of the core elements in his identity, as he became a leading campaigner on behalf of other Gulf War veterans, demanding an acknowledgement of liability from the British government. Other people attempt different ways of learning to live with the pains from their past – an increasingly common method is to join with groups of fellow victims with whom one can share the memory of the suffering, hoping for some kind of solace through re-experiencing the pain and loss within a supportive group context.

The fact that there is no single method of dealing with the past should sensitise us to the phenomenon that there is no singular 'past', it is not some once-and-for-all set of events with an independent existence. Our past is our historical memory or representation of our experiences. It is our *re-membered* past, and as such it is just one of a range of possible alternative memories that it is possible to hold. The point to be emphasised here is that in the context of efforts to achieve a peace that is 'just enough' to be durable, it is crucial that people construct and reproduce new memories shorn of the desires for revenge and retribution that can destroy a fragile peace.

FORGIVENESS AND BECOMING RECONCILED TO LOSS

In societies emerging out of violent division and war it is vital for the sake of peace that people manage to learn how to live with their sense of loss. A significant dimension of such a process is that people become *reconciled to* their situation, resigning themselves to a current condition that is far from their ideal for the sake of their future. In order for people to become *reconciled to* loss as a way of dealing with the pain of the past, it is necessary for them to reinterpret that past, look backwards through time with a lens that enables them to reconstruct their memories in a manner that eases the intensity of feelings of hatred and bitterness, thereby opening up the possibility for new relationships with those once deemed responsible for their suffering.

To explore this process, let me first refer to a phenomenon that Geiko Muller-Fahrenholz has termed 'deep remembering', when people remain trapped within a memory of the past that reproduces the old divisions and traumas.[12] This is particularly pervasive in Northern Ireland, as Clem McCartney has observed:

> For the people living in Northern Ireland the situation has proved so intractable because of a vivid awareness of past attitudes and behaviour and the fear that these will be replicated in the future.

Their concerns about the past and the future in turn govern and limit their present conduct and reconfirm the belief that opponents have learnt nothing from the past: They have not and will not change.[13]

By contrast with the 'deepness' of divisive memories in Northern Ireland, survivors of war in other parts of the world can display a greater willingness and capacity to reconstruct their memories. Thus, at the start of her book on truth commissions, Priscilla Hayner tells of a meeting in 1995 with a government official in post-genocide Rwanda. She asked him whether he wanted to remember or forget. He replied, 'We must remember what happened in order to keep it from happening again. But we must forget the feelings, the emotions, that go with it. It is only by forgetting that we are able to go on.'[14] A similar attitude was displayed by a Sierra Leonean human rights worker I met in 2002. He told me how, in some villages, people were accepting back into their community young people who had committed horrendous crimes in the different militias that had terrorised the civilian population for so many years of the civil war. When I expressed a certain incredulity he continued, 'Of course we welcome them back. We have to forget. It is difficult but we have to forgive. They were drugged you know.'[15]

In affirming the need to 'forgive and forget' my Sierra Leonean friend was acknowledging the need to redefine the past (the war crimes committed by these young men) and create a new memory for the sake of the future harmony of the community. He was able to do this, and justify his gift of forgiveness, by reference to the fact that they were not fully responsible for their actions – they were drugged. In so doing he highlighted a key feature of inter-personal forgiveness – the prepared-ness of the victim to distinguish between the perpetrator and the deed and thereby recognise the humanity of the other. It is in this manner, through a reframing of the past – the creation of a new memory – that forgiveness can open up the possibility of a new relationship between those that have been divided. As Hannah Arendt phrased it, 'Forgiveness serves to undo the deeds of the past.'[16] Agostino Giovanoli expressed a similar view when he wrote, 'Forgiveness is the start of a new memory, of a new kind of memory.'[17]

CONDITIONS THAT FACILITATE INTER-PERSONAL FORGIVENESS

As was remarked above, central to acts of forgiveness is the prepared-ness to distinguish between the wrong committed and the person responsible for that wrong. A number of factors would appear to make this redefinition of the perpetrator (and hence the construction of a new memory) more possible.

[1] Acknowledgement and apology

Admission of culpability and acceptance that what they did was wrong indicates that the perpetrator is aware of the offence they caused and is expressing a desire to reach towards a new relationship with the victim. To the extent that a perpetrator is prepared to acknowledge their guilt, then they are clearly attempting to establish a distance between their present self and the historical self that committed the wrong.

[2] The promise not to repeat the wrong

The acknowledgement of shame regarding the wrongs committed and the promise that they will not be repeated represents one more layer in the affirmation of the perpetrator's commitment to 'change their ways', distancing themselves even further from their old self and reassuring the victim about their future relationships.

[3] Offers to make amends – reparations

The willingness of a perpetrator to 'pay the price' and face the con-sequences of their past deeds, either by their preparedness to suffer and/ or their willingness to make reparations can symbolise in a very clear and unambiguous fashion their distance from the old self that committed the original wrong.

In addition to such offers and commitments made by the perpetrator, reference should also be made to two other significant background factors that heighten the likelihood of inter-personal forgiveness. One is the predisposition of the victim to forgive due to their personal philosophy or culture. To the extent that a victim, due to their religious or secular moral code, feels that they *ought* to forgive those that have committed wrongs against them, then they are more likely to respond constructively to the opportunities to establish a new relationship with the perpetrator.[18]

The second contextual factor is perhaps the most important of all – time. As Walter Benjamin observed:

> In order to struggle against retribution, forgiveness finds its power-ful ally in time … time not only extinguishes the traces of all misdeeds but also – by virtue of its duration, beyond all remem-bering or forgetting – helps, in ways that are wholly mysterious, to complete the process of forgiveness …[19]

CONDITIONS THAT FACILITATE SUCCESSFUL COLLECTIVE FORGIVENESS WORK

On the basis of this analysis of the factors that can facilitate inter-personal forgiveness, we can extrapolate and theorise about those conditions or processes that can heighten the capacity of communities emerging from the traumas of war and violent conflict to deal with the pains of the past in a manner which opens up possibilities for future reconciliation with former enemies.

Truth. At the core of confession and inter-personal apology is the acknowledgement of the victims' historical experience. Hence, the capacity of a community to create a new collective memory that allows for the relinquishment of the desire for revenge will be enhanced to the degree that former enemies acknowledge the wrongs perpetrated in the past.

Peace/security. A necessary condition for people to begin to forgive at either the inter-personal or the inter-communal level is the experience of a break with the past in the form of an identifiable end to the wrongs perpetrated. Expressions of regret and commitments towards the future by former enemies, at the interpersonal and inter-communal levels, offer the promise of future peace and security which, over time, will allow for the formation of new memories and new relationships. What is crucial however is that beyond words there are the necessary institutional changes to reassure people that 'the past is past', enabling them to experience a degree of personal and collective security sufficient to reassure them about the future actions of former enemies and wrongdoers.

Justice. The capacity of people to relinquish the desire for revenge fed by feelings of bitterness towards former perpetrators is enhanced to the extent that they feel genuine efforts have been made to 'make things right'. This notion of restitution is at the heart of common-sense notions of justice: people should not be allowed to act with impunity, they should be required to pay at least some price for the wrongs committed; whilst victims/survivors should receive some kind of compensation or reparation for the suffering endured.

Time. Dealing constructively with the past by means of forgiveness, whether at the interpersonal or collective level, requires time. The length of time necessary for new memories to be formed that allow for new relationships between those that were divided will vary from person to person and community to community according to the particular circumstances and culture.

FORGIVENESS AND RECONCILIATION

I have tried to argue that war is such an evil that one of the key characteristics of any 'just peace' should be its resilience. For a peace to be durable in the context of a post-civil war society it is important that key actors believe it to be sufficiently just as to deserve their commitment. The likelihood of this happening is increased to the extent that certain institutional changes take place, but alongside these there needs to be a process akin to forgiveness – the formation of new interpretations of the past, new memories that allow for the creation of constructive relationships with former enemies. It is this process of relationship-building that we can refer to as reconciliation work. An analytical distinction can be made between forgiveness and reconciliation work, in so far as the former is oriented towards the reframing of the past, whilst reconciliation work is oriented towards the future and the fostering of co-existence between those that have been divided. However, at the empirical level of the lived world it can be very difficult to distinguish between initiatives that are exclusively past or future-oriented. Despite this a number of observations seem relevant at this point concerning the relationship between past-oriented forgiveness work and future-oriented reconciliation work in the context of achieving a sustainable and just peace.

[1] Forgiveness might be a necessary but it is not a sufficient condition for future reconciliation in the full sense of the restoration of harmonious relationships between those that were divided. It is at least theoretically possible for former enemies to experience some kind of forgiveness process but without any concomitant desire to establish a shared mutually dependent relationship. They can agree to put past enmities behind them whilst deciding that there is insufficient basis for any shared future. They can enjoy a form of 'peace through separation'.[20]

[2] This sensitises us to the fact that the levels of forgiveness and reconciliation achieved over time are matters of degree. Louis Kriesberg, in a series of insightful publications, has identified a range of types of co-existence possible between members of different communities historically divided by destructive conflict. He has focused in particular upon two dimensions: the degree to which groups are integrated together in terms of interaction and interdependence, and the extent to which the relationship is mutually constructed or unilaterally imposed and sustained.[21]

[3] Forgiveness, and hence reconciliation, are not once-and-for-all irreversible processes. Whatever new memories and interpretations of the past are created in the process of forgiveness, they are formed on the basis of the old. Under certain circumstances these deeper memories can resurface, resurrecting the old resentment, bitterness and the desire to avenge past crimes and injustices suffered at the hands of the historical enemy.

TENSIONS BETWEEN THE CONSTITUTIVE DIMENSIONS OF A JUST PEACE

The resurfacing of deep memories invariably reflects a growing belief amongst key actors that the peace process is not 'just enough' to deserve their continuing commitment. Frequently the critique of the peace focuses on the lack of progress made in relation to one or more of the constitutive processes of peace/security, truth and justice.

Unfortunately the elements conducive to forgiving the past as the basis for future reconciliation do not rest easily together. Too active a pursuit of justice in societies emerging out of division can result in a return to repression and bloodshed. Too great a concern with avoiding a resumption of violence for the sake of peace and security can mean that truth and justice are forfeited through individual and collective amnesia. Likewise, if the value of truth is sought above all else, then this can come at the cost of justice – after all, why should perpetrators confess to their war-crimes if, as a consequence, they will face punishment?

In the following review of the main modes adopted by regimes to deal with the legacy of a past characterised by destructive conflict and accompanying human rights abuses we will see how the choices made and the relative value placed on the different constitutive elements of peace/security, truth and justice reflect to a significant degree the balance of power between the different parties to the peace settlement and the subsequent post-settlement peace-building process.

PRIORITISING JUSTICE: PURSUING THE JUST PEACE OF THE VICTOR

When the outcome of a violent conflict is the comprehensive defeat of one of the parties, then it is highly likely that the victors will prioritise some form of retributive justice as the main means of dealing with the past. The extent to which this happens will reflect the degree to which they enjoy the capacity and the will to punish the perpetrators of abuse amongst the vanquished, and their perception of the relative significance of any resultant threat to the peace and stability of the post-war society. The main problem with this approach to creating a just peace is that it can leave the vanquished nursing grievances about what they might consider a perverted form of *victor's* justice, thereby undermining any efforts at longer-term reconciliation between those divided by war and violence. Some features of this pattern can be found in the recent history of post-genocide Rwanda.

In this small central African country the minority Tutsis had been the dominant group. In the 1960s there was an uprising and the representatives of the majority Hutus took power. This regime was challenged in 1990 by the Tutsi-led Rwandan Patriotic Front (RPF) invading from Uganda. Peace talks were subsequently held in Tanzania in 1994. The assassination of the Rwandan president as he returned from signing the peace accords in Arusha in April 1994 served as a pretext for the launch of a genocidal attack against politically moderate Hutus and the Tutsi population, resulting in some 800,000 deaths over the next few months. As the RPF advanced there were reports of revenge killings and human rights atrocities against the Hutu population, some two million of whom fled as refugees to neighbouring countries. Another one million people were displaced inside Rwanda. Hundreds of thousands of survivors had lost their homes and property, and had witnessed extreme forms of brutality, including the rape and murder of their family members – an estimated 300,000 children were amongst the murder victims.[22]

Having experienced such a nightmare, there was an overwhelming cry for justice from significant sections of the survivors, a retributive justice involving the punishment of the *genocidaires*. As the Attorney General noted,

> Of course we cannot kill all those who deserve to die, it would not stabilise our society. But in the aftermath of genocide there was an overwhelming feeling that there must be accountability, people must be punished so it will not happen again.[23]

Thousands upon thousands were imprisoned in camps to await trial and punishment. However, the Rwandan state infrastructure was in ruins, and there had been mass involvement in the killing. It became increasingly apparent that there was no way that all those who had participated could be prosecuted and punished in accordance with due legal process. Several years after the genocide, in 2001, just over 2,500 suspects had been tried and sentenced, including some who were executed in public, but there were another 120,000 suspects still incarcerated and waiting to be processed through the courts.[24] As Richard Goldstone has observed,

> in a perfect society victims are entitled to full justice, namely trial of perpetrators, and if they are found guilty adequate punishment. That ideal is not possible in the aftermath of massive violence. There are simply too many victims and too many perpetrators – even the most sophisticated criminal justice system would be completely overwhelmed.[25]

Whilst the round-up of suspects was taking place in Rwanda itself the international community acted to set up the International Criminal Tribunal for Rwanda (ICTR) on 8 November 1994. It was mandated to prosecute 'persons responsible for genocide and other serious violations of international humanitarian law committed in the territory of Rwanda and Rwandan citizens responsible for genocide and other such violations committed in the territory of neighbouring states between 1 January 1994 and 31 December 1994'. The ICTR targeted the main instigators and architects of the genocide, who had fled from Rwanda and who were therefore beyond the reach of the Rwandan judicial system. It indicted 56 people, but by September 2003 it had only processed 21 suspects and sentenced nine of them, despite enjoying a budget of some $100 million a year – too slow a process in the eyes of many, who were also aggrieved that the suspects enjoyed the relative luxury of Western style prisons and escaped execution.[26]

In response to these dilemmas and aware that retributive justice alone would not further the cause of reconciliation within the country, the Rwandan state initiated a form of restorative justice known as *gacaca*, based on traditional processes for settling village disputes presided over by community elders respected for their moral integrity and calibre. Suspects have been categorised according to the severity of their presumed crimes. Whilst those accused of being significant architects of the killing still face the death sentence in a court of law, other suspects can be brought before a *gacaca* court to be judged by lay members of the community. If they confess and show repentance their prison sentences can be reduced and they are then required to participate in some form of community service as a means of atonement for their crimes.[27]

The introduction of *gacaca* met with opposition from certain sections of the victim/survivor population of Rwanda. There were well-founded fears that witnesses at the hearings would be exposed to intimidation, with a representative of one of the survivors' organisations complaining, 'We are extremely concerned to see justice. Gacaca will mean Hutus gathering to let other Hutus off.'[28] However, for the post-genocide regime there was the growing awareness that the pursuit of retributive justice was militating against the broader process of reconciliation. In a country as small and as densely populated as Rwanda there is no feasible alternative but for victims/survivors and perpetrators to live alongside each other. The hope invested in the *gacaca* system has been that this form of 'reconciliatory justice' would help repair the social fabric.[29]

Of course, for those survivors that lost their families in the slaughter nothing can fill the void of loss. At the same time the pursuit of a Tutsi defined 'just peace' has heightened the feeling of resentment amongst certain sections of the Hutu population who have witnessed the re-establishment of Tutsi political domination with a partial view of justice. There is anger that there have been no prosecutions of those Tutsis and RPF personnel responsible for revenge killings and other abuses after the genocide. One woman who lost her husband and her six sons in 1996 complained, 'Today they talk about *gacaca*, but it is only justice for Tutsi victims, not for Hutus.'[30]

Thus, the dilemma for Rwanda remains: how to achieve a sustainable peace that is 'just enough' to satisfy all sections of the population when the prime concern of the minority is for 'justice' and the majority demand is for democracy?[31] According to Mahmood Mamdani the prime prerequisite for reconciliation and a common future, a truly just peace, is a form of *political justice* whereby Tutsis relinquish their monopolisation of political power rather than continue to hold on to it out of fear of the majority. In his words,

> Rather than think that power is the precondition for survival, the Tutsi will sooner or later have to consider the opposite possibility: that the prerequisite to cohabitation, to reconciliation, and a common political future may indeed be to give up the monopoly of power. ... so long as Hutu and Tutsi remain alive as political identities, giving up political power may be a surer guarantee of survival than holding on to it.[32]

PRIORITISING PEACE: THE APPEAL OF COLLECTIVE AMNESIA

The history of post-civil war Spain under the dictator Franco bears out the observations made regarding the tendency for the outright victors in a civil war to impose their own version of a just peace on the post-war society, without too much concern for the preferences of the vanquished. The three-year Spanish civil war ended in 1939 and Franco was determined that the bloody contest should be remembered and memorialised as a war of victory over the evil forces of international socialism and secularism that would have destroyed Mother Spain. In the wake of victory came a regime of repression and the institution-alisation of revenge against the defeated. Tens of thousands were brought before special tribunals and sentenced to death or lengthy periods of imprisonment and forced labour. At the same time a blanket amnesty was extended to cover all acts perpetrated by Franco's forces during the war.[33]

Within a year of Franco's death in 1975 a process of political reform had been instituted in Spain. Because the divisions of the civil war had been reproduced throughout the years of dictatorship, there was widespread consensus that the time had come to heal the divide. A 'pact of oblivion' was agreed by all parties and groupings committed to the transition.[34] This decision to forget the past was the outcome of negoti-ations between elites that included those remnants of the old regime with the capacity to disrupt the peaceful transition if significant attempts were made to settle old scores and reveal the truth about the extent of human rights abuses perpetrated during the years of Franco's rule.

The prioritising of peace/security above all other aspects of a just peace is invariably the outcome when a civil war or period of severe internal repression has come to an end by means of a negotiated settlement between the parties and where the successor regime lacks the capacity and/or the will to pursue the values of justice and truth for fear of provoking those threatened by such moves. This prioritising of peace and security can receive wide endorsement, particularly if signifi-cant sections of the population were actively involved in or complicit with abuses during the period of violent conflict, and especially if those that were divided have no alternative but to live alongside each other in the post-settlement society. In such cases, and where the peace settlement has been arrived at by negotiation rather than military victory, 'leaving the past behind' by means of some kind of process of personal and collective amnesia can seem the most desirable option. This can appear as the only 'realistic' option if there are well-grounded fears that any attempts to bring to account those responsible for the worst abuses might provoke a renewal of the conflict with all the accompanying bloodshed and pain. Here the case of Mozambique comes to mind. Riven by many years of a murderous civil war between the government and the RENAMO rebels which divided members of the same family against each other, a peace settlement was finally negotiated in 1992. Since then observers have been surprised by the manner in which the people have foregone any attempt to seek retribution. Fighters returning from the war have been welcomed back to their home villages, with traditional healers playing a significant role in helping them cleanse themselves of the pollution of the past for the sake of a common future.[35]

A similar process of prioritising peace above justice and truth can be observed in the case of Cambodia. Between the years 1975 and 1978 the Khmer Rouge attempted to transform Cambodia into some perverted image of an agrarian socialist utopia. The result was the deaths of somewhere in the region of one million people from hunger, exhaustion, disease and beatings, including 100,000 executed as enemies of the revolution. In 1978 Vietnam invaded and drove the Khmer Rouge back towards the Thai border regions. A civil war then ensued between the Vietnamese-backed regime in Phnom Penh and the Khmer Rouge, supported by China and Thailand, until peace accords were signed in Paris in October 1991. Significant sections of the Khmer Rouge refused to disarm and sporadic fighting continued until key leaders defected in 1996 in exchange for an amnesty granted by King Sihanouk.

Whilst pressure groups amongst the Cambodian diaspora joined with human rights organisations within the country to demand that those most responsible for the 'auto-genocide' be brought to trial, the Prime Minister Hun Sen (who had himself been a Khmer Rouge cadre until his defection to the Vietnamese in 1978) urged that 'We should dig a hole and bury the past.' This was a view echoed by a Cambodian journalist writing in 1999: 'I know the Khmer Rouge are bad and criminals, but there are too many to convict and some remain strong. To safeguard the living it is better not to seek justice for the dead.'[36]

The emphasis on 'national reconciliation' and the avoidance of 'the spirit of revenge' which has characterised the Cambodian approach to dealing with the pain of the past is in part a consequence of agreements between the Cambodian political elite and the surviving leadership of the Khmer Rouge. It also reflects a genuine fear that the pursuit of justice against the surviving Khmer Rouge cadres would bring a renewal of bloodshed and division. Cultural factors are also relevant, with the Buddhist tradition of Cambodia emphasising that suffering is a conse-quence of bad acts committed in this or previous lives, and that the taking of revenge upon wrong-doers will only occasion future suffering.[37] But it is also important to realise that whilst each and every Cambodian family network lost people who were killed or who died unnecessarily during the terrible years of the Khmer Rouge, in those same families there are also likely to be people who participated in the killing or were complicit in allowing people to die from malnutrition and preventable disease. In such circumstances it is not surprising that there has been no great public demand for an uncovering of the past nor any overwhelming cry for justice against the perpetrators of the genocide. Where would it end? Who would remain untouched?

However, just because one generation might want to forget the past, it does not mean that subsequent generations will remain satisfied with leaving it covered up. Time remains a significant variable. Thus, in the case of Cambodia, half the population was born after the Vietnamese drove the Khmer Rouge out of Phnom Penh, and there is some evidence that they are beginning to voice their demands to know how such terrible events came to happen during those years in the 1970s. After much delay, and in response to considerable international pressure, steps are underway to establish a tribunal to bring to account the surviving leaders of the Khmer Rouge.[38]

PRIORITISING TRUTH: WHEN PEOPLE CANNOT FORGET

Over recent years there has been a growing interest in truth commissions as a means of dealing with the pain of the past and thereby laying the foundation for a just peace. Thus, such transitions from dictatorship towards more representative regimes that took place in Argentina (1983), Uruguay (1985) and Chile (1990) – and the settlements that brought a formal end to the civil wars in El Salvador (1992) and Guatemala (1994) – all resulted in the establishment of some form of truth commission as the officially sanctioned mode of dealing with the past. The more recent South African Truth and Reconciliation Commission has been elevated to iconic status as the model to be emulated by transition states the world over. Countries that have established truth commissions since 2000 include East Timor, Ghana, Nigeria, Panama, Peru and Sierra Leone.[39]

Typically the focus of concern of truth commissions is the acknowledgement of the wrongs inflicted upon the victims of abuse and violence. In a number of cases this exercise is implemented not only in pursuit of the value of truth but also as a necessary step towards the realisation of some system of compensation for victims. The hope is that through such a process of unveiling the past and receiving reparations former victims might be enabled to come to terms with their anger and bitterness and define the post-settlement peace as 'just enough' to merit their commitment.[40]

When one considers the situation that faced the civilian regimes that succeeded the military juntas in South America, and the unstable 'law and order' situation that confronted the new post-apartheid regime in South Africa, it would seem that the truth commission is the approach adopted by successor regimes that have come to power as a result of a negotiated process between the parties to the conflict, where the new regime lacks either the capacity or the will to prosecute the perpetrators of past abuses, but where the policy of collective amnesia is unacceptable because of the depth of division and level of bitterness in society and the demands articulated by active civil society organisations and groups.

Most criticisms of the truth commission approach to dealing with the past in the context of bringing about a just peace involve the charge that justice is sacrificed in the proclaimed quest for truth, and that the alleged reconciliation is false. At its crudest it is alleged that the criminals provide a version of the truth in return for amnesty, and the victims are then left to become reconciled *to* their loss. Sadly, this might be the price that has to be paid for the sake of peace and the restoration of human rights, at least in the short term. The Latin American regimes that inherited power from the military juntas opted for truth commissions and eschewed trials because they believed they had to make a choice, settling for truth and peace rather than justice. It was because of such criticisms that the South Africans introduced the element of *conditional* amnesty into their model. Any perpetrator of human rights abuses who sought an amnesty did not have to express regret or remorse, but to be free from the fear of prosecution they were required to confess their crimes and convince the Amnesty Committee that these had been 'political' in nature and were not committed out of personal malice or for private gain.

The conditionality of the South African amnesty system reflected the balance of power in the negotiations leading up to the peaceful transfer of power symbolised by the democratic elections of April 1994 and the inauguration of Nelson Mandela as president. A key factor in enabling this process to take place so smoothly was the 'sunset clause' in the Interim Constitution that guaranteed the positions of state employees, including those that might have been threatened by a purge following the transfer to majority rule. Without this concession it was clear that there would have been no negotiated settlement.[41] But, as the incoming government, the African National Congress and its allies, had sufficient power to frustrate the demands for a blanket amnesty, the result was a compromise.

Even without formal punishment there is still a kind of justice, a calling to account, involved in the public naming and shaming of those who abused their fellow-citizens. Moreover, those at the heart of the South African Truth and Reconciliation Commission articulated a broader restorative concept of justice that went beyond the narrow retributive demand for the punishment of culprits. Archbishop Tutu in particular has written and spoken much about the notion of *ubuntu*, the understanding that we are all part of one community, and that by enabling perpetrators to take their place once again within this community they can be helped to regain something of their lost humanity, and thereby enrich us all through the restoration of social harmony and wholeness.

Despite the rhetoric around *ubuntu* as a form of restorative justice, there is some evidence to indicate that as a result of the evidence of abuse and criminality revealed during the truth commission process in South Africa, there has been increased frustration amongst victims and survivors with the prioritisation of truth above justice and growing demands that perpetrators should be held to account. This disenchantment has been fuelled by the tardiness in implementing the recommendations of the Commission relating to the award of appropriate reparations to those who suffered at the hands of the apartheid regime.

RESTITUTION AND CHANGING DEFINITIONS OF A 'JUST PEACE'

With the passage of time the capacity of a peace once deemed 'just enough' to engender commitment amongst people will be weakened to the extent that they feel insufficient progress is being made to 'make things right'. For example, in the immediate aftermath of a civil war people might be prepared to accept, however reluctantly, that war criminals should be allowed to go free and that their own loss and pain should remain unacknowledged. This might be the necessary price to pay for a surface peace achieved with the end of organised killing and repression. However, if their commitment to the peace is to be sustained then it is crucial that they experience some grounds for hope in the future. Central to this is the perception that appropriate efforts are being made to deepen the peace. This might entail attempts to hold perpetrators to account and the acknowledgement of the suffering of their victims. It might also involve sustained efforts to make appropriate reparations to those denied their potential to fulfil themselves as human beings because of the war. But if people are to let go of the painful memories of the past and begin to orient themselves towards a new future, with or alongside those that once were enemies, it is crucial that a sustained effort is made to transform the institutional structures and circumstances of everyday life that embody and perpetuate the old divisions and feelings

To conclude, the necessary conditions for a sustainable just peace include:

1. The preparedness of survivors to forgive the past, in the sense of reframing their personal and collective narratives in a manner which allows them to acknowledge the humanity of former enemies and allows for the possibility of future co-existence.
2. The perception of key publics and opinion-leaders that the peace remains 'just enough' to merit their continued commitment over time.
3. The development amongst key sectors of all communities of a degree of trust necessary for them to anticipate a shared future.

For these conditions to be realised it is vital that people believe that the evils of the past will not return, as evidenced by their experience of a sustained deepening of the peace process along the dimensions of peace/security, truth and justice. In other words, people's perception of and commitment to a just peace must be founded upon their experience of 'things moving in the right direction'. This in turn requires institutional change. It is unrealistic to expect any sustainable progress towards co-existence so long as the members of once-divided communities live their everyday lives within the same institutional frameworks that remind them of the 'deep memories' which fuelled the violence that split them apart. Only with appropriate changes in the conditions of everyday life will the seeds of a durable culture of reconciliation flourish, one which embodies those values that facilitate inter-personal and collective forgiveness, thereby opening up the possibility of erasing those deep memories that can call into question the justness of any post-war peace process.

NOTES

1. Sebald (2003), pp. 19–20.
2. Ibid., pp. 28–9.
3. Oestreicher (2004).
4. See Eriksson, Wallensteen and Sollenberg (2003).
5. See, for example, Macrae (2000).
6. See the contributions in Berdal and Malone (eds), (2000).
7. See Keen (2003).
8. Licklider (2001), p. 697.
9. Of approximately 80 civil wars that took place between 1945 and 1993, half of those peace agreements brought about by a negotiated settlement collapsed, whilst only 15 per cent of those terminated by military victories were followed by a renewal of the violence. See ibid., p. 699.
10. See Walter (1997).
11. Sebald (2003), p. 41.
12. From Geiko Muller-Fahrenholz, 'Deep remembering: the art of forgiveness', a presentation given at the Centre for the Study of Forgiveness and Reconciliation, Coventry University, 12 October 2001.
13. McCartney (1999).
14. Hayner (2002), p. 1.
15. Personal conversation, Coventry Cathedral, 1 June 2002.
16. Arendt (1959), p. 213.
17. From his contribution to the commemorative events in 2000 for the thirtieth anniversary of the World Conference on Religion and Peace. See Giovandi (2001), p. 17.
18. People can feel pre-disposed to offer forgiveness not because of any particular moral code but because of a realisation that the refusal to do so will cause continuing distress and prevent them from 'moving on'. This kind of 'self-centred' or 'instrumental' forgiveness has been relatively under-researched in the literature on forgiveness, much of which has been dominated by theologians and religiously oriented writers, especially Christian.
19. Bullock and Jennings (eds) (1996), p. 287.
20. By way of an illustration, the morning I was revising this text (1 April 2004) I heard on the radio (BBC World Service) an extract from an interview with a Rwandan woman survivor of the 1994 genocide who referred to the *genocidaires*, saying 'I can forgive them, but I don't want to see them again.'
21. See Kriesberg (2001).
22. Melvern (2000), p. 222.
23. Quoted in *The Guardian*, 6 April 2001.
24. Kobukyaye (2001).
25. From Minow (1998), p. ix.

26. Kimani (2003b).
27. In so far as most of the suspects have been in prison since 1994, this means in effect that most people brought before a *gacaca* court are released immediately.
28. Quoted in *The Guardian*, 5 October 2001. In March 2004, nine people were sentenced to death for killing a survivor who was due to testify about their role in the genocide.
29. Rwandan president, Paul Kagame, assured members of parliament in June 2002, 'reconciliatory justice will be the basis for unity and the foundation for progress'. See *The Guardian*, 19 June 2002.
30. Quoted in Kimani (2003a).
31. Mamdani (2001), p. 274.
32. Ibid., p. 279.
33. This draws on material in Rigby (2001), especially pp. 40–3.
34. As one member of parliament put it, 'How can we be capable of reconciliation after years of killing each other if we don't have the capacity to forget our past forever?' Quoted in ibid., p. 55.
35. See Honwana (1999).
36. Quoted in *International Herald Tribune*, 22 January 1999.
37. 'Defeat your enemy by not taking revenge' was a saying quoted to me by one Cambodian. (Interview with Cambodian human rights activist, Phnom Penh, 28 June 2001.)
38. For a challenging review of the many facets to be addressed as part of any national reconciliation project in Cambodia, see Etcheson (2003).
39. For a reasonably up-to-date overview, see United States Institute of Peace Library (2004).
40. The various aphorisms displayed at the meetings of the South African Truth and Reconciliation Commission reflected the assumption about the healing powers of unveiling the past. They included the following: 'Truth hurts but silence kills', 'Revealing is healing', and 'Truth is the road to reconciliation.'
41. The deputy president of the Constitutional Court observed at the time, 'If the Constitution kept alive the prospect of continuous retaliation and revenge, the agreement of those threatened by its implementation might never have been forthcoming.' Quoted in Tutu (1999), p. 26.

CONCLUSION

Conclusion

IN DEFENCE OF JUST WAR THEORY

MARK EVANS

———◁▷———

With varying degrees of sympathy and criticism, the chapters in this book have scrutinised some of the key elements of just war theory and have thereby demonstrated how central they have been in arguments about the justification of war and its conduct. Even where they have found serious flaws, one might see from them how the elements in question could still continue to set the terms of such controversies – and the presence of conceptual and practical problems with them may suggest, not that they should be abandoned, but that further work needs to be done to refine them, to render them more robust and workable.

Still, the question of whether just war theory as a whole is ultimately defensible, an appropriate way of thinking about war, will not go away; clearly the very idea of just war theory still strikes many as deeply problematic. In this chapter, then, I examine some of the general criticisms which have been levelled against it. In the space allowed, I cannot hope to canvass all of the possible objections to the theory. But enough can, I think, be said in support of my conclusion: that, for all of its problems, just war theory presents in broad form a paradigm which, to all intents and purposes, is inescapable once we commit ourselves to the normative evaluation of war. And that commitment is one whose rejection is difficult to imagine: moral neutrality or indifference to the range of issues raised by war, a refusal to take a stand on them, is a baffling and perhaps inconceivable stance. This argument should not, however, allow us to forget the kinds of problem uncovered in these pages. I conclude, therefore, by raising two further such problems with the theory, consolidating the overall message of this book: that its

203

reappraisal of just war theory does not bring the debate about it to a conclusion but highlights instead how much more needs to be said.

SOME OBJECTIONS TO JUST WAR THEORY

[1] *What counts as a 'war' is far from clear-cut and therefore the appropriate applicability of just war theory will always be contestable.*

It has to be admitted that defining what kinds of conflict count as 'war' may be a difficult issue for at least two reasons. One is that the nature of warfare is diverse and changeable. Many analysts nowadays talk, for example, of 'new wars' – types of conflict which are qualitatively distinct (in terms of scale, technology used, types of cause and combatant, and so on) from 'old wars'.[1] This conceptual fluidity alone opens up room for perhaps continuous disagreement over its application. The second reason compounds this: the decision to call a military confrontation a 'war' often has specific rhetorical and ideological purposes that may themselves be deeply contested. To illustrate: the IRA characterised its military campaign against British rule in Ulster as a 'war' ('of liberation'), whereas the British government took strenuous pains to deny it that epithet in order to treat it as ('mere') criminality.

But if the definition of 'war' is often contentious, that is clearly no reason to discard just war theory altogether, because sometimes we have no problem at all in identifying some extended instances of violence as 'war'. Furthermore, we may wonder anyway what, morally speaking, actually hangs on the definitional issue. Should we not wish morally to justify *any* resort to *any* form of violence? And, if we do affirm this general demand, might not the appropriate justificatory theory look something very much like just war theory in some substantive respects? It would seem odd to claim that, for example, violence should be used proportionately and as a last resort only in war and not similarly in any other circumstance. Criteria such as these look to have applicability well beyond the realm of war however we might define it. True, some of these criteria – such as 'legitimate authority' – may be difficult, if not impossible or inappropriate, to operationalise in certain kinds of violent confrontation.[2] The need to ask 'is this conflict a war?' may still arise with respect to some – but, it would seem, certainly not all – of the questions just war theory poses in its search for moral justifications. But all violence should be justified with reference to 'just cause', 'last resort', 'proportionality', discrimination' and so on. Thus, it seems apposite to think of just war theory as a particular type of 'just *violence* theory', which may in large part mirror just war theory's moral criteria. The responsibility to respect the latter, then, is not substantially shirked by virtue of definitional quibbles.

[2] *Going to war, in which people will inevitably die or suffer serious injury, can never be morally justified.*

This is a rather basic way of stating the pacifist position. In fact, pacifism can be formulated in numerous and philosophically more nuanced ways.[3] Enough, however, can be said about pacifism in general to indicate how just war theory might ride through its objections.

First, it should stressed that it is logically possible to affirm just war theory and deny that any actual war thus far fought in human history has been morally justified. The theory does not venture any claim about the extent to which moral justifications have been present for actual wars; it could therefore be affirmed by what we might call a de facto pacifist, who does not rule out the notional possibility of a justified war in principle but thinks that as a matter of fact, wars have not been and typically never are justified. Even if it were true that moral justifications have been lacking in all wars to date, however, this would constitute no reason to think that just war theory is pointless. Judgements on the past and present may well not apply to the wars which may be yet to come.

But what about the pacifist who says that in principle wars could never be morally justified? We should distinguish this position from that of pacifism as a personal ethical ideal, in which one says 'on moral grounds *I* will never fight in a war but I recognise that it may be justified for others to do so'. Instead, it withholds moral credentials from any resort to war. Now, just war theorists agree with pacifists on many points of fundamental moral judgement. A just war is always fought against a major injustice and, if the latter is deemed to be what 'starts' the war, then of course they can both agree that it is wrong to start a war. The pacifist, of course, rejects the idea that war against that injustice could be justified. Yet just war theorists who agree with my charac-terisation of their position as given in the Introduction do not deny that many evils are attendant on the resort to war – but they say that, in a just war, such action is the *lesser* of two evils, which is what their pacifist opponents would deny. Even so, the awareness of the evil that is necessarily dealt out in war is built into just war theory's view of war as posing a moral tragedy.

What just war theorists want the pacifists to explain is why they think a resort to war in the face of grave injustice is necessarily the *greater* of two evils. (Here I am ascribing the same 'tragedy' conceptualisation to the pacifist attitude; I think it would serve itself rather poorly if it thought there was never any moral problem arising at all from the anti-war stance.) For example, why do pacifists regard it as necessarily better to allow the deaths of innocents at the hands of an unjust aggressor without waging a war in their defence (a war that we must assume will indeed cause the deaths of innocents as well)? On what grounds do pacifists 'live with' the killings by the unjust aggressors rather than the killings they would cause were they to go to war against the unjust aggressors, particularly if it is reasonable to assume that a war would reduce the overall number of casualties (as is likely to have been the case had there been a concerted and suitably timely military intervention in Rwanda in 1994)? Do they not, then, become morally complicit (and compromised) 'bystanders' to evil?[4]

In response, some pacifists deploy a 'moral integrity' argument: essentially, regardless of the number and nature of casualties, they say that one's own moral integrity would be crucially undermined if one participated in the evil of killing or actively supported it when committed by others. Now, I would certainly not want to dismiss altogether the ethical importance of such integrity, but one does wonder just how comprehensively determinate it can be of morally justifiable behaviour. For example, let us grant that in the face of a violent threat to your own life it might be that, when the only alternative is for you to kill others, morality demands self-sacrifice, or martyrdom: 'preserve one's moral integrity and do not commit evil to save your own skin' sums up the maxim here. But it is hardly obvious that you must automatically invoke the martyrdom requirement on behalf of *others* who might otherwise be spared violent death if (but only if) only *you* took up arms and fought to save them. To insist again, nobody need doubt the tragic nature of the dilemma with which we are faced when innocents are being slaughtered, but a concern with one's integrity such as the pacifist might manifest in such instances can become distastefully narcissistic when people who could have been saved are left to face certain death.

Unsurprisingly in the light of reflections such as these, not all pacifists are strictly absolutist in their prohibition of war. But it is then hard to see what might distinguish them from the just war theory position, certainly when (as it is in the Introduction) it is conceptualised around an ideal-level notion of just peace and laden with strict and demanding tests of a war's justifiability.

[3] *Such is the nature of actual decisions to go to war, and the decisions taken in the conduct of war, that the criteria of just war theory are not in fact going to be respected.*

Realists typically insist that 'strategic' as opposed to 'moral' considerations explains the behaviour of political actors as far as war-making decisions go and, further, they see no moral problem with this in so far as they believe there to be no appropriate room here for moral norms. Now, just war theory is in part a reaction against this view: even if it is true that wars have not as a matter of fact exhibited much in the way of respect for moral considerations, that point has no bearing on the appropriateness of insisting that moral judgements about them *should* be made.

In fact, few political leaders, military commanders or diplomats today actually own up to being 'pure' realists. One should not underestimate the role that morality has actually played in decision-making about many wars.[5] As we have already seen, people very often feel constrained to offer moral arguments for their decisions to go to war and how they choose to wage it. (And it is probably a piece of a priori cynicism, rather than verified fact, when we think that they are *all* necessarily 'constrained' thus and hence unwilling adherents to morality.) This is particularly important in just war theory as I stated it in the Introduction: a just war is one that has to be justified publicly. And even if political and military leaders are actually impervious to the demands of morality, and use its terms only hypocritically, they are not the only agents at stake in just war theory. Citizens use it as well, to support or – more pertinently perhaps – oppose their leaders. Here, to illustrate this point, we can continue the debate against pacifism. For just war theory is as amenable to anti-war as it is to pro-war arguments. To be sure, it was originally designed to constrain decision-making about war, but this implies an obvious flip-side function. A peace movement which opposes a government that has gone to war can hold it to account according to its criteria as well. Just war theory can provide such a movement with the moral basis of its opposition to war without committing it to outright and generalised pacifism. The archetypal realist position, flawed as it already is, seems to be oblivious to this democratic, citizen-based rather than leader-based, aspect of politics in its dismissal of morality's relevance.[6]

[4] *Just war theory is too abstract to deal with the brutal concrete particularities of conflict: reality is always far too messy.*

The charge of 'abstraction' is often levelled at many types of moral theory, and it is frequently unclear what it is intended to mean. This unclarity is usually exposed neatly when one asks what a 'non-abstract' moral theory is supposed to look like. But one way of formulating it more clearly is to claim that just war theory's criteria are derived in abstraction from the realities of war and therefore naïvely and unrealistically pretend to be able to control a phenomenon that in fact always resists morality's demands. It is its unworldliness, in the sense of being divorced in its origins from reality, that renders just war theory inapplicable, so this argument runs.

However, it is wrong to think that the theory is necessarily the 'ivory-tower' product of 'armchair' philosophers and other kinds of dreamer who have no knowledge of the harsh realities for which they are attempting to legislate. The criteria of just war theory are in fact best understood as extrapolations from powerful intuitive moral reactions to various facets of actual wars, codified as general principles in order for us to be able to make consistent and defensible judgements about the morality of specific conflicts. Just war theory can be, and has been, revised in *reflective equilibrium*: extrapolated general principles may be tested against considered judgements in specific situations (and vice versa), with revisions on either side, or both sides, to establish a satisfactory coherence between our individual estimations and the principles which inform them. So, for example, we make a judgement about whether War A has a just cause and then whether War B has a just cause and, in assessing the similarities and differences in these judgements, we draw from them a general principle about what counts ('in general') as a just cause. The generality of principle, then, does not imply 'abstraction' in the sense of utter isolation from concrete specificities.[7]

In Chapter 3, I suggested that the content of humanitarian morality, which could inform the theory's account of justice, need not be regarded as fixed, ahistorically frozen. The idea of reflective equilibrium can accommodate this flexibility: the process of revising specific judgements and general principles can be an ongoing process as experiences are accumulated, new facts come to light, fresh theoretical interpretations of relevant factors are proffered, and so on. We can, say, learn from historical experience (as just war theorists have actually done, of course). And we can philosophically re-evaluate our concepts. For example, the idea of 'self-defence' is often approached in international relations theory through the concept of 'security', defined as the freedom from whatever poses an existential threat to the nation-state. In recent times, this notion has dramatically broadened from a traditional 'military-threat' understanding of (in)security to include economic, environ-mental and cultural threats. Although this particular concept may have become rather too permissive for just war purposes, we can never-theless appreciate the fluidity of the key notions from this example, and just war theorising can readily accommodate this phenomenon.[8]

Another way of formulating the 'abstraction' charge can concede that the theory's precepts reflect moral experience in the face of actual war, but it insists on the ultimate futility of attempting to rein in war by moral precepts. For instance, one might say that *jus ad bellum* judgements are sometimes (perhaps very often) difficult to make accurately at the time because heat-of-the-moment judgements of proportionality and discrimination often lack the necessary information and cool-headed restraint they demand. Further, it could be argued that wars often evolve and proceed in such chaotically unpredictable ways that many of the judgements required by the theory as a whole are necessarily no better than (poorly) informed guesswork. With the increased know-ledge and enhanced reflection that comes with hindsight, we can see just how imperfect are those judgements. In response: it is unclear exactly what might follow from this. The avowed imperfections of on-the-spot judgements may yet not be enough to say that such judge-ments should not therefore be required, that we shouldn't even bother to try to make them. Alternatively, the theory might require us to say that, if our judgements are going to be so flawed, then the war in question is to be judged as decisively unjust precisely because we simply cannot translate the demands of justice into faithful concrete practice.

In fact, however, we should not overestimate the force of the 'unpre-dictability' and related arguments. We are sometimes able to make some very easy judgements about likely consequences that would definitely bar the justice of military action: the devastating consequences of nuclear war are typically to the fore in arguments against the justice of that type of war. It is not merely by virtue of 20/20 hindsight that the critics of the 2003 invasion of Iraq challenge the justice of that war with reference to the evident chaos in what is supposedly its aftermath: plenty of opponents argued well before its outbreak that such problems were likely. By the same token, however, some judgements in support of action may be relatively straightforward to make: tragically, estimations of how relatively few troops could have spared the lives of hundreds of thousands in Rwanda in 1994, which were made at the time, are still widely accepted today as realistic.[9]

Non-ideal theory, of which just war theory is an example, is by definition attuned to failures with respect to the application of moral demands. It simply insists that it is still possible to distinguish between a moral and a non-moral way of thinking and acting in difficult situations, and that the moral should be preferred as much as possible. It may still be extremely difficult to stick consistently to moral rules and laws in the awful circumstances of war, but it would seem to be a grave error to think that such rules should therefore be totally ignored, which would leave war completely unregulated morally. Heuristic principles, acting as guidelines or rules of thumb, remain justified so long as they can make some substantive moral difference to thinking and behaviour. They do not undermine themselves with unrealistically stringent expectations about the degree to which they can be clearly satisfied in practice.

[5] *The 'moralism' objection.*

It is striking that, among certain sections of the political left in particular, a perspective persists today which, whilst apparently fuelled by passionate normative concern in its critique of Western militarism, thinks that just war theory is a form of what is (pejoratively) dubbed 'moralism' or 'moral judgementalism'.[10] The basic complaint here is that judgements about 'right' and 'wrong', 'good and evil', which just war theory enjoins us to make, are actually unhelpful in orienting appropriate responses to the events in question. A pithy example of this is a piece by Andrew Chitty which replies to some just war-based arguments concerned to evaluate the US-led response to September 11th.[11] Here are the five main elements of his specific way of stating the critique, with commentary on each.

[a] *Moral judgementalism encourages overly rapid and ill-informed analysis and decision-making.* Now the rush to moral judgement in the aftermath of events such as September 11th may well lead to insensitive, ill-informed and inappropriate responses not least in the media. But this surely requires not abandonment of moral theory but simply its judicious and careful application to derive *considered* judgements. A 'rush to judgement' is not an inevitable feature of just war theory; in so far as it would not represent proper 'theorising', it would indeed seem inimical at least to its intention.

[b] *The language of moral condemnation of events such as September 11th, and with which just war judgements are voiced, is cynically employed by political and military decision-makers to justify decisions (in this case, the wars in Afghanistan and Iraq) that have not actually been based on moral considerations at all.* This is at heart another rehearsal of the basic realist position which we have already discussed. As stressed back in the Introduction, the fact that just war theory's precepts can be used hypocritically, cynically and otherwise incorrectly is no reason to reject them. A theory should be reasserted in the face of its abuse, not packed away as redundant – especially if no better alternative is forthcoming.

[c] *Moralism in general tends to encourage violence.* The claim here is that outraged declamations of 'evil', heightened senses of 'injustice' and righteous talk of 'crusades' in response to perceived injustices help to fuel a dash to war, as was evident in the weeks following the September 11th attacks and the consequent war in Afghanistan. In response: once again, the use of moral theory in general seems to be attacked here due to the unfortunate proclivities of some to misuse it. When we consider again just how detailed just war theory is, how many fine judgements it requires one to call before war is sanctioned, it is evident that it is structured precisely to resist such hurried resorts to arms (the 'last resort' criterion, for example, is particularly pertinent in this regard).

[d] *The relevant historical and political contextual factors in understanding the roots of a conflict must be taken into account. Once they are, it becomes much more difficult to pass any kind of sensible and determinate moral judgement.* What we might call 'historical-political understanding' is often proposed in leftist critiques such as this as the substitute for moral theory, the implication being that a proper empirically based analysis

renders moral judgements of 'right' and 'wrong' just too simplistic to be justified on their own terms. The mystery, however, is why moral theory's use should be regarded as essentially incompatible with such understanding. *Bad* applications of moral precepts may pay no heed to relevant contextual issues. But a proper use of just war theory requires a full grasp of the context in which a conflict breaks out in order to arrive at the kinds of balanced judgement it demands. True, this may make such judgements more difficult to draw but this is not in fact a necessary general truth about them. It is quite possible, for example, to understand the various grievances which motivated al-Qaeda's attacks on September 11th and yet refute its claim that they were morally justified on various scores.

[e] *Arguing about moral judgements is ultimately fruitless.* This would seem to be the upshot of criticism [d], but it could also be supported by, for example, the charge that there is a radical value-pluralism which renders us incapable of agreeing on the content of 'justice' and whatever other moral concepts just war theory needs to employ. Such a viewpoint has considerable resonance today: many do indeed believe that our moral experiences point towards this pluralist thesis. It is, however somewhat mysterious as to what succour historical-political under-standing might think it can reasonably draw from this. Despite what might seem to be their firmer empirical base, theories of history and social explanation have proven to be equally contested and arguments between them could therefore be equally 'fruitless'. (To take up criticism [b] again, historical-political understanding does not obviously seem significantly less prone to cynical abuse either: the history of Marxism in political practice proves this.)

One might anyway wonder how a critical posture is possible (in this case, an anti-war-on-terror position) without it being in some *substantive* sense 'morally judgementalist'. On what basis does one make evaluatively critical judgements if not moral considerations? The facts that we garner as we deepen our historical-political understanding do not 'speak for themselves' in yielding critiques that are intended to evaluate in terms of what ought and ought not to be the case. We make evaluative judgements when we select and interpret the facts (and the differences in possible approach accounts for the claim that historical-political understanding is also prone to reasonable disagreement in its judgements). So, if we have had to make such judgements from the very start, it seems strange to talk about trying to avoid them – particularly when the critique, in Chitty's case, is hardly intended to be dispassionately neutral with respect to its object. It, too, is motivated by considerations of what is right and wrong and it is puzzlingly self-deceptive not to treat this as moral judgementalism, burying this feature behind an ostensibly 'non-moralising' approach, just because some others examples of such have been overly crude in their moralising.

A few further thoughts in response to the gist of some of the foregoing, before moving on. Such is the stringency of the theory's criteria, and the consequent rarity of genuinely just wars, that it may be plausible to assume the question of how a just war is just is fairly straightforward for sincere and 'right-minded' thinkers. Most wars fall obviously short on one or more counts. Some, however, do not: a defensive war against genocidal fascist aggression probably does not present any great problems of moral indeterminacy. However, many conflicts – such as that between Israel and the Palestinians – do appear to be much more morally intractable. But if just war theory does not ultimately guide us towards determinate answers to the justice of situations such as the latter, I am inclined to propose that this is evidence not of the inadequacy of the theory (as if there could be an adequate alternative theory that would yield determinate answers) but of the injustice of the conflict: neither side should be fighting if the justice of the conflict is so opaque.

Furthermore, even when moral arguments do seem to us to be inconclusive, the point of such argument is not thereby vitiated. For moral argument can also act as a mechanism for self-disclosure and self-clarification: one can work out and articulate where one stands on the issues in question. Such debate can also prompt mutual reevaluations: it need not be (as criticism [e] above might imply) the mere trading of fixed and intractable viewpoints. One might even venture that the democratic bias in just war theory, which I identified in Chapter 3, encourages a respect for other views, a preparedness to debate and revise one's opinions when they are confronted by others.

A NEW CHALLENGE TO *JUS IN BELLO*

From the selective review of critiques just completed, I do not wish to give the impression that I believe just war theory has all the answers to all the challenges it may face. To reinforce whatever other issues for further analysis readers may believe to have been suggested by the previous chapters, I add two further ones of my own which have received comparatively little attention but thereby attest to the fact that just war theory has not exhausted the need for much deeper scrutiny.

The first takes up the claim, emphasised by Walzer in particular, that in a just war there is 'moral equality' among both the soldiers and the civilians.[12] The 'moral equality of soldiers' thesis holds that the rights and responsibilities of combatants are to be regarded as equal regardless of the side on which they fight. By extension, the 'moral equality of civilians' insists that the moral status of a civilian is not affected by the side on which they find themselves. So, for example, even if one's government has launched an unjust war, one's moral standing is not to be regarded as inferior to one's counterpart, whether soldier or civilian.

Now, as a matter of fact both aspects of the equality norm seem rather routinely to be violated in war. Recently, the ongoing controversy over the US's incarceration of what it claims to be terrorists from Afghanistan at Camp Delta, at Guantanamo Bay in Cuba, has highlighted the issue: the obfuscation over their legal status gave the Bush administration evasive leeway to ignore certain legal obligations pertaining to their treatment which are ultimately founded on some such norm that prescribes how prisoners should be treated regardless of what side they are on. Further, the phenomenon of casualty phobia, identified in Chapter 4, exhibits obvious favouritism towards one's own soldiers in war which modern military technology (such as high-altitude aerial bombardment) has been able to accommodate to a considerable degree. Minimising the casualties on one's own side is typically preferred even when the strategies to deliver that outcome result in such higher casualties on the enemy side that the total number of dead on both sides is considerably in excess of what would result from alternative strategies. (The air war against the Iraqis in 1991, prior to the ground war to liberate Kuwait, is a good example of this: untold thousands of troops were killed in huge air attacks to ease the path of the allied armies.)

The rationale behind such preferences may be perfectly under-standable, of course. But this amounts to a de facto evaluation of one's own soldier's life as worth more than one of the enemy's. The assump-tion is that it is morally justified to kill more soldiers on the other side if that helps to save some of the lives of your own – and the point is that this seems to be embraced in much military policy as a moral precept in its own right (and hence justified), rather than something that may be excusable but not justified.

More disturbingly, this inegalitarianism manifests itself in attitudes towards civilian casualties as well, when they fall under the category of the double-effect principle (see 2(i) in the Introduction). Peter Singer offers a powerful example. During the 2003 Iraq war, a civilian house in Basra was bombed because it was believed to be the refuge of 'Chemical Ali', the nickname of a notorious member of Saddam Hussein's regime. He was unscathed, but one of the bombs hit the home of a family who had no connection with the regime; three adults and seven children were killed. The head of the family survived to tell *The New York Times*: 'I consider what was done to be a crime of war. How would President Bush feel if he had to dig his daughters out of the rubble?' Now this is the kind of deeply regrettable incident that the double-effect principle permits just war theory to regard as possibly still *justified*. But, as Singer says, the question posed by the family head is a good one: would Bush have felt such an action justified if his daughters, or even any fellow Americans, were the foreseeable but unintended victims?[13] (What if 'Chemical Ali' was found holed up, and well-armed, in an American neighbourhood? Would air strikes still be regarded as an entirely appropriate way of dealing with him?[14]) The example exposes a common assumption that even civilians on the enemy side count for less, in terms of their justified liability to death, than those on one's own side. Is *this* assumption something that just war theory should want to justify?

On behalf of the theory, one might respond here that these actual manifestations of unequal treatment merely show that the incidents in question are *unjust* wars; just war theory does not allow one to treat the lives of soldiers and civilians on the side of justice as worth more in the senses relevant in these examples than those on the side of injustice. But it might be objected that if such favouritism for one's own side is indeed perfectly 'natural' and understandable, then the theory should regard it as unavoidable. We would have to be saints not to exhibit such partiality for one's own side and, as the whole point of a just war theory is that it is not for saints, it is unreasonable to expect just warriors to have to respect it.

However, the actual point of the theory is precisely to resist the powerful and emotive tendencies that bundle people towards the moral abyss during wartime and it is hardly clear that there is a *physical* impossibility (as opposed to a deep-seated reluctance for which one can nevertheless be held morally responsible) at play in this favouritism. Certainly, like some of the other criteria, 'discrimination' may be difficult to operationalise and its upshot may well be to treat its victims in an unequal fashion. But is there really no case at all to sanction an explicit allowance of such?

An ostensibly uncomplicated way of granting this 'inegalitarian permission' invokes a consequentialist argument: since it is better on the whole if the just side and not the unjust side wins, it must on balance be better for someone on the just side to survive if at the expense of someone on the unjust side, and not vice versa. So the life of the former is indeed worth more than the life of the latter according to a justice-based yardstick. But this is not a congenial line of argument for just war theory to take, as its intention is exactly to avoid the sweeping-away of the significance of individual lives in some monolithic utilitarian calculus. Even if we did decide to modify the theory to permit this argument, its generalised character is far too abstract for it to be reliable. The actual contributions of specific individuals to desired end-states are highly variegated and may not in fact be easily quantified with reference to whether they are soldiers or civilians, or even whether they are on the side of justice and injustice (there is no a priori guarantee that the life of one just warrior is *always* more likely to secure a better outcome than the life of an unjust warrior and hence 'worth more').

It is therefore tempting to think that just war theory should have nothing to do with the idea of unequal treatment – and I certainly struggle to think how it could be justified with reference to the 'innocent' (which could include, for example, forcibly conscripted combatants). A just-warring side should, *ceteris paribus*, face up to its full responsibilities and recognise that, if Strategy A would kill only 100 of their soldiers but 1,000 civilians unintentionally on the other side and Strategy B would kill 500 soldiers but claim only 500 victims on the other side, then it is actually Strategy B that morality requires. But I think it is not so obvious that the idea should not apply to *any* combatants either. Consider: are the lives of the men of the *Einsatzgruppen*, sweeping through the Western Soviet Union and murdering defenceless Jews in their thousands, really on the same moral par as the lives of soldiers who might have resisted them?

The 'moral equality' principle seems to be descended from an earlier 'warrior ethic' that emphasised respect for combatants and which was based upon a chivalric code to be honoured regardless of the cause being fought, of whether one was a comrade in arms or an enemy. But, even if this was ever appropriate, it seems decidedly misplaced when we consider the nature of the injustices, such as a military campaign of genocide, that might prompt a just war. Surely the justice of the cause *does* inform our conception of the moral standing of those fighting it? And in a theory that strains to keep moral values in view in order to restrain war and its conduct, it seems frankly perverse and perhaps self-defeating to disregard crucial moral distinctions when it comes to the assessment of the moral standing of combatants qua embodiment of, or vehicle for, the cause for which they fight. Particularly given that one cannot escape personal moral responsibility for committing a crime against humanity by the 'I-was-only-following-orders' defence as well, fighting for such an unjust cause does indeed appear to mark a very significant moral distinction between the combatants on just and unjust sides.

A STRUCTURAL QUESTION ABOUT THE THEORY

If I am right that the unequal-treatment principle may need to be acknowledged in some way, then there is clearly work to be done in thinking through how just war theory can do so. In touching on how this may proceed I raise the second problematic issue I have selected as indicative of what further refinement the theory might require.

It would seem clear for just war theory that any inegalitarianism to permit favouritism on one's own side should be employed very sparingly; it would be unwise to ditch the equality principle altogether or even deny it *pro tanto* primacy. But it might be thought that even this introduces a liberality that the theory must not brook: should it not instead require each of its criteria to be met in full before justificatory credentials are bestowed on a war? The case for this is that the theory urges great caution in war-making decisions and hence none of its tests are to be taken lightly in any instance. True, this might make it extremely demanding. Perhaps very few wars would pass muster on its terms, but the theory might regard this as actually a very good thing given its avowed reluctance to sanction war.

If we think that room should therefore be made for the unequal-treatment principle, one of three modifications to the theory might be proposed. First, we could insert an 'exemption clause', which permits the suspension of a criterion in a particular instance when it proves to be an obstacle to meeting a cause of justice which is otherwise so overwhelming. Now we already have an example of such with the supreme emergency exemption, of course. And in Chapter 3, I proposed an argument to the effect that the legitimate-authority criterion could in effect be suspended on occasion as well. Moreover, it is not difficult to think of other scenarios in which exemptions might apply. Having introduced *jus post bellum* stipulations into the theory, for example, it might be necessary to concede that an inattention to them cannot always dissolve the moral justifiability of a war. Would a war to rescue people from genocide be unjustified if the rescuers thereafter shirked *jus post bellum* requirements, even if those people would have been butchered had there been no war?

There seems, then, to be a strong *prima facie* case for an exemption clause. The theory would not wish to make it applicable to all the criteria, of course: there would be no question of suspending the 'just cause' requirement, obviously, and other criteria – such as 'last resort' – also seem to be 'unsuspendable'. But a point in favour of the clause's insertion is that the heuristic character of the theory does not sit too well with an insistence that its criteria must be met equally in full, not least because they do not all seem to be easily quantifiable such that we could definitively identify when they were 'equally satisfied'. To be sure, we are obligated to *consider* each criterion as seriously as every other – we should do our best to meet them in practice when wondering whether to go to war and/or how it should be fought – but that is *not* to say that, when we come to ask the overall question 'is this a just war?' we should give them equally decisive weight in formulating the answer.

The upshot of this approach would be to introduce a hierarchy among the theory's criteria, distinguishing those which can be suspended from those more important criteria that are exceptionless in application. Given that this order of priority cannot be left as arbitrary, to be determined according to whatever suits whoever on any one occasion, we end up with an even more internally complex theory. Our parsimonious instincts might flinch at adding extra layers to it, though perhaps if that proves necessary to satisfy our moral intuitions, we should say 'so be it'. But it would seem that this theoretical manoeuvre could still introduce a further and more damaging degree of indeterminacy in judgements about a war's justice. For consider: differential weighting may allow us to say that a war is *maximally* just if it meets all of the criteria. But if, as the hierarchy argument suggests, it could still be just without them all being met, then do we not have to say in the latter case that a war is *sufficiently* but *not* maximally just? In which case, 'justice' starts to become a matter of degree which makes its judgements even more open than its heuristic character already allows. Its ability to assert the authority of objective morality against the subjective opinions and preferences of warring sides could therefore be significantly diminished.

The second and third modifications would propose that these difficulties arise because too many criteria have been packed into the theory to start with: the more complex it becomes, the more such difficulties are likely to arise. So, one response is to jettison the idea that we should consider all the relevant moral criteria together to make a singular, overall judgement of whether a war is just or not. Once again, we should still do our best to meet them all in our decision-making and practice. But when we come to the question of 'is this a just war?', and except in the rare, and perhaps impossible, situation of a war maximally satisfying all the relevant moral considerations, we make do with saying that a war is just with respect to criterion X but not, or not maximally, with respect to criterion Y, and so on. In other words, we do not try to answer the *general* question of 'is this a just war?' by weighing up all of these individual judgements about specific facets of justice to come up with a compound measure of justice.

Unlike the 'hierarchy' argument, this approach explicitly breaks up just war theory into distinct considerations of justice. This might make it crucially less obvious why we should nevertheless try to respect all the criteria in our decision-making about when and how to fight a war, for that would imply that they still ought to be treated as part of a single moral theory. Further, although these 'micro-judgements' are often heard when people debate a war's justification, surely we cannot rest content with them. A war may satisfy X and not Y, but we do still want to know the answer to the general question: 'Is it therefore justified? Should it be fought, or should it have been fought, or not?' We typically feel impelled to compare the weightings of these individual estimations to make an overall judgement, not least because perhaps every war ever fought could well meet at least one of the criteria. If we agree it would be morally absurd to reduce a war's justifiability to just one criterion, we must *necessarily* incorporate them into a single theoretical framework – and the question must then be whether we would not in fact end up recreating just war theory, or something very much like it, as we strive to unify these considerations as we think best.

This last observation also counts against the third modification, which would simply discard all but what it judged to be the most weighty criterion/criteria altogether. There are, of course, plenty of simpler 'normative' alternatives to just war theory: 'an-eye-for-an-eye' is a kind of moral theory that could form a 'principled' justification for war, for example. But when we bring morality to bear on this question, the powerful – and I think devastating – objection to this modification is that we very rapidly become dissatisfied with such simplified justificatory theories. War is terrible: the possibility of its justification must surely rest, then, on considerations that do full justice to its implications. And it is the number and complexity of *those* that lead us away from the 'simplification' strategy, and again it must be wondered whether we are not inevitably led towards a recreation of just war theory when we seek to do justice to the full range of moral issues that war forces upon us.

JUST WAR THEORY: A FLAWED BUT INESCAPABLE FRAMEWORK?

Despite these, and other, challenges to just war theory, then, the defensive case promised in the title of this chapter essentially runs as follows: the real challenge to just war theory's critics is whether, in so far as we still wish to think normatively about war (and I think that we cannot avoid doing so), we can conjure up any principles and beliefs, and put them into a coherent structure, in a way that does not lead us right back to just war theory. For all of its problems, the theory seems to raise all of the questions it is appropriate to raise about the morality of war and it organises them in an integrated structure that it seems *hard* to better. But it is not obviously pointless still to try to do so.

A final word about the specifically normative-philosophical approach that I have taken to the morality of war here. I do not pretend that, in its rather abstractive character, it alone suffices. I have embraced the importance of history, and other empirically based theories, in informing its judgements. And the more artistic literature on war – reportage, prose, poetry – can often depict the issues at stake far more vividly than can this particular mode of discourse.[15] But it would be unfortunate to conclude from the difficulties raised in the foregoing discussion that the philosophical approach of just war theory has sufficient severe limitations as to diminish its utility. We need this approach to help us tackle these problems. And if philosophy continues to struggle with them, perhaps we should conclude that such is to be expected from a *non-ideal* theory. We should not assume that a non-ideal world is one that a moral theory, even a non-ideal one, can always deal with comprehensively and consistently. These problems may be the mark of a non-ideal world and not of an inadequate and substitutable theory for the non-ideal world. And *that* is no reason not to embrace the theory, if there is none better, and no reason not to continue philosophising to try to develop one that is better. Such philosophy tries to map, and mark out a route in, the non-ideal world, helping us to understand and appreciate its terrain and orient ourselves within it, paying as much attention to moral principle as possible. Without any such map, as moral beings we are surely lost.

NOTES

1. See, for example, Kaldor (1999).
2. We should not, however, exaggerate this 'inapplicability' point in excusing combatants from the demands of just war theory. It might be thought that a guerrilla group campaigning on behalf of, say, a minority against a majoritarian state is, by dint of its technical illegality, not a 'legitimate authority' and therefore not appropriately subject to the theory's strictures. But it is not difficult to rework the criterion to pose pertinent questions about the *moral* legitimacy of this group's campaign: do the people it claims to represent really support it and their violent methods? Even if there is a just and consciously felt grievance, who or what gave *this* group the right to be the ones to do something about it? This question has been often posed of, say, the IRA in Ireland, or ETA in the Basque country and not least by some of the people on whose behalf they have claimed to be fighting.
3. See, for example, Norman (1995).
4. For a discussion of 'bystanding' and individual responsibility, see Evans (2004).
5. See Crawford, N. C. (2002) for extended defence of this claim.
6. Walzer (1992), chapter 1, remains a classic extended discussion of 'realism'.
7. For an extended discussion of reflective equilibrium, see Daniels (1996), especially chapters 1 and 2.
8. For a summary of the 'security' debate, see Baylis (2001).
9. Romeo Dallaire, the UN military commander in Rwanda, submitted a plan for just five thousand extra troops. See Power (2003), chapter 10.
10. I say 'persists' because the 'anti-moralism' standpoint seems highly redolent of the venerable Marxist hostility to the idea of morality as anything other than ideologically complicit and in fact dispensable in social criticism. For a leftist critique of this view, see Cohen (2000), chapter 6.

11. See Chitty (2002).
12. Walzer (1992), pp. 35–41, 136.
13. Singer (2004), pp. 51–2.
14. The same question is frequently asked of how Israeli governments have dealt with Palestinian militants who are attacked in their family homes, living with children, the aged and other innocents.
15. For discussion of this point, see Zehfuss (2004).

BIBLIOGRAPHY

Aldrich, G. H. (2002), 'The Taliban, al-Qaeda, and the determination of illegal combatants', *American Journal of International Law* 96 (4), pp. 891–8.

Aquinas, T. [1266–73] (1954), *Summa Theologica*, ed. A. P. d'Entrèves, Oxford: Blackwell.

Archard, D. (1993), *Children, Rights and Childhood*, London: Routledge.

Arendt, H. (1959), *The Human Condition*, New York: Doubleday Anchor.

Aristotle [*c.* 350 BC] (1955), *Ethics*, trans. J. A. K. Thomson, London: Penguin.

Augustine [413–26 AD] (2001), *Political Writings*, eds E. M. Atkins, R. J. Dodaro, Cambridge: Cambridge University Press.

Bailey, S. (1972), *Prohibitions and Restraints in War*, Oxford: Oxford University Press.

Baylis, J. (2001), 'International and global security in the post-cold war era', in J. Baylis, S. Smith (eds), *The Globalization of World Politics*, Oxford: Oxford University Press, pp. 253–76.

Bellamy, C. (1999), *The State of the World's Children 1996*, Oxford: Oxford University Press.

Berdal, M. , Malone, D. (eds) (2000), *Greed and Grievance: Economic Agendas in Civil Wars*, Boulder, CO and London: Lynne Rienner.

Best, G. (1994), *War and Law Since 1945*, Oxford: Clarendon Press.

Betts, R. K. (1982), *Surprise Attack*, Washington, DC: Brookings Institute.

Betts, R. K. (2002), 'The soft underbelly of American primacy: tactical advantages of terror', *Political Science Quarterly* 17 (1), pp. 19–36.

Betts, R. K. (2003), 'Striking first: a history of lost opportunities', *Ethics and International Affairs* 17 (1), pp. 17–24.

Blair, T. (1999), 'Doctrine of the International Community' speech before the Economic Club of Chicago, Chicago Hilton Hotel, 22 April, at www. globalpolicy.org/globaliz/politics/blair.htm.

Boyden, J. (1990), 'Childhood and the policy makers: a comparative perspective on the globalisation of childhood', in A. James, A. Prout (eds), *Constructing and Reconstructing Childhood: Contemporary Issues in the Sociological Study of Childhood*, London: Falmer Press, pp. 190–216.

Boyden, J. (2003), 'The moral development of child soldiers: what do adults have to fear?', *Peace and Conflict: Journal of Peace Psychology* 9 (4), pp. 343–62.

Boyden, J., Levison, D. (2000), *Children as Economic and Social Actors in the Development Process*, Working Paper 2000: 1, Stockholm: Expert Group on Development Issues.

Boyle, J. (2002), 'Traditional just war doctrine and humanitarian intervention', American Political Studies Association conference proceedings, at www. apsaproceedings.cup.org/Site/abstracts/003/003020Boyle Joseph.htm.

Brocklehurst, H. (2003), 'Kids 'r' us? Children as political bodies', *International Journal of Politics and Ethics* 3 (1), pp. 79–92.

Brocklehurst, H. (in press), *Who's Afraid of Children? Children, Conflict and International Relations*, Aldershot: Ashgate.

Brocklehurst, H., Phillips, R. (eds) (2003), *History, Nationhood and the Question of Britain*, Basingstoke: Palgrave Macmillan.

Brown, J. (1988), '*A* is for atom, *B* is for bomb: civil defense in American public education, 1948–1963', *The Journal of American History* 75 (1), pp. 68–90.

Brown, M. (ed.) (1996), *Debating the Democratic Peace*, Cambridge, MA: MIT Press.

Brownlie, I. (1963), *International Law and the Use of Force by States*, Oxford: Clarendon.

Bull, H. (1977), *The Anarchical Society*, London: Macmillan.

Bullock, M., Jennings, M. (eds) (1996), *Walter Benjamin: Selected Writings volume 1 1913–1926*, Cambridge, MA: Harvard University Press.

Bush, G. W. (2002), 'Remarks by the president at the 2002 graduation exercise of the United States Military Academy, West Point', at www.whitehouse. gov.news/releases/2002/06/20020602–3.htm.

Cairns, E. (1996), *Children and Political Violence*, London: Blackwell.

Carlsson, I. (1989), 'The importance of children's rights', in *Making Reality of Children's Rights: Final Report, Stockholm Conference on the Rights of the Child*, Stockholm: Radda Barnen, pp. 22–8.

Carlton-Ford, S. , Hamill, A. , Houston, P. (2000), 'War and children's mortality', *Childhood* 7 (4), pp. 401–19.

Carmola, K. (2004), 'Outsourcing combat: casualty phobia and the externalization of war crimes', in M. Evans (ed.), *Ethical Theory in the Study of International Politics*, New York: Nova Science Publishers Inc., pp. 123–44.

Chalk, F. , Jonassohn, K. (eds) (1990), *The History and Sociology of Genocide*, New Haven, CT: Yale University Press.

Chesterman, S. (2002), *Just War or Just Peace: Humanitarian Intervention and International Law*, Oxford: Oxford University Press.

Chitty, A. (2002), 'Moralism, terrorism and war: reply to Shaw', *Radical Philosophy* 111, pp. 16–19.

Christopher, P. (1994), *The Ethics of War and Peace*, Englewood Cliffs, NJ: Prentice-Hall.

Churchill, W. (1986a), *The Second World War Volume 3: The Grand Alliance*, New York: Mariner Books.

Churchill, W. (1986b), *The Second World War Volume 6: Triumph and Tragedy*, New York: Mariner Books.

Clark, I. (1988), *Waging War: A Philosophical Introduction*, Oxford: Oxford University Press.

Clausewitz, C. von. [1832] (1976), *On War*, trans. M. Howard, P. Paret, Princeton, NJ: Princeton University Press.

Clenenden, C. C. (1961), *The United States and Pancho Villa: A Study in Unconventional Diplomacy*, Ithaca, NY: Cornell University Press.

Coates, A. J. (1997), *The Ethics of War*, Manchester: Manchester University Press.

Cockburn, G. (2000), *Meaningful Youth Participation in International Conferences: A Case Study of the International Conference on War-Affected Children*, Winnipeg, MB: Canadian International Development Agency.

Cohen, G. A. (2000), *If You're an Egalitarian, How Come You're So Rich?*, Cambridge, MA: Harvard University Press.

Commission on Global Governance (1995), *Our Global Neighbourhood*, New York and Oxford: Oxford University Press.

Commission on Human Security (2003), *Human Security Now*, New York: Communications Development Incorporated.

Committee Established to Review the NATO Bombing Against the Federal Republic of Yugoslavia (2000), 'Final Report to the Prosecutor', 16 June, at www.un.org/icty/pressreal/nato061300.htm.

Conetta, C. (2004), 'Disappearing the dead: Iraq, Afghanistan and the idea of "new warfare"', Project on Defense Alternatives, at www.comw.org/pda/0402rm9.html.

Cook, C. , Hanieh, A. , Kay, A. (2004), *Stolen Youth: The Politics of Israel's Detention of Palestinian Children*, London: Pluto Press in Association with Defence for Children International.

Costello, P. J. M. , (2000), *Thinking Skills and Early Childhood Education*, London: David Fulton.

Craig, G. A. (1955), *The Politics of the Prussian Army 1640–1945*, Oxford: Oxford University Press.

Crawford, J. (2002), *The International Law Commission's Articles on State Responsibility: Introduction, Text, and Commentaries*, Cambridge: Cambridge University Press.

Crawford, N. C. (2002), *Argument and Change in World Politics: Ethics, Decolonisation and Humanitarian Intervention*, Cambridge: Cambridge University Press.

Crawford, N. C. (2003a), 'Fear and the slippery slope to preventive war', *Ethics and International Affairs* 17 (1), pp. 30–6.

Crawford, N. C. (2003b), 'Just war theory and the US counterterror war', *Perspectives on Politics* 1 (1), pp. 5–25.

Dallaire, R. (2003), *Shake Hands with the Devil: Humanity's Failure in Rwanda*, New York: Random House.

Daniels, N. (1996), *Justice and Justification*, Cambridge: Cambridge University Press.

Denny, D. A. (2003), 'US air force uses new tools to minimize civilian casualties', United States Mission to the European Union, at www. useu. be/ Categories/GlobalAffairs/Iraq/Mar1803CivilianCasualties. html.

Department of Foreign Affairs and International Trade, Canada (1998), 'Notes for an address by the Honourable Lloyd Axworthy, Minister of Foreign Affairs, to a meeting of the Mid-America Committee "Global action, continental community: human security in Canadian foreign policy"', 9 September, at webapps.dfaitmaeci.gc.ca/minpub/Publication.asp?FileSpec=/ Min_Pub_ Docs/101090.htm&bPrint= True& Language=E.

Detter Delupis, I. (1987), *The Law of War*, Cambridge: Cambridge University Press.

Dinstein, Y. (1995), *War, Aggression and Self-Defence*, Cambridge: Cambridge University Press.

Dodge, C. P. , Raundalen, M. (1991), *Reaching Children in War: Sudan, Uganda and Mozambique*, Bergen, Norway: Sigma Forlag.

Dower, N. (1998), *World Ethics: The New Agenda*, Edinburgh: Edinburgh University Press.

Doyle, M. (1983a), 'Kant, liberal legacies and foreign affairs, part I', *Philosophy and Public Affairs* 12 (3), pp. 205–35.

Doyle, M. (1983b), 'Kant, liberal legacies and foreign affairs, part II', *Philosophy and Public Affairs* 12 (4), pp. 323–53.

Doyle, M. (1997), *Ways of War and Peace*, New York: Norton.

Elshtain, J. B. (1992), 'Epilogue: continuing implications of the just war traditions', in *Just War Theory*, ed. J. B. Elshtain, Oxford: Blackwell, pp. 323–33.

Elshtain, J. B. (1996), 'Commentary: political children', *Childhood* 3 (1), pp. 11–28.

Elshtain, J. B. (2003), *Just War Against Terror: The Burden of American Power*, New York: Basic Books.

Enloe, C. (1993), *The Morning After: Sexual Politics at the End of the Cold War*, London: University of California Press.

Eriksson, M., Wallensteen, P., Sollenberg, M. (2003), 'Armed conflict 1989–2002', *Journal of Peace Research* 40 (5), pp. 593–607.

Etcheson, C. (2003), 'Beyond the Khmer Rouge tribunal', *Phnom Penh Post* 12 (22) (24 October–6 November).

Evans, M. (2002), 'Selectivity, imperfect obligations and the character of humanitarian morality', in A. Moseley, R. Norman (eds), *Human Rights and Military Intervention*, Aldershot: Ashgate, pp. 132–49.

Evans, M. (2004), 'World citizenship and the ethics of individual responsibility', in M. Evans (ed.), *Ethical Theory in the Study of International Politics*, New York: Nova Science Publishers, pp. 35–54.

Falk, R. (1995), *On Humane Governance: Toward a New Global Politics*, Cambridge: Polity.

Farson, R. (1974), *Birthrights*, London: Collier Macmillan.

Fiala, A. (2002), 'Terrorism and the philosophy of history: liberalism, realism and the supreme emergency exemption', *Essays in Philosophy* volume 3, pp. 1–15.

Foucault, M. (1979), *Discipline and Punish: The Birth of the Prison*, New York: Vintage Books.

Freeman, M. (1983), *The Rights and Wrongs of Children*, London: Frances Pinter.

Freeman, M. (1996), *Children's Rights: A Comparative Perspective*, Aldershot: Dartmouth.

Frost, M. (2002), *Constituting Human Rights: Global Civil Society and the Society of Democratic States*, London: Routledge.

Fullinwider, R. (1975), 'War and innocence', *Philosophy and Public Affairs* 5 (1), pp. 90–7.

Galtung, J. (1996), *Peace by Peaceful Means*, London: Sage.

Giovanoli, A. (2001), 'Commemorative Symposium: Conflict Resolution and Religious People', in *Dharma World* 28 (March/April).

Goodwin-Gill, G. , Cohn, I. (1994), *Child Soldiers*, Oxford: Clarendon.

Grotius, H. [1631] (1925), *The Laws of War and Peace*, trans. F. W. Kelsey, Indianapolis: Bobbs-Merrill Co.

Halsan, A. (2001), 'Underage and Under Fire: An Enquiry into the use of child soldiers 1994–8', *Childhood* 8 (3), pp. 340–60.

Hart, R. (1992) *Children's Participation: From Tokenism to Citizenship*, Florence: UNICEF Child Development Centre.

Hayden, P. (2002), *John Rawls: Towards a Just World Order*, Cardiff: University of Wales Press.

Hayden, P. (2005), *Cosmopolitan Global Politics*, Aldershot: Ashgate.

Hayden, P. (2001) (ed.), *The Philosophy of Human Rights*, St Paul, MN: Paragon House Publishers.

Harvey, R. (2003), *Children and Armed Conflict: A Guide to International and Humanitarian Human Rights Law*, Essex University and the International Bureau of Children's Rights: The Children and Armed Conflict Unit.

Hayner, P. (2002), *Unspeakable Truths: Facing the Challenge of Truth Commissions*, London: Routledge.

Held, D. (1995), *Democracy and the Global Order*, Cambridge: Polity.

Henkin, I. , Pugh, R. , Schachter, O. , Smit, H. (eds) (1993), *International Law: Cases and Materials* 3rd edn, St Paul, MN: West Publishing Co.

Herz, J. H. (1951), *Political Realism and Political Idealism*, Chicago: University of Chicago Press.

Holmes, R. L. (1989), *On War and Morality*, Princeton, NJ: Princeton University Press.

Holzgrefe, J. L. , Keohane, R. (2002), *Humanitarian Intervention: Ethical, Legal, and Political Dilemmas*, Cambridge: Cambridge University Press.

Honwana, A. (1999), 'The collective body: challenging western concepts of trauma and healing', *Track Two* 8 (1), at ccrweb.ccr.uct.ac.za/two/8_1/p30_collective_body.

Howard, M. (1994), *The Laws of War*, New Haven, CT: Yale University Press.

Howard, M. (2002), 'What's in a name? How to fight terrorism', in *Foreign Affairs* 81 (1), pp. 8–13.

Human Rights Watch Africa (1995), *Easy Prey: Child Soldiers in Liberia*, New York: Human Rights Watch Africa.

International Commission on Intervention and State Sovereignty (2001), *The Responsibility to Protect*, Ottawa: International Development Research Centre.

Johnson, J. T. (1987), *The Quest for Peace: Three Moral Traditions in Western Cultural History*, Princeton, NJ: Princeton University Press.

Johnson, J. T. (1999), *Morality and Contemporary Warfare*, New Haven, CT: Yale University Press.

Jones, C. (1999), *Global Justice: Defending Cosmopolitanism*, Oxford: Oxford University Press.

Kaldor, M. (1999), *New and Old Wars*, Cambridge: Polity.

Kant, I. (1991a), *Political Writings*, ed. H. Reiss (2nd edn), Cambridge: Cambridge University Press.

Kant, I. [1785] (1991b), *The Metaphysics of Morals*, trans. M. Gregor, Cambridge: Cambridge University Press.

Kant, I. [1780] (1999), *Metaphysical Elements of Justice*, trans. J. Ladd, Indianapolis, IN: Hackett Publishing Company.

Keane, J. (2003), *Global Civil Society?*, Cambridge: Cambridge University Press.

Keen, D. (2003), 'Conflict, trade and economic agendas', *CCTS Newsletter* 19, at www.c-r.org/ccts/ccts19/agendas. htm.

Kegley, C. W. , Raymond, G. (2003), 'Preventive war and permissive normative order', *International Studies Perspectives* 4, pp. 385–94.

Kellogg, D. (2002), 'Reaping the whirlwind: terrorism, supreme emergencies and the abandonment of the *jus in bello* restrictions on attacking enemy civilians', unpublished paper, University of Maine.

Kimani, M. (2003a), 'Refusing to give up refugee status: Rwandans in Tanzanian camps', *Internews Reports* (15 April), at www.internews.org/activties/ICTR_reports/ICTRnewsApr03. html.

Kimani, M. (2003b), 'When justice is not enough', *Internews Reports* (1 September), at www.internews.org/activities/ICTR_reports/ICTR newsSEp03.html#0901b.

Knight, W. A. (2004), 'Children and Armed Conflict: Impact, Protection and Rehabilitation', at www.arts.ualberta.ca/childrenandwar/research_ methodology.php.

Kobukyaye, F. (2001), *Justice and Reconciliation in Post-Genocide Rwanda*, unpublished MA dissertation, Coventry University.

Kriesberg, L. (2001), 'Changing forms of coexistence', in M. Abu-Nimer (ed.), *Reconciliation, Justice and Coexistence*, Lanham MD: Lexington Books, pp. 47–64.

Lackey, D. (1989), *The Ethics of War and Peace*, Englewood Cliffs, NJ: Prentice-Hall.

Lake, A. (1994), 'Confronting backlash states', *Foreign Affairs* 73 (2), pp. 45–55.

Lang, A. F. Jr (1999), 'Responsibility in the international system: reading US foreign policy in the Middle East', *European Journal of International Relations* 5 (1), pp. 67–107.

Lang, A. F. Jr (2002), *Agency and Ethics: The Politics of Military Interventions*, Albany, NY: SUNY Press.

Lang, A. F. Jr (ed.) (2003), *Just Intervention*, Washington, DC: Georgetown University Press.

Lang, A. F. Jr, Pierce, A., Rosenthal, J. (eds) (2004), *Ethics and the Future of Conflict*, Upper Saddle River, NJ: Prentice-Hall.

Larson, E. (1996), *Casualties and Consensus: The Historical Role of Casualties in Domestic Support for U. S. Military Operations*, Santa Monica, CA: RAND.

Licklider, R. (2001), 'Obstacles to peace settlements', in C. A. Crocker, F. O. Hampson, P. Aall (eds), *Turbulent Peace: The Challenges of Managing International Conflict*, Washington DC: United States Institute of Peace, pp. 697–718.

Lopez, G. A. (2002), 'Iraq and just war thinking', *Commonweal*, 27 September, pp. 14–15.

Lu, C. (2002), 'Justice and moral regeneration: lessons from the Treaty of Versailles', *International Studies Review* 4 (3), pp. 3–25.

Luban, D. (1980), 'Just war and human rights', *Philosophy and Public Affairs* 9 (2), pp. 160–81.

MacLean, G. (1998), 'The changing perception of human security: coordinating national and multilateral responses', paper presented at the conference on 'The United Nations and the New Security Agenda', 8 May, at www.unac.org/en/link_learn/canada/security/perception.asp.

Macrae, J. (2000), 'Humanitarianism: facing new challenges', *Great Decisions: 2000*, New York: Foreign Policy Association, pp. 87–96.

Mamdani, M. (2001), *When Victims Become Killers: Colonialism, Nativism and the Genocide in Rwanda*, Oxford: James Currey.

Marks, M. (2001), *Young Warriors: Youth Politics, Identity and Violence in South Africa*, Johannesburg: Witwatersrand University Press.

Matthews, G. B. , (1984), *Dialogues with Children*, Cambridge, MA: Harvard University Press.

McCartney, C. (1999), 'Striking a balance: the Northern Ireland peace process', *Accord* 8, pp. 10–12.

McGreal, C. (1995), 'Africa's child troops fuelled by drugs and revenge', *The Guardian*, 21 February.

Meintjes, S., Pillay A., and Turshen M. (2002), 'There is no aftermath for women', in S. Meintjes, A. Pillay, M. Turshen (eds), *The Aftermath – Women in Post-Conflict Transformation*, London: Zed Books.

Melvern, L. (2000), *A People Betrayed: The Role of the West in Rwanda's Genocide*, London: Zed Books.

Minow, M. (1998), *Between Vengeance and Forgiveness*, Boston, MA: Beacon Press.

Moellendorf, D. (2002), *Cosmopolitan Justice*, Boulder, CO: Westview Press.

Morgenthau, H. J. (1954), *Politics Among Nations*, 2nd edn , New York: Alfred A. Knopf.

Murphy, C. N. , Weiss, T. G. (2000), 'International peace and security at a multilateral moment: what we seem to know, what we don't, and why?' in S. Croft, T. Terriff (eds), *Critical Reflections on Security and Change*, London: Frank Cass, pp. 116–41.

Nagel, T. (1972), 'War and massacre', *Philosophy and Public Affairs* 1 (2), pp. 123–44.

Nardin, T. (1983), *Law, Morality and the Relation of States*, Princeton, NJ: Princeton University Press.

National Security Council (2002), *The National Security Strategy of the United States of America*, Washington DC: Office of the President.

Netherlands Red Cross (2001), *Protecting Civilians in 21st Century Warfare: Target Selection, Proportionality and Precautionary Measures in Law and Practice*, The Hague: Wolf Legal Productions.

New English Bible with Apocrypha (1970), Oxford and Cambridge: Oxford University Press and Cambridge University Press.

Norman, R. (1995), *Ethics, Killing and War*, Cambridge: Cambridge University Press.

Nussbaum, M. (1999), *Sex and Social Justice*, Oxford: Oxford University Press.

Nussbaum, M. and Sen, A. (eds) (1993), *Quality of Life*, Oxford: Oxford University Press.

Nuttall, J. (1993), *Moral Questions: An Introduction to Ethics*, Cambridge: Polity.

Oestreicher, P. (2004), 'The legacy of Dresden', *The Guardian*, 3 March.

O'Hanlon, M. (2003), Testimony on national counterterrorism strategies before the Subcommittee on National Security, Emerging Threats and International Relations, House Committee on Government Reform, 3 March, at www.brook. edu/dybdocroot/views/testimony/ohanlon/20030303.pdf.

Orend, B. (1999), 'Kant's just war theory', *Journal of the History of Philosophy* 37 (2), pp. 323–55.

Orend, B. (2000a), *Michael Walzer on War and Justice*, Cardiff: University of Wales Press.

Orend, B. (2000b), *War and International Justice: A Kantian Perspective*, Waterloo, ON: Wilfrid Laurier University Press.

Orend, B. (2002a), *Human Rights: Concept and Context*, Peterborough, ON: Broadview Press.

Orend, B. (2002b), 'Justice after war', *Ethics and International Affairs* 16 (1), pp. 43–56.

Otunnu, O. (1999), 'Protection of children affected by armed conflict: note by the Secretary General', United Nations General Assembly, 1 October, 99–28333.

Otunnu, O. (2000), 'The impact of armed conflict on children: filling knowledge gaps, draft research agenda. ' A Proposal by The Special Representative of the Secretary-General For Children and Armed Conflict, at www.mofa.go.jp/policy/human/child/survey/annex2.html.

Pascal, B. [1660] (1961), *Pensées*, trans. J. M. Cohen, Harmondsworth: Penguin.

Perle, R. (2003), 'The War Behind Closed Doors', at www.pbs.org/wgbh/pages/frontline/shows/iraq/interviews/perle.html.

Peters, K. , Richards, P. , Vlassenroot, K. (2003), 'What happens to youth during and after wars? A preliminary review of literature on Africa and an assessment of the debate', The Hague: RAWOO (The Netherlands Development Assistance Research Council), 1–48.

Peterson, V. S. (ed.) (1992), 'Security and sovereign states: what is at stake in taking feminism seriously?', in V. S. Peterson (ed.), *Gendered States: Feminist (Re)visions of International Relations Theory*, Boulder CO: Lynne Rienner, pp. 31–64.

Pogge, T. (2002), *World Poverty and Human Rights*, Cambridge: Polity.

Power, S. (2003), *A Problem from Hell: America and the Age of Genocide*, London: Flamingo.

Prunier, G. (1995), *The Rwanda Crisis: History of a Genocide*, New York: Columbia University Press.

Rachels, J. (2002), 'Punishment and desert', in H. LaFollette (ed.), *Ethics in Practice: An Anthology* (2nd edn), Oxford: Blackwell, pp. 466–74.

Ramsey, P. (1965), *War and the Christian Conscience: How Shall Modern War Be Conducted Justly?*, Durham, NC: Duke University Press.

Rawls, J. (1972), *A Theory of Justice*, Oxford: Oxford University Press.

Rawls, J. (1999a), *The Law of Peoples*, Cambridge, MA: Harvard University Press.

Rawls, J. (1999b), *Collected Papers*, ed. S. Freeman, Cambridge, MA: Harvard University Press.

Reisman, W. , Antoniou, C. (eds) (1994), *The Laws of War: A Comprehensive Collection of Primary Documents Governing Armed Conflict*, New York: Vintage.

Rice, C. (2002), 'A balance of power that favors freedom', Wriston Lecture October 1, at www. manhattan-institute.org/html/wl/2002.htm.

Rieff, D. (1995), *Slaughterhouse: Bosnia and the Failure of the West*, New York: Simon and Schuster.

Rigby, A. (2001), *Justice and Reconciliation: After the Bloodshed*, Boulder, CO: Lynne Rienner.

Roberts, A. (2002), 'Counter-terrorism, armed force, and the laws of war', *Survival* 44 (1), pp. 7–32.

Roberts, A. , Guelff, R. (eds) (2000), *Documents on the Laws of War*, Oxford: Oxford University Press.

Rodin, D. (2002), *War and Self-Defense*, Oxford: Clarendon.

Ronzitti, N. (2000), 'Is the non liquet of the final report by the committee established to review the NATO bombing campaign against the Federal Republic of Yugoslavia acceptable?', in *International Review of the Red Cross* 840, pp. 1017–28.

Ruddick, S. (1990), *Maternal Thinking: Towards a Politics of Peace*, Boston, MA: Beacon Press.

Rumsfeld, D. (2001), 'News Conference', at www.defenselink.mil.news/Nov2001/t11302001_1130sd.html.

Sanger, D. E. (2002), 'Beating them to the prewar', *The New York Times*, 28 September, p. B7.

Schabas, W. (1997), *The Abolition of the Death Penalty in International Law*, 2nd edn , Cambridge: Cambridge University Press.

Schafer, J. (2001), 'Guerrillas and violence in the war in Mozambique: de-socialisation or re-socialisation?', *African Affairs*, 100, pp. 215–37.

Schall, J. V. (2001), 'On the justice and prudence of this war', *The Catholic University Law Review* (Fall), pp. 1–13.

Sebald, W. G. (2003), *The Natural History of Destruction*, London: Hamish Hamilton.

Sen, A. (1999), *Development as Freedom*, New York: Alfred A. Knopf.

Shaw, M. (2003), *War and Genocide: Organized Killing in Modern Society*, Cambridge: Polity.

Shewmaker, K. E. (ed.) (1983), *The Papers of Daniel Webster: Diplomatic Papers volume 1 1841–1843*, Hanover, NH: University Press of New England.

Shue, H. (1996), *Basic Rights: Subsistence, Affluence, and US Foreign Policy*, 2nd edn, Princeton: Princeton University Press.

Simmons, A. J. (1991), 'Locke and the right to punish', *Philosophy and Public Affairs* 20 (4), pp. 311–49.

Singer, P. (2001) 'Caution: children at war', *Parameters*, Winter 2001–02, pp. 40–56, at http://carlisle-www.army.mil/usawc/Parameters/01winter/singer.htm.

Singer, P. (2004), *The President of Good and Evil*, London: Granta.

Slaughter, A.-M. (2003), 'Good reasons for going around the UN', *New York Times*, 18 March.

Stockholm Initiative on Global Security and Governance (1991), *Common Responsibility in the 1990s*, Stockholm: Prime Minister's Office.

Teichman, J. (1986), *Pacifism and the Just War*, Oxford: Blackwell.

Totten, S. , Parsons, W. , Charny, I. (eds) (1997), *Century of Genocide*, New York: Garland.

Tutu, D. (1999), *No Future Without Forgiveness*, London: Rider.

United Nations (1994), *Human Development Report 1994*, New York and Oxford: Oxford University Press.

United Nations Children's Fund (1995), *The Convention on the Rights of the Child* London: UK Committee for UNICEF.

UNICEF (1989), 'Convention on the Rights of the Child', at www.unicef. org/ crc/crc.htm.

US Catholic Bishops (1992), 'The Challenge of Peace: God's Promise and Our Response', in *Just War Theory*, ed. J. B. Elshtain, Oxford: Blackwell, pp. 77–168.

United States Department of Defense (2001), *Quadrennial Defense Review*, Washington, DC: US GPO.

United States Institute of Peace Library (2004), 'Truth Commissions Digital Collection' at www.usip.org/library/truth.html.

Van Bueren, G. (1998), 'Opening Pandora's box', in G. Van Bueren (ed.), *Childhood Abused: Protecting Children Against Torture, Cruel, Inhuman and Degrading Treatment and Punishment*, Dartmouth: Ashgate, pp. 51–73.

Vitoria, F. (1991), *Political Writings*, eds A. Pagden, J. Lawrance, Cambridge: Cambridge University Press.

Walter, B. F. (1997), 'The critical barrier to civil war settlement', *International Organization* 51 (3), pp. 335–64.

Walzer, M. (1971), 'World War II: why was this war different?', *Philosophy and Public Affairs* 1 (1), pp. 3–21.

Walzer, M. (1973), 'Political action: the problem of dirty hands', *Philosophy and Public Affairs* 2 (2), pp. 160–80.

Walzer, M. (1992), *Just and Unjust Wars*, New York: Basic Books.

Walzer, M. (2004), *Arguing About War*, New Haven, CT: Yale University Press.

Weigel, G. (1987), *Tranquillitas Ordinis: The Present Failure and Future Promise of American Catholic Thought on War and Peace*, Cambridge: Cambridge University Press.

Zehfuss, M. (2004), 'Writing war, against good conscience', in *Millennium* 33 (1), pp. 91–121.

INDEX